GOING SOLO

**Center Point
Large Print**

**This Large Print Book carries the
Seal of Approval of N.A.V.H.**

GOING SOLO

THE EXTRAORDINARY RISE AND SURPRISING APPEAL OF LIVING ALONE

ERIC KLINENBERG

CENTER POINT LARGE PRINT
THORNDIKE, MAINE

This Center Point Large Print edition
is published in the year 2012 by arrangement with
The Penguin Press,
a member of Penguin Group (USA) Inc.

The text of this Large Print edition is unabridged.
In other aspects, this book may vary
from the original edition.
Printed in the United States of America
on permanent paper.
Set in 16-point Times New Roman type.

ISBN: 978-1-61173-451-5

Library of Congress Cataloging-in-Publication Data

Klinenberg, Eric.
Going solo : the extraordinary rise and surprising appeal of living alone
/ Eric Klinenberg. — Large print ed.
p. cm.
ISBN 978-1-61173-451-5 (library binding : alk. paper)
1. Living alone—United States. 2. Single people—United States.
   3. Single people—United States—Psychology. I. Title.
HQ800.4.U6K56 2012b
306.81′5—dc23
                                                      2012008667

For Lila, Cyrus, and Kate

CONTENTS

INTRODUCTION:
THE SINGLETON SOCIETY

IN THE BEGINNING of the Old Testament, God creates the world one day at a time: The heavens and the earth. Water. Light. Day and night. Living species of every kind. After each creation, God declares: "It is good." But the tone changes when God makes Adam. Suddenly, God pronounces the first thing that is not good, *lo tov*: "It is not good that the man should be alone."[1] So God makes Eve, and Adam is no longer on his own.

In time, injunctions against being alone moved from theology to philosophy and literature. In *Politics*, Aristotle wrote, "The man who is isolated, who is unable to share in the benefits of political association, or has no need to share because he is already self-sufficient, is no part of the polis, and must therefore be either a beast or a god." The Greek poet Theocritus insisted that "man will ever stand in need of man," and the Roman emperor and Stoic philosopher Marcus Aurelius proclaimed that "human beings are social animals."[2]

So, too, are other animals. (Aristotle, alas, was only half right.) Beasts will indeed live on their own when conditions favor it, particularly when there is a shortage of food. Otherwise most species fare better in groups. Collective living carries some costs, including competition for status and occasional outbursts of violence. But the benefits—protection from predators, co-operative hunting, efficient reproduction, among others—can easily outweigh them. Our closest animal relatives, the apes, are typically social and live in stable units. Even orangutans, which are notoriously solitary, live with their mothers during their first seven or eight years, and as the Dutch primatologist Carel van Schaik has discovered, orangutans living in a calorically rich swamp forest in Sumatra are "every bit as sociable" as their cousins, the chimpanzees.[3]

Orangutans are not the only misrepresented creatures. Hermit crabs, it turns out, are actually quite social, living in communities of up to one hundred because they cannot thrive alone. One manual for prospective pet owners advises that "it's best to always have at least two hermit crabs in a tank—if possible at least two of each species." Not because they need protection or help with food gathering, but for a simpler reason: When alone, hermit crabs get stressed and unhealthy. Their bodies fail them. They may even lose a leg or a claw.

Isolation can also be unbearably stressful for people, as policy makers in different historical eras have recognized. In the ancient world, exile ranked among the most severe forms of punishment, exceeded only by execution. (Though some called exile a fate worse than death.) During the late eighteenth and nineteenth centuries, modern prison systems popularized the use of solitary confinement because, as the English jurist William Paley put it, isolation "would augment the terror of the punishment" and thereby deter crime.[4] Today, the United States alone detains roughly 25,000 people in "supermax" prisons where, one prominent psychologist writes, inmates "experience levels of isolation . . . that are more total and complete and literally dehumanized than has been possible in the past."[5] A common phrase used to describe this condition conveys one widespread belief about being cut off from others: It is, say both critics and advocates of solitary confinement, a "living death."

Nothing better expresses the human interest in collective living than the formation of families. Throughout history and in all cultures, families, not individuals, have been the fundamental building blocks of social and economic life. And for good reason. As evolutionary biologists argue, living with others offered a competitive advantage to members of the first human societies because it provided security, access to food, and a means of reproduction. Through

11

natural selection, argue the social scientists Nicholas Christakis and James Fowler, our species developed a genetic disposition to establish close social ties.[6]

In 1949, the Yale anthropologist George Peter Murdock published a survey of some 250 "representative cultures" from different eras and diverse parts of the world. He reported, "The nuclear family is a universal human social grouping. Either as the sole prevailing form of the family or as the basic unit from which more complex familial forms are compounded, it exists as a distinct and strongly functional group in every known society. No exception, at least, has come to light."[7]

Since then, scholars have challenged Murdock's argument, identifying domestic arrangements, such as the kibbutz, that don't fit into his nuclear model. Yet their counterexamples are always alternative collectives, typically including more people than the conventional family. Though this debate remains unsettled, there's one thing both sides would agree on: Human societies, at all times and places, have organized themselves around the will to live with others, not alone.

BUT NOT ANYMORE.

During the past half century, our species has embarked on a remarkable social experiment. For the first time in human history, great numbers of people—at all ages, in all places, of every political persuasion—have begun settling down as singletons.* Until recently, most of us married young and parted only at death. If death came early, we remarried quickly; if late, we moved in with family, or they with us. Now we marry later. (The Pew Research Center reports that the average age of first marriage for men and women is "the highest ever recorded, having risen by roughly five years in the past half century.")[8] We divorce, and stay single for years or decades. We survive our spouses, and do whatever we can to avoid moving in with others—even, perhaps especially, our children. We cycle in and out of different living arrangements: alone, together, together, alone.

Not long ago, it might have made sense to treat living on our own as a transitional stage between more durable arrangements, whether coupling up with a partner or moving into an institutional home. This is no longer appropriate, because today, for the first time in centuries, the majority of all American adults are single. The typical American will spend more of his or her adult life unmarried than married, and for much of this time he or she will live alone. Naturally, we are

---

*In this book, I use the term "singletons" for people who live alone. "Singles" may or may not live alone (some live with a romantic partner, or roommates, or children), and so not all singles are singletons.

adapting. We are learning to go solo, and crafting new ways of living in the process.

Numbers never tell the whole story, but in this case the statistics are startling. In 1950, 22 percent of American adults were single. Four million lived alone, and they accounted for 9 percent of all households. In those days, living alone was by far most common in the open, sprawling Western states—Alaska, Montana, and Nevada—that attracted migrant workingmen, and it was usually a short-lived stage on the road to a more conventional domestic life.

Today, more than 50 percent of American adults are single, and 31 million—roughly one out of every seven adults—live alone. (This figure excludes the 8 million Americans who live in voluntary and nonvoluntary group quarters, such as assisted living facilities, nursing homes, and prisons.)[9] People who live alone make up 28 percent of all U.S. households, which means that they are now tied with childless couples as the most prominent residential type—more common than the nuclear family, the multigenerational family, and the roommate or group home. Surprisingly, living alone is also one of the most stable household arrangements. Over a five-year period, people who live alone are more likely to stay that way than everyone except married couples with children.[10]

Contemporary solo dwellers are primarily

women: about 17 million, compared to 14 million men. The majority, more than 15 million, are middle-age adults between the ages of thirty-five and sixty-four. The elderly account for about 10 million of the total.* Young adults between eighteen and thirty-four number more than 5 million, compared to 500,000 in 1950, making them the fastest-growing segment of the solo-dwelling population.[11]

Unlike their predecessors, people who live alone today cluster together in metropolitan areas and inhabit all regions of the country. The cities with the highest proportion of people living alone include Washington, D.C., Seattle, Denver, San Francisco, Minneapolis, Chicago, Dallas, New York City, and Miami. One million people live alone in New York City, and in Manhattan, more than half of all residences are one-person dwellings.

DESPITE ITS PREVALENCE, living alone is one of the least discussed and, consequently, most poorly understood issues of our time. We aspire to get our own places as young adults, but fret about whether it's all right to stay that way,

---

*In this book, I use the terms "old people" and "the elderly" to refer to those age sixty-five and above. The reasons for this have more to do with the statistics on aging, which typically classify people as elderly once they reach age sixty-five, than on an argument about the age when one becomes old.

even if we enjoy it. We worry about friends and family members who haven't found the right match, even if they insist that they're happy on their own and will find someone in due course. We struggle to support elderly parents and grandparents who find themselves living alone after losing a spouse, and we are puzzled about what to do if they tell us they prefer to remain home alone.

In all of these situations, living alone is something that each person or family experiences as the most private of matters, when in fact it is an increasingly common condition and deserves to be treated as a subject of great public significance. Unfortunately, on those rare occasions when there is a public debate about the rise of living alone, commentators tend to present it as an unmitigated social problem, a sign of narcissism, fragmentation, and a diminished public life. Our morally charged conversations tend to frame the question of why so many people now live on their own around the false and misleading choice between the romanticized ideal of *Father Knows Best* and the glamorous enticements of *Sex and the City*. In fact, as we'll see, the reality of this great social experiment in living alone is far more interesting—and far less isolating—than these conversations would have us believe.

The rise of living alone has been a transformative social experience. It changes the way we understand ourselves and our most intimate relationships. It shapes the way we build our cities and develop our economies. It alters the way we become adults, as well as how we age and the way we die. It touches every social group and nearly every family, no matter who we are or whether we live with others today.

THIS "WE" IS MORE EXPANSIVE than you might imagine. It's tempting to treat the soaring rates of living alone as a peculiar American condition, an expression of what the literary critic Harold Bloom called the nation's "religion of self-reliance." After all, Americans have long taken pride in self-sufficiency. Thomas Jefferson called individualism "the great watchword of American life," and the historian David Potter wrote that Americans view it as a "sacred term." In *Habits of the Heart*, sociologist Robert Bellah and his coauthors distinguish between two traditions of American individualism. "Utilitarian individualism," best exemplified by Benjamin Franklin, is based on the belief that society flourishes when each person pursues his or her interests first; this notion has inspired America's libertarian streak. "Expressive indi- vidualism," as exemplified by Walt Whitman, advocates cultivating and "celebrating" the self (as the poet put it in the first line of the first edition of *Leaves of Grass*). This view has inspired America's ongoing search for identity and meaning. Though these two strains of individualism promote different values and agendas, together they offer Americans a well of cultural resources for putting the self before society. We draw from them often.

Consider Ralph Waldo Emerson, one of America's first public intellectuals. In his powerful essay "Self-Reliance," Emerson warned that "society everywhere is in conspiracy against the manhood of every one of its members," and he offered advice for those seeking relief: "Absolve you to yourself, and you shall have the suffrage of the world."[12] Emerson's neighbor Henry David Thoreau made the case for self-reliance in more dramatic fashion, moving into a cabin he built near Walden Pond. "It is as solitary where I live as on the prairies," he wrote. "I have, as it were, my own sun and moon and stars, and a little world all to myself." Thoreau insisted that there was no loneliness in such a setting: "There can be no very black melancholy to him who lives in the midst of Nature and has his senses still . . . I have never felt lonesome, or in the least oppressed by a sense of solitude, but once . . . when, for an hour, I doubted if the near neighborhood of man was not essential to a serene and healthy life. To be alone was something unpleasant . . ." Until, in an instant: "I was suddenly sensible of such sweet and beneficent society in Nature . . . as made the fancied advantages of human neighborhood insignificant, and I have never thought of them since."

The wisdom of Emerson and Thoreau has inspired generations of American individualists to chart their own paths out of society. Lone rangers on the Western frontier. Cloaked detectives in the shadowy urban streets. Adventurers going "into the wild" to discover themselves. All are icons of American popular culture, symbols of our romantic fantasy of an unfettered self. So it would be easy to conclude that the contemporary urban singleton is just the latest variation on this theme.

It just wouldn't be right.

Americans have never fully embraced individualism, and we remain deeply skeptical of its excesses. De Tocqueville found here both a creeping individualism "which disposes each citizen to isolate himself from the mass of his fellows and withdraw into the circle of family and friends" *and* an abiding moral code that binds citizens to each other in civic organizations and associations of all kinds. Transcendentalists such as Emerson and Thoreau espoused the virtues of solitude. But the escape, for them, always preceded a return to society, and the insights borne of solitude were meant to promote the common good.[13]

In fact, reports of the transcendentalists' individualism have been greatly exaggerated. Most of the leading figures in that movement—Emerson and Thoreau, as well as Bronson Alcott, Elizabeth Peabody, and Margaret Fuller—were deeply engaged in civic and political life. Thoreau was hardly alone, or self-sufficient, during the two years (from 1845 to 1847) he spent on and off at Walden Pond. His cabin, as modern visitors know, sat on land owned by Emerson and was less than two miles from Concord. Thoreau could walk to town in less than thirty minutes, and he returned often to see family and friends, sometimes spending hours downing drinks in the local pub. The human traffic went in two directions. Thoreau was happy to receive visitors, particularly his mother, who came frequently to deliver home-cooked meals.[14]

Who could blame her? Anxiety about the fate of people who live alone, particularly family or close friends, has always shadowed America's interest in self-reliance. In the early colonial towns of New England, local authorities prohibited young men from living independently, lest they use this liberty for licentious pursuits. And as the historian David Potter noted, "In our literature, any story of the complete isolation, either physical or psychological, of a man from his fellowman, such as the story of Robinson

Crusoe before he found a human footprint on the beach, is regarded as essentially a horror story."[15]

So, too, are reports that document the decline of American "communities"—another of our sacred terms. The titles of the most popular sociology books in U.S. history—*The Lonely Crowd, The Pursuit of Loneliness, The Fall of Public Man, The Culture of Narcissism,* and *Habits of the Heart*—raise the specter of individualism run amok. As does one of the most influential works of recent scholarship: Robert Putnam's *Bowling Alone,* which argues that many of our contemporary problems—poor health, failing schools, distrust, even unhappiness—result from the collapse of community life.[16] Americans are attracted to arguments like these precisely because we remain, at heart, a "nation of joiners," just as we were when De Tocqueville visited nearly two centuries ago.

American culture is not the driving force behind the incredible rise in living alone.

IF YOU'RE NOT PERSUADED, consider another piece of evidence: Today Americans are actually *less* likely to live alone than are residents of many other nations, including those we generally regard as more communal. The four countries with the highest rates of living alone are Sweden, Norway, Finland, and Denmark, where roughly 40 to 45 percent of all households have just one person. By investing in each other's social welfare and affirming their bonds of mutual support, the Scandinavians have freed themselves to be on their own.

They have good company. In Japan, where social life has historically been organized around the family, about 30 percent of all households now have a single dweller, and the rate is far higher in urban areas. Germany, France, and the United Kingdom have famously different cultural traditions, but they share a greater proportion of one-person households than the United States. Same for Australia and Canada. And the nations with the fastest growth in one-person households? China, India, and Brazil.[17] According to the market research firm Euromonitor International, at the global level the number of people living alone is skyrocketing, having risen from about 153 million in 1996 to 202 million in 2006—a 33 percent increase in a single decade.[18]

So what *is* driving the widespread rise in living alone? Unquestionably, both the wealth generated by economic development and the social security provided by modern welfare states have enabled the spike. Put simply, one reason that more people live alone than ever before is that today more people can afford to do so. Yet there are a great many things that we can afford to do but choose not to, which m[ ] economic explanation is just one piece [ ] puzzle. We cannot understand why so ....any people in so many places are now living alone unless we address a difficult question: Of all the ways that the relatively privileged citizens of the most developed nations could use their unprecedented affluence and security, why are they using them to separate from each other?

IN ADDITION TO ECONOMIC PROSPERITY and social security, the extraordinary rise in living alone stems from the world-historic cultural change that Émile Durkheim, a founding figure of sociology, called "the cult of the individual." According to Durkheim, the cult of the individual grew out of the transition from traditional rural communities to modern industrial cities, where the individual was gradually becoming the "object of a sort of religion," more sacred than the group. A Frenchman who wrote his major works in the late nineteenth century, Durkheim did not envision the radical economic individualism later endorsed by figures such as Milton Friedman, Ayn Rand, or Margaret Thatcher (who famously declared, "There is no such thing as society"), nor did he share their conviction that liberating individuals from the state was the most effective way to generate wealth and vance the common good. But he wasn't entirely pessimistic, either. Durkheim argued that the modern division of labor would bind citizens organically. After all, individuals could achieve "independence" and "liberty" only if they were supported by the key modern social institutions—the family, the economy, and the state—which meant they had a clear self-interest in joining together to promote the common good.

The Austrian economist Joseph Schumpeter didn't think individuals would see things this way. In his 1942 book *Capitalism, Socialism, and Democracy*, Schumpeter observed that modern capitalism promoted "the rationalization of everything in life," and predicted that a cold, calculating culture would ultimately lead to the "decomposition" of the collective. "As soon as men and women learn the utilitarian lesson and refuse to take for granted the traditional arrangements that their social environment makes for them, as soon as they acquire the habit of weighing the individual advantages and disadvantages of any prospective course of action . . . they cannot fail to become aware of the heavy personal sacrifices that family ties and especially parenthood entail . . ." Schumpeter predicted the gradual "disintegration of the bourgeois family" form, because free-thinking men and women would opt for lives "of comfort, of freedom from care, and opportunity to enjoy alternatives of increasing attractiveness and variety."[19]

The transition would take some time, though, since the cult of individualism still had to contend with deep cultural attachments to commitment. For most of the twentieth century, even the most modern societies expected individuals to marry and judged them harshly if they "failed" to do so. Schumpeter may well have seen singles as rational, but in a survey of Americans conducted in 1957, more than half the respondents said that unmarried people were "sick," "immoral," or "neurotic," while about a third viewed them "neutrally." These positions did not hold. By 1976, a generation later, only one-third of Americans acknowledged that they had negative views about the unmarried, while half were neutral and one in seven actually approved. Today, with single adults out-numbering married ones, pollsters don't even bother asking whether Americans approve of being unmarried. Though the stigma of living alone is not entirely gone, there's no question that our cultural attitudes about singlehood and family life have changed.[20]

According to contemporary wisdom, the search for success and happiness depends less on tying oneself down to another than on opening up the world of possibilities so that one can always pursue the best option. Freedom. Flexibility. Personal choice. These rank among our most cherished modern virtues. Today, writes the demographer Andrew Cherlin, "one's primary obligation is to oneself rather than to one's partner and children," which means the contemporary cult of the individual has intensified far beyond what Durkheim had envisioned.[21]

Not long ago, someone who was dissatisfied with his or her spouse and wanted a divorce had to justify that decision. Today it's the opposite: If you're not fulfilled by your marriage, you have to justify staying in it, because of the tremendous cultural pressure to be good to one's self.

Our commitment to places is even weaker. We move so often that some sociologists call modern neighborhoods "communities of limited liability," places where people make connections without expecting those links to be deep or lasting.[22] The same is true in the workplace, where employers no longer reward productive employees with career-long positions, and we all know that being self-regarding, self-motivated, and entrepreneurial is the only way to stay afloat. "For the first time in history," write the German sociologists Ulrich Beck and Elisabeth Beck-Gernsheim, "the individual is becoming the basic unit of social reproduction."[23] Everything revolves around it.

• • •

THE CULT OF THE INDIVIDUAL SPREAD gradually across the Western world during the nineteenth and early twentieth centuries. But it made its deepest impressions on modern societies in the West and beyond only in the second half of the twentieth century, when four other sweeping social changes—the rising status of women, the communications revolution, mass urbanization, and the longevity revolution—created conditions in which the individual could flourish.

Begin with the rising status of women, whose advances range from gains in education and massive incorporation into the paid labor force to the right to control their domestic, sexual, and reproductive lives. Consider, for instance, that in 1950 there were more than two men for every woman on American college campuses, whereas today women make up the majority of undergraduate students as well as of those who earn a bachelor's degree.[24] Or the fact that, between 1950 and 2000, the number of working women counted by the U.S. Bureau of Labor Statistics rose from 18 million to 66 million while the proportion of women working jumped from 33 percent to 60 percent.[25] Most other advanced nations have experienced similar changes during the past half century, such that today the level of men's and women's participation in higher education and the paid workforce is more balanced than ever before.

Women's assertion of control over their own bodies has also changed the terms of modern relationships, resulting in delayed marriage, a longer transition to adulthood, and increased rates of separation and divorce. In the United States, divorce rates have climbed steadily since the mid-nineteenth century, but in the 1960s they began to rise sharply, and by 2000 marriages were twice as likely to end in divorce as they were in 1950.[26] Today, neither breaking up with a spouse nor staying single means settling for a life of unwanted abstinence. Rather than settling down, great numbers of young adults indulge in the opportunities afforded by easy access to contraception and freedom from family supervision. The Stanford sociologist Michael Rosenfeld argues that middle-class people in their twenties and thirties now look forward to a "second adolescence" in which they seek out new experiences—from serial dating to interracial and same-sex relationships—and refrain from commitment unless they find their "true romantic love." The new permissiveness around sexual experimentation is an important feature of what Rosenfeld calls our "age of independence." Living alone gives us time and space to discover the pleasures of being with others.[27]

The second driving force behind the cult of the individual is the communications revolution, which has allowed people throughout the world to experience the pleasures of social life—not to mention vast amounts of entertainment—even when they're home alone. The telephone, for instance, is the most common device that we use to stay connected. Home phone service in the United States first became available during the late nineteenth century, yet most Americans were either unwilling or unable to get it. In 1940, only one in three American households had phone service, but demand surged after World War II, with household penetration reaching 62 percent by 1950 and roughly 95 percent today.[28] The television penetrated into American households far more rapidly. In *Bowling Alone*, Robert Putnam reports that between 1948, when the device came on the market, and 1959, home ownership rates for TV went from 1 percent to 90 percent, a pace unmatched by any other major communications technology, including the radio, the VCR, the personal computer, and the mobile phone. Over the past decade, the Internet has further transformed our communications, combining the more active, interpersonal features of the telephone with the more passive, mass communications features of the television. Individual users can not only communicate instantly, at all hours, with friends and strangers, they can also express themselves to a potentially unlimited audience via a blog, a homemade video posted on YouTube, or a social networking site. For those who want to live alone, the Internet affords rich new ways to stay connected.

In the modern world, most people who live alone have another way to connect with each other: simply leaving their home and participating in their city's robust social life. Mass urbanization is the third enabling condition for the rise of the singleton society, in part because it has led to a booming subculture of singles who share similar values, orientations, and ways of life.

Subcultures thrive in cities, which tend to attract nonconformists who are able to find others like themselves in the dense variety of urban life. (That's why we tend to associate subcultures with particular places, from the bohemians of Greenwich Village to the surfers of Manhattan Beach.) When a subculture gets established and becomes visible, it can grow enough to influence or even transform the culture at large. The historian Howard Chudacoff argues that, in the late nineteenth and early twentieth centuries, single men in cities such as Chicago and New York created a new collective lifestyle built around drinking clubs, civic associations, apartment houses, and relatively liberal sexual mores. By the late twentieth century, what was once a distinctive bachelor subculture was such a big part of urban culture in general that the concept lost its salience. Singles, including those who lived alone, didn't have to confine themselves to particular buildings, clubs, neighborhoods, or cities. A growing number of places—gyms, coffee shops, clubs, residential complexes—and services—cleaning, food preparation, home delivery—were being developed with their needs and interests in mind. With some notable exceptions, they could find people who understood their experiences and shared their concerns just about anywhere. Together, as Ethan Watters argues in *Urban Tribes*, they could help each other live alone.[29]

The fourth change that has amplified the cult of the individual is also a collective achievement, but it is rarely experienced that way. Because people are living longer than ever before—or, more specifically, because women often outlive their spouses by decades, rather than years— aging alone has become an increasingly common experience. In 1900, about 10 percent of the widowed elderly in the United States lived alone; by 2000, 62 percent did.[30] Today it's not unusual for women to spend a quarter or a third of their lives in a place of their own, and men are spending a greater share of their adult years living alone, too.

Aging alone is not easy. The ordinary

challenges of growing old—adjusting to retirement, managing illnesses, enduring frailty, watching friends and family die—can become extraordinary hardships for someone who spends most of the time alone. Yet it is not always miserable, either. A survey in England, for instance, found that old people who lived alone had higher life satisfaction, more contact with service providers, and no more cognitive or physical impairments than those who lived with others. And according to a recent review of the literature on aging, studies of the entire elderly population have found that "those living alone are healthier than those living with adults other than a spouse, or even, in some cases, than those living with a spouse."[31] Indeed, in recent decades old people have demonstrated a clear preference for living alone rather than moving in with family or friends or to an institutional home.[32] This, again, is not merely an American phenomenon. From Japan to Germany, Italy to Australia, aging alone has become common, even among ethnic groups that have long exhibited a clear preference for keeping multi-generational homes.[33] Today few people believe that aging alone is an ideal outcome, but most of those who are single as they get older do everything possible to maintain a place of their own.

The question is why. Or more precisely: Why

do so many of us find living alone so much more appealing than other available options? Why has it become so common in the world's most affluent societies? What makes it so compelling for the young, the middle-aged, and the old?

We have embarked on this massive social experiment in living alone because we believe it serves a purpose. Living alone helps us pursue sacred modern values—individual freedom, personal control, and self-realization—whose significance endures from adolescence to our final days. It allows us to do what we want, when we want, on our own terms. It liberates us from the constraints of a domestic partner's needs and demands, and permits us to focus on ourselves. Today, in our age of digital media and ever expanding social networks, living alone can offer even greater benefits: the time and space for restorative solitude. This means that living alone helps us discover who we are, as well as what gives us meaning and purpose.

Paradoxically, living alone might be exactly what we need to reconnect. After all, for most people living alone is a cyclical condition, not a permanent one. Many, though by no means all, of those who live alone ultimately decide they want the intimacy of a domestic partner, whether a lover, family member, or friend. But they, too, know that today none of our arrangements are binding or permanent. We are unmoored from tradition yet uncertain how to remake our lives, and in contemporary societies it has become increasingly common for people to move through different experiences—single, solo, married, separated, partnered, and back—while anchored only by the self.

This means that each person who lives alone is subjected to extraordinary pressures, and at times it can be hard to stave off self-doubt about whether one is living the way one should. But it doesn't mean that those who live alone are condemned to feel lonely or be isolated. On the contrary, the evidence suggests that people who live alone compensate by becoming more socially active than those who live with others, and that cities with high numbers of singletons enjoy a thriving public culture.[34]

IT'S IMPORTANT, even urgent, that we find new and better ways to assist those who suffer from social isolation. But sweeping laments that associate living alone with the end of community and social decline divert attention from this project and do nothing for the people and places that most need help.

Living alone and being alone are hardly the same, yet in recent years journalists, professors, and pundits have routinely conflated them, raising fears that the rise of living alone signals the ultimate atomization of the modern world.

Exhibit A is *The Lonely American*, in which Jacqueline Olds and Richard Schwartz, a married couple who teach psychiatry at Harvard Medical School, warn that "increased aloneness" and "the movement in our country toward greater social isolation" is damaging our health and happiness. The book opens with two blockbuster findings that are meant to support this conclusion. The first, drawn from an article published in an academic journal, reports that between 1985 and 2004 the number of Americans who said they had *no one* with whom they discussed important matters tripled, reaching nearly a quarter of the population.

A quarter of the population! This is an incredible statistic, and the authors of *The Lonely American* were hardly the first to note it. The finding, which came from research by social scientists at Duke University, ran in headlines and framed talk show conversations for weeks after its initial publication. And it would indeed be disturbing, deeply so, if it were reliable. In fact, the social scientists who authored the original article were skeptical of their own numbers, and they cautioned readers—to no avail, alas—that they had probably overstated the prevalence of social isolation. Berkeley sociologist Claude Fischer is even more dismissive. After scrutinizing the evidence, he reported that the paper's claims about

Americans' isolation are implausible, anomalous, and inconsistent with all other research, and he attributes the problem to flaws in the social survey on which it is based. "Scholars and general readers alike should draw no inference from the [survey] as to whether Americans' social networks changed substantially between 1985 and 2004," Fischer concludes. "They probably did not."[35]

The Lonely American is even less careful with its second big claim: that by 2000 about one-quarter of all American households consisted of only one person, and that this reveals how lonely and disconnected we have become. In fact, there's little evidence that the rise of living alone is responsible for making more Americans lonely. Reams of published research show that it's the quality, not the quantity of social interactions, that best predicts loneliness. What matters is not whether we live alone, but whether we feel alone. There's ample support for this conclusion outside the laboratory. As divorced or separated people often say, there's nothing lonelier than living with the wrong person.[36]

This point has also failed to register with the experts who regularly appear in the media to promote marriage and denounce the culture of singlehood. Take *The Case for Marriage*, in which authors Linda Waite and Maggie Gallagher report that, compared to married people, those who live alone (including divorced, widowed, and single people) are less likely to be happy, healthy, and wealthy. "Marriage is good for everyone," they declare, whereas being unmarried "chops almost ten years off a man's life," and "will shorten a woman's life span by more years than would being married and having cancer or living in poverty."[37]

These cautions may well come from good intentions, but they vastly overstate what the research shows. For instance, there is good evidence that people who never marry are just about as happy as people who are currently married, but also significantly happier and less lonely than people who are widowed or divorced. We also have good evidence that bad marriages produce undue stress, strain, and sickness for those who suffer through them; one recent study reports that "individuals in low-quality marriages exhibit an even greater health risk than do divorced individuals."[38] Moreover, as several critics of *The Case for Marriage* have noted, studies comparing the fate of married and unmarried people suffer from a serious problem that makes intuitive (not to mention statistical) sense: namely, that the mental, physical, and financial health of married people may well be the *cause* of their enduring marriage, not the *consequence* of it.

Marriage proponents are not the only ones whose activism can hinder their analysis. On the other side of the spectrum, singles advocates—or defenders, as is often the case—must work so hard to debunk the myths and stereotypes about the unmarried that they have little time or incentive to address the challenges of going solo.[39] For although, as the psychologist Bella DePaulo writes in *Singled Out*, singletons endure all kinds of prejudice and discrimination and "still live happily ever after," they do not do so easily, or always. (After all, who does?) It is important to understand why.

Living alone may not be the social problem that it's generally made out to be, but it generates all kinds of challenges for those who do it, and for those who care for them. The fact that no previous human societies have supported large numbers of people who lived alone means that we have no historical examples to learn from, no precedents to mimic or avoid. This makes understanding what it means to live in a society of singletons all the more important, and our first order of business is to analyze how we got here.

This book begins with a brief account of how the collective project of living alone grew out of the culture of modern cities, not the monastic or transcendental traditions, as we often assume. Cities allowed for the expression of individual eccentricities and permitted the experiments with new ways of living that small towns and villages suppressed. The urban environment, from the hotel residence to the apartment house and the social club, created places where young people who wanted to prolong the transition to adulthood could indulge in all kinds of new experiences while living in places of their own. Eventually middle-age and older adults made use of these same urban amenities, and helped develop new ones, too. By the late twentieth century, they had turned downtown areas throughout the developed world into adult playgrounds, where bars, restaurants, entertainment zones, and a booming commercial street culture encouraged singletons to comingle rather than hunker down at home.

Cities created the conditions that make living alone a more social experience, but they did not provide any answers to the difficult questions that those who pioneered the new lifestyle encountered. The core chapters of this book address these challenges, proceeding in the chronological order through which they typically appear. (This means that the early parts of the book focus on the experiences of younger and more financially secure solo dwellers, while the later parts focus on older and more frail ones.) Drawing on extensive interviews and observations, each chapter explores how people who live alone manage the most common problems that stem from their situation: Learning how to live alone after spending one's early life in a shared household, and struggling to balance one's investment in professional development with one's social and personal needs. Remaking one's life as a singleton after spending years in a marriage or domestic partnership, with little knowledge about how life after separation will feel. Organizing with others to promote the welfare and status of people who live alone as a group. Protecting oneself from the demands of the workplace, the reach of social media, the pull of troubled friends or family members, or what is, for some, the unmanageable pressure of collective life. Aging alone after the loss of a long-term companion. Facing up to the fact that since any one of us could live alone someday, it's in everyone's interest to make it a healthier, happier, more socially engaging experience. And that's a challenge we can only overcome together.

I'VE DONE ENOUGH WRITING and public speaking about the rise of living alone to know that you might already be wondering why I care about this issue, and what the stakes might be for me. After all, most libraries and bookstores are full of polemical tomes in which married people make the case for marriage, or single people make the case for being single, or cynics argue against love altogether. My interest in living alone stems less from my private life (I'm now married with two young children, but was once quite happy living alone) than from a personal response to something I discovered in my research. During the late 1990s, when I was working on a book about the devastatingly lethal Chicago heat wave of 1995, I learned that hundreds of people in America's "city of neighborhoods" had died alone and at home, out of touch with friends, family, and neighbors, and beyond the reach of the local safety net. They died not only because of the weather, but also because they had grown dangerously isolated while the rest of the city turned away from them. Silently, and invisibly, they had developed what one city investigator who worked with them regularly called "a secret society of people who live and die alone." The heat wave was the morbid birth announcement of this society, and the question, once several hundred dead bodies showed up in the center of Chicago and entered public consciousness, was how we would treat the solitary people who'd survived.

Soon after *Heat Wave* was published, someone from the Robert Wood Johnson Foundation asked if I would be interested in following up that study with a larger one, on living alone in America. At first I was reluctant, because my introduction to the topic had been so grim and difficult. But I recognized that I had come to it through its bleakest angle, and decided that by learning the story of how and why so many of us have come to live alone, I might also discover something fundamental about who we are and what we value today. I proposed a research project and, after the foundation agreed to support it, hired a team of research assistants to help with the investigation.[40]

We started in Manhattan, the nation's most popular place for living alone, and eventually expanded to other major American cities: Los Angeles, Chicago, Washington, D.C., Austin, and the San Francisco Bay Area, as well as to other nations where living alone has grown prevalent, such as Sweden, England, France, Australia, and Japan. By the end of this seven-year study, we had conducted in-depth interviews with more than three hundred singletons of all social classes and life stages—though, it's important to note, most people who live alone are financially secure enough to do it, which means our interviews, as well as the analysis I offer here, focus mainly on the experiences of the middle class. To supplement what we learned from these interviews, we also observed places where people live alone together, including residential buildings for affluent young professionals, single-room occupancy dwellings, and assisted living facilities for the elderly. We mined the archives for historical research, social surveys, and market studies about the lifestyles of singles and solo dwellers (since some studies lump them together, for some issues we had to do so as well); and we interviewed scores of others—including caregivers, government officials, architects, and artificial intelligence designers—who are concerned about the fate of the growing number of Americans who live on their own.

We all came to the project with preconceived ideas about what we would discover. Some of us lived alone in our twenties or thirties and viewed having our own place as a mark of distinction or a reward for professional success. One of us worried about widowed grandparents in distant cities who spent untold hours on their own. Another was relieved that their mismatched parents had finally separated and embraced their independence. Another was concerned about the fate of female friends who lived alone and wondered whether they would ever have children. And another was fixated on the plight of the sick and the isolated poor.

A fundamental principle of social research is that we acknowledge our preconceptions but strive to move beyond them. We did our best to honor this rule, and I ask that you do the same as you read this book. I know that this is no simple request. For you, too, possess knowledge of issues related to living alone, and you may have some strong views of your own. Many times during the course of my research, friends and colleagues who felt passionate about this issue urged me to address their own pressing questions.

Some of these questions are deeply personal: Does the rise of living alone stem from or contribute to a growing sense of distrust—of others, of intimate relationships, or of commitments in general? Has it become a strategy of self-defense for those who fear rejection and the pain of separation? Or does it represent a more risky and adventurous lifestyle, one best suited for those who are willing to continually put themselves on the line?

Some questions are sociological: Does living alone mean something different now that we're hyperconnected, through cell phones, social media, and the like? Has the fast growth of living alone among young adults led them to prioritize their personal development and avoid participating in communities and groups? Or has it paved the way for new "urban tribes" to replace the traditional families that, as so many of us know from experience, often break apart? Do the social networks formed by contemporary solo dwellers survive when participants marry, move, grow old, or become ill? If not, what happens to those who stay on their own?

Some questions are political: Will the growing ranks of people who live alone develop a collective identity and, as some prominent strategists believe, establish themselves as a lobbying group or voting bloc? Or will solo living give rise to political atomization, with each person promoting his or her own interests or looking out for his or her own needs? Will the nations where aging alone has become rampant invest in social programs that help those who become isolated, frail, and sick? What fate awaits us if we don't?

For many of us, the mere thought of living alone sparks anxieties about isolation, and not without reason. But although it's clear that for certain people, in certain conditions, living alone can lead to loneliness, unhappiness, sickness, or worse, it's also clear that it need not have such disastrous effects.

Today more and more people are seeking ways to flourish despite—or is it because of?—the solitude they can achieve at home: young professionals who can afford to have their own places and prefer domestic autonomy to having roommates; singles in their thirties and forties who refuse to compromise in their search for a partner, in no small part because they recognize and enjoy the benefits (personal, social, and sexual) of living alone; divorced men and women whose previous experiences in relationships ended the fantasy that romantic love is a reliable source of happiness and stability; elderly people who, following the death of a spouse, rebuild their lives through new friendships, social groups, and activities, and take pride in their ability to live alone.

Though each of these situations is distinctive, those who confront them share a common challenge: They must not only solve the puzzle of how to live alone, but also of how to live well. In this they are in good company, and all of us—no matter where we are or whether we live with someone at this moment—can learn from their answers.

1.
GOING SOLO

O N SEPTEMBER 30, 2007, the Non-Committals won the championship of the Brooklyn Kickball Invitational Tournament, defeating Prison under the lights of Greenpoint's McCarren Park. The teams were comprised mostly of young middle-class adults in their twenties and thirties who played regularly in a local league, but competitors came from as far as Providence, Washington, D.C., Atlanta, and Toronto. Today there are booming kickball clubs in Maui, Miami, Dallas, Denver, San Diego, and Seattle. The World Adult Kickball Association, which hosted seventy-two teams and 1,500 players at its 2009 Founders Cup in Las Vegas, calls the game "the new American pastime." That's clearly a misnomer, however, since the group has also helped organize leagues in England and India and is eagerly seeking additional outposts.

It's hard not to interpret the surprising popularity of this childhood game as a symbol of the historically new life stage that sociologists call second adolescence. This period of pro-longed development on the path to adulthood is growing increasingly common in affluent nations, where young adults are growing ever more committed to Non-Committal Living, as the Brooklyn champs would put it. In Chicago, for instance, one organization's ads for a kickball league claim, "Recess was never this much fun!" and its campaign for a dodgeball league—what else?—promises, "As an adult you can relive the glory days on the playground!" In some places, games reproduce the college fraternity experience as well as elementary school days. During "sloshball" competitions, ESPN reports, players must hold a beer at all times and runners cannot advance until they shotgun a beer. In New York City, games are played in the epicenter of Brooklyn hipster culture, and instead of engaging in frat house behavior, participants act like natives, going straight from the ball field to the barroom, where they'll listen to indy rock bands till early the next day. At season's end they gather in Greenpoint for the Kickball Prom.[1]

Playing children's games on weekends is not the only way that today's young adults revisit adolescence. They stay in school longer than did previous generations, knowing that the job market rewards them for being both well trained and flexible, and guessing that it's unwise to commit too hastily to a career path or to a corporation that will not commit to them. They delay marriage and having children and spend years engaging in casual sex or serial dating, often remaining skeptical that an intimate relationship can last a lifetime. They chat on instant message and social network sites, play video games, share music online. Those younger than twenty-five even move back in with their families, frequently enough to be labeled the "boomerang generation" by journalists and sociologists.

But viewed historically, the "boomerang" label is undeserved, as is the view that by indulging in a second adolescence young adults are neglecting to grow up. "It is widely believed that young adults are more likely to live with their parents now than ever before," writes sociologist Michael Rosenfeld.[2] But in fact, he notes, compared to previous generations they are far more likely to establish themselves in a home of their own. While it's true that the prevalence of people ages twenty-five to thirty-four living with their parents has gone up since 1960, the increase has been modest: from 11 percent to 14 percent for men, and from 7 percent to 8 percent for women.[3] The more significant change in the culture of young adults involves breaking away from their family home. Consider, for instance, that only 1 percent of people ages eighteen to twenty-nine lived alone in 1950, while 7 percent do today, or that 11 percent of people ages twenty to twenty-nine lived apart from their parents back then, whereas today more than 40 percent do. (Not all of them live alone, but leaving home is a necessary condition for doing so.)[4] "The increase in this type of living arrangement has grown astonishingly since 1970," observe demographers Elizabeth Fussell and Frank Furstenberg Jr., marking "a new sort of independence from family with significant social meaning."[5]

This is an understatement. In recent decades a growing number of twenty- and thirtysomethings have come to view living alone as a key part of the transition to adulthood. In the large urban areas where it is most common, many young professionals see having one's own home as a mark of distinction and view living with roommates or parents as undesirable at best.

Living alone offers several advantages: It grants sexual freedom and facilitates experimentation. It gives time to mature, develop, and search for true romantic love. It liberates young adults from difficult roommates, including good friends who turn out to be better friends when they are not always in the next room. It enables them to socialize when and how they want to, and to focus on themselves as much as they need.

Why did the practice of living alone grow so popular among young adults, and how did it turn from a sign of social failure to a rite of passage and a reward for success? To answer these questions we need to look more closely at how the public life of cities and, more specifically, the subculture of singles encouraged new forms of individualism. For the urban bohemians who first experimented with solo living in neighborhoods like Greenwich Village did something that they hadn't intended: They pioneered a lifestyle whose broad appeal would ultimately bring it into the mainstream. We also need to examine the private lives of families, because changes in the way we relate to one another inside the home have led more of us to grow comfortable in a place of our own. First, though, we should step back to see what we might call the "old" cult of the individual, if only to establish how different it is from the individualism we find in cities today.

THE CONTEMPORARY VIEW of living alone as a productive experience grew out of a rich historical legacy. The monastic tradition, which has roots in ancient China, Egypt, and Syria, valorized asceticism as a path to knowledge and a meaningful life. According to monastic teachings, separating from society is the most powerful way to get closer to the divine. This is why the fourth-century hermit Abba Moses issued his famous instruction: "Go, sit in your cell, and your cell will teach you everything."

In practice, however, few hermits were true solitaries. Whether in the desert or on the outskirts of a town, they typically lived in settlements shared by other men and congregated with them for a variety of purposes. The historian Peter Brown writes that in Egypt, where "the theory and practice of ascetic life reached its highest pitch of articulateness and sophistication . . . [g]roups had to reproduce exactly, on the fringe of the desert, the closed-in, embattled aspect of the fortified villages"; he notes further that "the monastery of Pachomius was called quite simply The Village." In ancient China, writes the Asia scholar Aat Vervoorn, the earliest versions of eremitism were secular and philosophical rather than religious, and the lifestyle involved not renouncing society so much as "a lack of regard for those things of the world that are common objects of human action, such as wealth, power, and fame."[6]

Over the centuries, these traditions have evolved and mutated as much as they have traveled. Today we find traces of the old cult of the individual in romantic ideals that emphasize solitude as a return to nature, in the spirit of Thoreau or John Muir; as a path to the sacred, as for Thomas Merton or Hesse's Siddhartha; or, as the psychologist Anthony Storr put it, as a return to the creative self.[7] These are all influential perspectives, and they no doubt fed the stream of ideas that gave rise to the belief that living alone is important for becoming an autonomous adult. But they also share a decidedly antiurban and antisocial bias, and are in many ways antithetical to the practice of living alone in the city. To find the sources of our contemporary ways of settling down, we must look beyond the traditions of the monastery and toward those of the modern metropolis.

"The metropolis," wrote the German sociologist Georg Simmel, "assures the individual of a type and degree of personal freedom to which there is no analogy in other circumstances." Simmel was born in Berlin in 1858, when the population was about 460,000, and during his lifetime he witnessed it grow to more than 2 million people. Many of his contemporaries, particularly those who participated in the romanticist movement against modernity, lamented the moral and cultural changes wrought by urbanization. But Simmel doubted that the less urban life was more virtuous or meaningful. He rebuked those, like Nietzsche and Ruskin, who believed that cities crushed the individual spirit. "Small-town life," he argued, "imposed such limits upon the movements of the individual in his relationships with the outside world and on his inner independence and differentiation that the modern person could not even breathe under such conditions." The city, by contrast, offered possibilities for "social evolution," because in it "the individual's horizon is enlarged" and he "gains a freedom of movement beyond the first jealous delimitation" of the family or the religious community. In the city, the individual could participate in any of the emerging social groups, or subcultures, that matched his preferences and interests.[8]

What evolved from this new social landscape, Simmel claimed, was a new, "metropolitan type" of individual, with a rational and intellectual orientation to the world, a deep psychological life, and a cool, blasé attitude that he designated as "reserve." City dwellers were hardly inhibited. On the contrary, Simmel insisted that modern urban culture liberated residents and allowed them to cultivate the very parts of themselves that the village had repressed. "Individual freedom," he wrote, "is not only to be understood in the negative sense as mere freedom of movement and emancipation from prejudices and philistinism. Its essential characteristic is rather to be found in the fact that the particularity and incomparability which ultimately every person possesses is actually expressed, giving form to life . . . We follow the laws of our inner nature—and this is what freedom is."[9]

For city dwellers at the turn of the twentieth century, being liberated from the tight grip of the family, the constraints of religious traditions, and the surveilling eyes of a small-town community was exhilarating. It's often argued that modern urban culture helped usher in an era of great creativity and aesthetic experimentation, giving rise to avant-garde movements such as surrealism, Dadaism, and the Bauhaus. But modern cities induced extraordinary innovations in what Simmel called the everyday techniques of living, too, because they rewarded residents who gave up old habits and acculturated to the new social scene. While the aesthetes declared that they were treating "art as life," even the less eccentric urbanites began to experience life as art, remaking themselves, their communities, and their homes to suit their "inner natures," pushing back against "the concrete institutions" that the city and the state were already rebuilding.

From today's perspective, the act of taking a place of one's own does not appear especially "peculiar" or "extreme" (to use Simmel's terms), but at the turn of the century it was a bold and provocative way to use one's social liberties. Not that young single adults were uncommon in the late nineteenth century, when young workers were abandoning their native towns to seek jobs in metropolitan areas. In 1890, the proportion of young single men (ages fifteen to thirty-four) living in large American cities was higher than it would be until about 1990, and at the time the average age of first marriage was also higher than it would be for another century, roughly twenty-six for American men and twenty-two for American women. The fact that these are averages means that many delayed marriage until they were even older. In 1900, fully one-third of all native-born American white men between the ages of twenty-five and thirty-four were single, as were half of all native white men that age in New York City. Hardly any of these bachelors lived alone, however. About half of all unmarried men, and a greater proportion of unmarried women, lived with their family (just as they do in parts of Southern Europe and in many developing nations today). Nearly all of those who left their family home to work in a distant neighborhood or city rented a room from another family or, to the growing dismay of social workers and sociologists, moved into a rooming house.[10]

ROOMING HOUSES, which were known as "plain hotels for plain people," were precursors to the small, private apartments that would ultimately house single urban residents. They were popular among people in skilled trades who made a steady but modest income and wanted to escape surveillance, but their abundance and accessibility made them attractive for many migrants to the city. "Hotel life," writes the architectural historian Paul Groth, could be "virtually untouched by the social contract and tacit supervision of life found in a family house or apartment unit shared with a group."[11] This fact aroused great anxiety among moral reformers of all stripes, who feared that living outside a family home would lead to isolation and a host of social problems.

Solo living was said to be dangerous for men because it made them selfish and vulnerable to wanton impulses, and for women because it made them lonely, hysterical, and depressed. As early as 1856, the poet Walt Whitman authored "Wicked Architecture," an essay in which he listed the personal consequences of boarding-house life as: "listlessness; emptiness; sloth; nerves; dyspepsia; flirtations; prodigality; vain show; perhaps—often, might we not say?—immorality, nay, infamy." Fifty years later, a well-known Protestant minister warned that the rooming house system was "stretching out its arms like an octopus to catch the unwary soul." And in his classic 1929 field study *The Gold Coast and the Slum*, University of Chicago sociologist Harvey Zorbaugh lamented that the typical rooming house has "no dining room, no parlor, no common meeting place. Few acquaintanceships spring up in a rooming-house . . . The keeper of the rooming-house has no personal contact with, or interest in, his roomers."[12]

Along with many of his contemporaries in the social sciences, Zorbaugh argued that living without a domestic partner was one of the key urban conditions that generated "personal disorganization" and "social anomie." To illustrate the point, he offered statistics that showed a concentration of suicides in the neighborhoods where boardinghouses were common as well as a series of horrific stories from the "world of furnished rooms." In the story of a "charity girl," a young woman from Emporia, Kansas, moves into a rooming house when she arrives in Chicago at age twenty-two to attend music school. She reports that it is impossible to make friends there, and within a few months of her arrival " 'my loneliness amounted almost to desperation.' " The "charity girl" endures a series of horrors. Her mother dies. Her father won't talk to her because she has moved to the city. Her music teacher blithely tells her she's not good enough to really make it. And she has no one to comfort her, not even the other souls who share her home. " 'I began to look at my life in Chicago. What was there in it, after all? My music was gone. I had neither family nor friends.' " For Zorbaugh, this was a parable about the dangers of urbanization. " 'The city is like that,' " he quoted her as saying, and added his own conclusion: "Such complete anonymity could be found nowhere but in the city of today, and nowhere in the city save in the rooming-house."[13]

Some city dwellers relished this anonymity, however, because it liberated them to live by their own "inner laws." In another classic study from the University of Chicago, *The Ghetto*, sociologist Louis Wirth explained that in the early twentieth century a number of Jewish hotels popped up in Chicago to house Jews who wanted to escape the confines of their local community. During the same era in New York City, writes one historian, "the first full-blown generation of American moderns" moved to Greenwich Village so they could enjoy "life without a father" (to use Gertrude Stein's phrase) and forge "a community of dissidents who prided themselves on living a life apart." Villagers took up a great variety of personal, political, and aesthetic causes. But, as Ross Wetzsteon argues in his neighborhood history *Republic of Dreams*, they were motivated by one common aspiration: "the liberated self."[14]

The Village of the early twentieth century was famous for its intellectuals, artists, activists, and eccentrics, including celebrated figures such as Georgia O'Keeffe, Emma Goldman, Eugene O'Neill, Alfred Stieglitz, Walter Lippmann, Claude McKay, and Eleanor Roosevelt. But even the more ordinary Villagers enjoyed the freedoms available in what the historian

Christine Stansell calls "the cradle of liberated personae," a place where "closeted identities can come out of their hiding places" and all variety of individuals could "foster more fully realized selves." Women's ability to find work in the paid labor market was a key part of this self-actualization, because it gave them a degree of financial autonomy, as well as a way to break out of the domestic sphere. The community, Stansell continues, nurtured "a population of single women supporting themselves outside traditional family situations . . . Ladies went to work by themselves every day. They rode streetcars alone," and their discussions focused "on how women might live outside traditional domestic roles." Whether in New York, Chicago, London, or Paris, experiments like these spawned a new story line in the day's novels. "The pleasures and dangers of being alone in the city excited the imagination of female contemporaries," writes Judith Walkowitz. "Heroines," adds Stansell, "lit by the high ambitions of their generation, set out to prove themselves in the world, rejecting romantic love, determined to find new stories for themselves beyond marriage."[15]

The bohemian culture of the Village was not entirely due to the spirit of its residents. The neighborhood's spatial arrangements—its narrow, windy streets; its intimate cafés, salons, and saloons; its great central gathering place,

Washington Square Park—provided both privacy for personal experimentation and a zone for self-expression and public display. At the beginning of the twentieth century the area had a great number of tenement buildings that warehoused large families. But over the next few decades builders developed an ample supply of small, relatively inexpensive residential units in rooming houses and apartment buildings, which enabled the modern men and women of "the place where everything happens first" to live alone. In 1917, the year that Marcel Duchamp and friends ascended the Washington Square Arch and declared the area "a free and independent republic," the writer Anna Alice Chapin identified a building nearby as "the first all-bachelor apartment house erected in town. It is appropriately called 'the Benedick' [from Shakespeare's *Much Ado About Nothing*], after a certain young man who scoffed at matrimony." By the 1920s developers were converting single-family houses and tenements into one- or two-room apartments, and women as well as men rushed to fill them.[16]

The sources of this demand are not hard to identify. Between 1920 and 1930, the population of children under age fourteen in the Village dropped by around 50 percent. By 1930, about half of the adult men in the Village were unmarried, as were 40 percent of all women.

These changes were consistent with the general population trends for New York City, but they happened faster in the Village, and in more exaggerated fashion. In a decade, the community of families had turned into an urban enclave for adults, particularly for singles. A growing vanguard lived alone, and the rest of the city would soon follow its lead.[17]

Like the bohemians, gay men at the turn of the twentieth century also moved to cities and sought housing that would free them from supervision and social control. The historian George Chauncey has documented how gay friends in New York City helped each other identify places where landlords and neighbors were tolerant, recruiting other gay men for adjoining units, lest someone more judgmental and intrusive move in. Rooming houses were especially attractive, not only because they maintained a culture of privacy, but also because they allowed residents to pay by the day or week, which made them easy to abandon if something went wrong. Chauncey reports that certain hotel residences in Manhattan attracted large numbers of gay men, as did the apartment houses where, as one analyst put it, "your neighbor is just a number on the door." Entire neighborhoods—in Greenwich Village, Chelsea, Hell's Kitchen, the East Fifties and Sixties—became gay enclaves, organized around bars, cafeterias, cheap restaurants, literary societies, and community centers that helped men support each other in the quest to define themselves. By the 1920s, these areas had established reputations as places where people of all sexual persuasions could come together to enjoy their autonomy, without worrying too much about whether anyone else was watching.[18]

In fact, before long, people went to New York City's bohemian, bachelor, and gay neighborhoods precisely so that they could watch, if not participate in, their distinctive subcultural scenes. It is well known that during the Harlem Renaissance middle-class whites traveled uptown for a taste of the neighborhood's exotic jazz clubs and intoxicating nightlife; so too did they go downtown to sample the Village's bohemian offerings. The Village attracted visitors at all hours, but at night its busy streets and buzzing cultural institutions transformed the area into a theater of the new, modern lifestyle, and an adventuresome audience from the city and beyond flocked to the site. This is precisely what happens when a city's public life is robust: Strangers meet in a densely packed, diverse social environment. The stage and street merge. A new public geography develops. And then, as Richard Sennett argues in *The Fall of Public Man*, "the imaginative limits of a person's consciousness [a]re expanded . . . because the imagination of what is real, and therefore believable, is not tied down to a verification of what is routinely felt by the self."[19] The idea that one could live quite socially while keeping a place of one's own shifts from being strange and unimaginable to being tantalizing and concrete.

Just as white middle-class exposure to African American music, dance, art, and literature during the Harlem Renaissance began to nudge blacks from the margins to the mainstream of U.S. popular culture, so too did the middle-class engagement with the world of bachelors and bohemians plant the seeds for the slow growth of new ideals about how to live. This is not to say that great numbers of Americans, or even New Yorkers, suddenly abandoned their aspirations to settle down in a traditional relationship. In fact, between the 1920s and the 1950s the dominant practice among young adults involved making a quick and early start to domestic life, and the average age of first marriage dropped by about two years for men (from 24.6 to 22.8) and one year for women (from 21.2 to 20.3). But during those same decades an alternative lifestyle—modern, independent, and single—was sprouting up in cities like New York, Chicago, Los Angeles, San Francisco, and Seattle. "New Women," as the most liberated called themselves, were at the forefront of the change.

• • •

"THE SINGLE WOMAN, far from being a creature to be pitied and patronized, is emerging as the newest glamour girl of our times . . . She is engaging because she lives by her wits. She supports herself. She has had to sharpen her personality and mental resources to a glitter in order to survive in a competitive world and the sharpening looks good. Economically, she is a dream. She is not a parasite, a dependent, a scrounger, a sponger or a bum. She is a giver, not a taker, a winner and not a loser."[20]

In 1962, a forty-year-old named Helen Gurley Brown published these words in her slim, sensational bestseller *Sex and the Single Girl*. Brown, who went on to edit *Cosmopolitan* for more than three decades, had humble origins. She spent her early childhood in the Ozark Mountains of Arkansas, but moved to Los Angeles at age ten after her father died. She was raised by her mother; her family was poor, and her sister had polio. Brown, who supported them, developed a firsthand appreciation for the struggles and aspirations of working women in her generation. She attended a small business college, found clerical work in a talent agency, and shifted into advertising when she was hired as a secretary. She gradually moved up the ranks, becoming one of the industry's most accomplished copywriters before branching out into journalism.

Sex and the Single Girl, which came out a year before Betty Friedan's *The Feminine Mystique*, was the kind of feminist tract that scandalized and alienated a great many feminists. For it was written not against what Friedan famously called "the problem with no name"—inequality of the sexes, generated through discrimination at home, in the courts, in politics, and in the workforce—but for women who felt oppressed by the overwhelming social pressure to settle down early, forgoing years of experimentation, growth, and pleasure to get a marriage license for a domestic life that they might not need or want. Brown insisted that young women should enjoy their best years without a husband. "A single woman's biggest problem is coping with the people who are trying to marry her off!" she argued, while marriage should be "insurance for the worst years of your life."

Brown's book was "not a study on how to get married but how to stay single—in superlative style."[21] She offered her own life as Exhibit A. *Sex and the Single Girl* opens with Brown's account of how, by delaying marriage until age thirty-seven, she wound up with a smart and sexy husband who worked in the movie business, two Mercedes in the driveway, and a big house overlooking the Pacific Ocean. It was not easy to maintain her autonomy, Brown admitted. During her twenties and early thirties she watched her contemporaries rush into wedlock, often settling for men whose flaws were readily apparent. "Although many's the time I was sure I would die alone in my spinster's bed, I could never bring myself to marry just to get married." Instead, she worked doggedly to advance in her career. She developed a fierce aggression and a unique style that she was willing to "get out in the open." None of this, according to Brown, required great beauty, wealth, or a high-voltage personality. It simply demanded guts, conviction, and the fortitude to live alone.

Brown did mean alone. "Roommates," she insisted, "are for sorority girls. You need an apartment alone even if it's over a garage." The benefits of going solo were innumerable. With a home of one's own, a single woman could have time and space to cultivate her self without the social pressure of family or friends. She could work late without worrying anyone, "furnish her mind" through reading, change her appearance as she saw fit. Most of all, she gained privacy, and with that the freedom to experience a more adventurous, libidinous life. The single girl "has a better sex life than most of her married friends," Brown claimed (albeit without providing any evidence). "She need never be bored with one man per lifetime. Her choice of partners is endless and they seek her."[22]

The private apartment, writes the literature

scholar Sharon Marcus, became a powerful symbol of the new urban culture during the 1960s because it "offered the single girl an eroticized arena in which to exercise her creativity and promote her own creative comforts."[23] But few single women expected to maintain this arena for long. Brown, after all, proposed living alone not as a means to subverting marriage but rather as a means to improving it. "Serving time as a single woman," she counseled, "can give you the foundation for a better marriage if you finally go that route." It could also prepare a modern woman for the possibility that, even if she married, she would one day find herself on her own again, since "a man can leave a woman at fifty (though it may cost him some dough) as surely as you can leave dishes in the sink."[24]

Indeed, when Brown wrote *Sex and the Single Girl*, a nascent cultural movement was pushing men to do precisely this, promoting a new bachelor lifestyle that repudiated marriage and family altogether. The movement had an outlet in *Playboy* magazine, an iconic leader in Hugh Hefner, its publisher and editor, and a totem in the bunny ears that signaled men's endorsement of a new way of living. "I don't want my editors marrying anyone and getting a lot of foolish notions in their heads about 'togetherness,' home, family, and all that jazz," said Hefner. His magazine did everything possible to discourage readers from getting those notions, too.

Playboy condemned conventional domestic life but embraced a new kind of masculine domesticity. "Throughout the 1950s and 1960s," writes Bill Osgerby in the *Journal of Design History*, "*Playboy* spotlighted a series of luxurious 'Playboy Pads'—both actual buildings and fantasy blueprints—tailored to the outlook and tastes of the hip 'man about town.' " In *The Hearts of Men*, Barbara Ehrenreich argues that the magazine's ideological project involved "reclaiming the indoors as a realm for masculine pleasure." Its not so subtle message to readers: Abandon, all ye who open these pages, your suburban home, your station wagon, your controlling wife. Return to the great city. Get a place of your own and fill it with modern luxuries: fine liquor, modern art, hip clothing, a stereo, leather furniture, a king-size bed, and the greatest pleasure of all—beautiful, available women.[25]

"*Playboy* loved women," Ehrenreich writes. "Large-breasted, long-legged young women, anyway—and it hated wives." Marilyn Monroe graced the cover of its first issue, which also included an attack on alimony and a story about "Miss Gold Digger of 1953." Hundreds, eventually thousands of women posed nude for its centerfold spreads and photo features.

Producers of high-end men's products bought ad space so that their brands would be associated with the lifestyle Hefner advocated.

Real women were welcome in a playboy's private home, particularly if they were the "fun-loving," nubile, liberated kind that the magazine celebrated. Hefner surrounded himself with "bunnies," first in a Chicago apartment and eventually in the famous Los Angeles mansion, and he took on several lovers at a time. His policy was always straightforward: Women could visit, spend a night or many more. But they shouldn't get too comfortable, seek emotional commitment, or expect him to settle down. His bed may have been open, but in the end it was his alone.

NOT THAT HE HAD TO MAKE IT. By the 1970s both sexes benefitted from the dramatic expansion of the service economy, including home cleaning, child care, elder care, food delivery, even laundry. Drawing on data from the Bureau of Labor Statistics, the sociologist Susan Thistle has shown that, since the 1970s, "the conversion of women's domestic tasks into work done for pay has . . . been the area of greatest job growth." There's a simple reason for this: Record numbers of women have been moving into the paid labor market. In 1950, about one in three of all adult women participated in the civilian labor market; by 1980, more than one half did.[26]

Women with more education entered the workplace at an even faster rate. Employment for those who had completed some college went from 51 percent to 67 percent during the 1970s, and from 61 percent to 74 percent among those who had earned a college degree. As these women left their invisible jobs as uncompensated domestic workers they generated new demand for other people, mainly women, who could replace them. The personal services industry has grown ever since.

Although women's wages lagged behind men's (and still do), their rapid entry into the paid labor market made it far easier for them to achieve independence than ever before. The average age of first marriage, which rose slowly during the 1960s, jumped considerably in the 1970s, from twenty-one to twenty-two for women and from twenty-three to twenty-five for men. Adults didn't only delay marriage during the tumultuous decade, they also terminated it at unprecedented rates. In 1970, about 700,000 American couples divorced, a high figure compared to the 393,000 divorces in 1960 and the 385,000 in 1950. But 1980 was unprecedented, with roughly 1.2 million divorces. Demographers calculated that the divorce rate had jumped 50 percent during the 1970s, and they marveled at the startling fact that 25 percent of all marriages that took place in 1970 had been terminated by 1977.[27]

The nation had experienced a divorce revolution, and the transformation wasn't due solely to women's increased participation in the labor market. It was also fueled by an emerging moral code that placed one's obligation to care for the self on par with, if not above, one's commitment to family. "Beginning in the 1950s," argues Barbara Dafoe Whitehead in *The Divorce Culture*, Americans "became more acutely conscious of their responsibility to attend to their own individual needs and interests . . . People began to judge the strength and 'health' of family bonds according to their capacity to promote individual fulfillment and personal growth," rather than on more traditional measures, such as income, security, or class mobility.[28] Scholars in Europe identified a similar shift. The British sociologist Anthony Giddens argues that once women achieved economic independence, couples began to seek "pure relationships," which are "free floating" and not anchored in traditional financial or social constraints. The modern marriage, he writes, "becomes more and more a relationship initiated for, and kept going for as long as, it delivers emotional satisfaction to be derived from close contact with another."[29] When it fails to do so, as marriage often does during hard times, individuals feel an obligation to justify sustaining it, because divorce is a readily available option. By the 1970s, more people began to act as if their quest for personal happiness—whether as a playboy, a liberated woman, or simply a "single"—trumped all other obligations. During that decade, writes David Sarasohn, "the freedom to hop from one relationship to the next was as essential as anything in the Bill of Rights."[30] Finding a place of one's own was the best way to achieve it.

During the 1960s and '70s the housing market aided the search for autonomy, with inventory expanding much faster than the population, particularly in central cities, where middle-class families were fleeing.[31] The urban crisis, as it came to be known, proved itself an opportunity for unmarried adults seeking their own apartments in metropolitan settings. In most big cities, middle-class individuals could easily find affordable rental units, and as they clustered together in places of their own they forged neighborhood cultures organized around single life: Lincoln Park in Chicago. The Marina District in San Francisco. West Hollywood in Los Angeles. Belltown in Seattle. These weren't bohemias or gay enclaves, but places for urban professionals, the young and never married as well as divorcees. They were full of apartment buildings, both new and newly renovated, to meet the needs of an increasingly individuated marketplace. Solo living was suddenly in vogue.

Consider how many people were doing it. In 1960, about 7 million Americans lived alone, but by the end of the decade more than 4 million others had joined them, making for some 11 million one-person households in the United States. During the 1970s the ranks rose faster and higher than ever before, topping 18 million in 1980.[32] The increase was particularly sharp in cities. In Manhattan, for instance, the proportion of residential units with just one resident went from 35 percent in 1960 to 46 percent in 1980, and the proportional rise was even greater in Los Angeles, Chicago, Dallas, Seattle, and San Francisco. The numbers of people living alone has continued to increase since the 1970s. It rose slowly during the 1980s and 1990s, then soared in the 2000s. Today more than 5 million Americans under thirty-five have places of their own.

MANY OF THE YOUNG ADULTS who live alone were brought up to do so. Not explicitly, since all children share their home with a family or adults of some sort, and schools do not promote living alone as a goal. But today an unprecedented number of children around the world develop the capacity and desire to live independently through another, historically novel experience: growing up in a room of one's own.

Traditionally, most children in the same family shared a room with each other, if not with their parents. This was true, of course, for the children of immigrant families who lived in urban tenements, and of African American children whose families packed into apartments after migrating to the northern states. But, until recently, it was also true of native-born white middle-class families, and even of some affluent ones. According to the U.S. Census, in 1960 the average family household had 2.4 children and 0.7 bedrooms per child. Since then, American families have become smaller and homes have grown larger. By 1980 the average household had 2 children and 1 bedroom per child, and in 2000 it had 1.9 children and 1.1 bedrooms per child—meaning it is common for American kids to have not only their own room, but perhaps even some claim on another one. Indeed, the size of a typical American home more than doubled between 1950 and 2000, rising from 983 square feet to more than 2,200.[33] Today in many middle-class communities parents feel negligent if they don't provide a private bedroom for each of their children. Adults who love living in city centers will leave for the suburbs so they can give their children private space. Once a luxury, in recent years it has become an entitlement of middle-class life.

Whether in cities or suburbs, today's children

also spend an unprecedented amount of time home alone, preparing their own snacks or meals and planning their own leisure time, because it's increasingly common for both of their parents to spend their weekdays at work. According to "Latchkey Kids," a report by the William Gladden Foundation, by 2005 somewhere between 10 million and 15 million American children under age sixteen were regularly taking care of themselves after school or during summer vacations. "More children today have less adult supervision than ever before in American history," the report claims, and many "begin their self-care at about age eight."[34]

The rise of latchkey kids and private rooms within the home is an international phenomenon. In Europe, the dramatic decline in fertility rates over the past fifty years has transformed the experience of domestic space. Between 1960 and 2000, the average number of people per household fell from 3.1 to 2.3 in England, from 3.1 to 2.4 in France, from 3.8 to 2.6 in Germany, from 3.6 to 2.6 in Italy, and from 2.8 to 2.1 in Denmark. The trends are similar in Canada, where between 1960 and 2005 the average household size dropped from 4 to 2.5; in Japan, where from 1975 to 2005 it went from 3.3 to 2.5; and in the United States, where it plummeted from nearly 5 in 1900 to 3 in 1950 and 2.6 in 2000.[35] In nearly all of these nations, the shrinking family has coincided with the extraordinary physical growth of the house and the apartment. By the late twentieth century, people throughout the developed world could be together at home with their family, but also alone.

Today, of course, we no longer need private rooms to separate into individual environments. Entire families can sit together, and even share a meal, while each member is immersed in an iPhone or a laptop rather than in conversation with those nearby. But the availability of a domestic private sphere for each person in a middle-class residence changed the norms of family interaction long before the advent of social media. In her comparative study of child-rearing practices among different class groups in the United States, sociologist Annette Lareau noticed that in the typical middle-class family, each child has his or her own room, and "except for times when they share meals (this happens only once every few days), parents and children are rarely all together in the same room." Instead, family life is organized around the needs and interests of each individual, parents and children included. The children do not belong to the same sports teams, play the same instruments, or hang out with the same friends, so the family develops a schedule that allows each one to be dropped off and picked up on his or her own. The parents do everything to promote "the individual development of each child," and in the process the children "learn to think of themselves as special and as entitled." But they also grow hostile toward and competitive with their siblings. For although the middle-class children rarely engage in face-to-face interaction with each other, Lareau observes, "references to 'hating' a family member are common and elicit no special reaction."[36] Things are calmer when everyone keeps to himself.

In an influential 1958 essay, the psychologist and pediatrician Donald Winnicott argued, paradoxically, that "the capacity to be alone is based on the experience of being alone in the presence of someone, and that without a sufficiency of this experience the capacity to be alone cannot develop." Specifically, Winnicott was referring to the infant and mother relationship, and to the developmental process through which a young child learns to feel secure on his or her own and self-contained when with others, because the reliable presence of the mother conveys the sense that the environment is benign and allows for healthy attachments. This process may well still be important, but children who grew up in the decades after Winnicott published his essay have had more opportunities to cultivate an ability to be alone—and not only because so many had private bedrooms.

One striking cultural change related to the rise of private bedrooms concerns the way child psychologists advise parents to help their infants sleep. For most of human history, mothers and infants slept together; today, the great majority of the world's mothers and children still do. The biological anthropologist James McKenna, who directs the Mother-Baby Behavioral Sleep Lab at Notre Dame University, argues that in the process of evolution mothers developed an innate capacity to attend to the needs of their sleeping children, even when they themselves are in deep sleep. While many cultures have used cradles to support sleeping babies, the crib was not widely marketed to or used by middle-class families until the twentieth century. Initially, babies who slept in cribs were placed near their mothers, close to or right next to the family bed. But in late 1946 a pediatrician named Benjamin Spock published *The Common Sense Book of Baby and Child Care*, in which (among other things) he advised parents to place newborns in rooms of their own so that they could learn to sleep independently, while also giving Mom and Dad some privacy and peace.[37]

It's hard to measure the impact of a few lines in an advice book, but this, of course, was no ordinary publication. *The Common Sense Book of Baby and Child Care* went on to sell more than 50 million copies in thirty-nine languages, placing it among the bestselling books of all time. By the 1950s, "Dr. Spock" had become the modern world's clear authority on child care and development, and his views on a great variety of issues—including sleep training for infants—commanded the attention of countless doctors and parents. In 2000, the chairwoman of the U.S. Consumer Product Safety Commission was using her office to advise all parents to avoid sleeping with children under the age of two. And she did so with the full support of Dr. Spock's successors: "sleep scientists" and child psychologists whose views on the value of individuating sleeping infants could be extreme.

In the 1986 bestseller *Solve Your Child's Sleep Problems*, for instance, Richard Ferber reports, "We know for a fact that people sleep better alone in bed." Parents, he acknowledges, may be tempted to give in to their infants' desires to be near them when they slumber, and some may even "feel this is in their children's best interests." But he believes they are mistaken: "Sleeping alone is an important part of his learning to be able to separate from you without anxiety and to see himself as an independent individual." Ferber has tough words for parents who resist his advice: "If you find that you prefer to have your child in your bed, you should examine your own feelings very carefully," since it's possible that "instead of helping your child you are using him to avoid facing and solving your own problems . . . If these problems cannot be simply settled, then professional counseling may be required."[38] Some parents were indeed put off by the harshness of the "Ferber method," but millions of others bought his books and steeled themselves for the experience of "Ferberizing" their children. In the process, they helped acculturate the next generation to the experience of being alone.

After growing up in a private bedroom with plenty of personal time, an increasing number of young adults want to maintain the condition when they leave home for the first time—even, or perhaps especially, if they are going to college. Housing officers at universities throughout the country report that a great majority of their entering students have never shared a bedroom and that many have trouble adjusting to life with a roommate during their first year. Once that year is finished, they're willing to pay extra to restore their privacy. On today's university campuses, the newest dormitories have an ample supply of single rooms, as well as suite-style units where students share a common area but have a private room with a bed and desk. Most colleges developed their housing stock before students began requesting singles, however, and today demand for private sleeping quarters far exceeds the supply.

For example, in 2006, Miami University housing director Lucinda Coveney acknowledged that the school had been consistently unable to accommodate most requests for single residences and announced plans to build hundreds of new single-room units. "We need to meet the needs of the modern student," she told the school paper. "A lot of students want that environment and privacy . . . We understand these residence halls were built a long time ago and we're working to try to make on-campus living more attractive." In 2008, George Washington University reported that it had received 286 applications for five single-room units in one of its dorms, and promised that it would add three hundred single units to its supply when it completed construction and renovation of new facilities. In 2009, Boston University opened a high-rise with luxurious "apartment-style" dorms for undergraduates, featuring a large number of one-person units (called singles) and suites in which each resident has a private room. In previous eras, graduating seniors packed into communal houses to share their final year of college near close friends. Today, a new spirit is emerging. "I applied by myself because my friends were all too cheap to live here," a resident of the BU dorm told the *Boston Globe*.[39] Now she could live without them, too.

• • •

AT LEAST ONE MOTHER with a child in BU's luxury dorm recognized that her son would have a hard time maintaining his lifestyle after he left the university. "You graduate facing a terrible job market and having to live with rats in Brooklyn," she told him in the fall of 2009.[40] She could have added one more thing: Regardless of their preferences, all but the most affluent young adults who move to big cities to make it on their own soon discover that they'll also have to live with roommates. And this is significant, because the distinction between living with roommates and having a home of one's own has acquired great cultural significance. For the current generation of young people, it's the crucial turning point between second adolescence and becoming adult.

Take Justin,* who was an aspiring journalist with a fresh degree from a Big Ten school when he got recruited to work in New York City at a job that came with transitional corporate housing. On first glance, Justin appears shy and guarded. He's physically slight, with curly brown hair, deep-set eyes, and a soft, gentle

---

*Justin is a pseudonym, as are the names of all the singletons who appear in this book, except those who are public figures. Granting anonymity to the subjects of social science research is the standard way of protecting them, and universities typically require scholars to do so.

voice that's often hard to hear. He's personable, and funny, once he gets comfortable, but since this can take a while he found that meeting people in New York was more difficult than he'd anticipated. Living alone didn't help. Fortunately, several of his college friends had also moved there, and through them he found a shared apartment where the roommates enjoyed going out together just as they had when they were in school. Justin hadn't soured on going solo, but he knew he wasn't ready and that he could try again when the time was right.

It can be fun to have roommates when you're young and single, as anyone who's watched *Friends* or *Three's Company* surely knows. Roommates provide companionship, so you don't have to feel alone when you wake up in the morning or come home after a rough day. When you move to a new city, they can help you meet people, invite you to parties, and add to your social network. They may share in the cooking, cleaning, and shopping, which means you don't have to do everything. And they help pay the rent, which means you can live in a better neighborhood or save money for going out. For years, Justin enjoyed all these benefits, so much that he endured a seemingly endless series of transitions—people moving in and out, being forced to search for new apartments, relocating to different neighborhoods—so that he could keep sharing a place with people his age. But after five years Justin found himself focusing on the costs of this situation. For, as anyone who's watched *Friends* or *Three's Company* also knows, often—too often—having roommates is no fun at all.

Is there anyone who has lived with roommates and not escaped with tales of woe? Review, among the many stories cataloged in the "trouble with roommates" findings from my research: The roommate, once a friend, who stops paying his rent or his share of the bills. The roommate who steals. The roommate with bad taste. The roommate who never leaves home. The roommate who goes silent. The roommate who blogs about you. The roommate with the TV addiction. The roommate with a drinking problem. The roommate who eats your food. The roommate who won't do the dishes. The roommate who smells. The roommate who hates your girlfriend. The roommate who hits on your girlfriend. The roommate who becomes your girlfriend, and then breaks up with you . . . and refuses to move out.

Justin's experiences were hardly catastrophic, but he had his share of difficulties. In one apartment, he and a roommate got on each other's nerves and the atmosphere quickly became stressful. Justin dreaded seeing him in the living room or at the table. He started avoiding home, or rushed straight to his room when he got there. It was awful, he remembers: "When you don't feel close to your roommates, in some ways that's lonelier than living alone because your isolation is strikingly in front of you. It totally sucks." So he moved, again to a place with roommates. The new place was better, but Justin felt himself still longing for more privacy. With roommates, he explains, "When you bring a girl home, not only will the girl notice your roommates, but your roommates will notice her." The social life at home becomes a burden, sometimes an unbearable one. The conversation the next morning can be even worse. As Justin hit his late twenties, he had plenty of friends and enough money to afford a one-bedroom apartment downtown if he cut out some other expenses and gave up any hope of accumulating savings. The choice was easy. He decided to live alone.

The experience was transformative. "Now I can't imagine living with a roommate," Justin explains. "I would not be happy." He's older, and in his social circle, he says, once you're past your mid-twenties there's an expectation that you'll either live with a partner or have a place of your own. There's a stigma around having roommates as a grown-up, he reports. "I might be embarrassed to admit it. I mean, I feel like an adult now and it's hard to imagine. Having roommates feels sort of unadult."

2.
THE CAPACITY TO
LIVE ALONE

I HAVE ALWAYS LIVED SINGLE, and never yearned to live any other way," writes Bella DePaulo, the psychologist, author, and singles advocate. DePaulo grew up in Dunmore, Pennsylvania, a small town where children learned that getting married was all but obligatory. Before she went to college, it never occurred to her that she could opt out, but as an adult she recognized that this was exactly what she wanted. "I don't think there was a specific moment when I realized I LIKE living single. This is who I am. It's not going to change," she explains. "To get to that point, I think I had to understand a bigger point—it is fine (good, even) to live the life that is most meaningful to you, even if your way is not the most conventional one."[1]

One need not grow up in a small town like Dunmore to have trouble imagining the possibility of living alone someday. The ideal of achieving security in a marriage or with an intimate partner remains fundamental to our culture, and it is instilled in the minds of our

87

young. Children in modern societies may well have more private space than they did in previous eras, but they are still raised in homes where there is at least one adult and often other children, too. Our early experiences living with others shape our expectations, establishing the shared household as a norm, if not an ideal. They also form our characters, leading us to develop skills, techniques, and models for sharing domestic space that we carry into adulthood, consciously or not.

Hardly anyone lives alone until they are grown up, however, which means that those who go solo quickly discover that doing it well requires a lot of learning. Thoreau, Siddhartha, or Helen Gurley Brown may be inspiring, but there is no guidebook for domestic autonomy, at least not the contemporary kind. Living alone is challenging, no matter how excited one is to do so, not only because it entails facing oneself in an intimate setting, but also because it puts people in novel situations and generates a distinctive set of personal needs. Some of these challenges are pragmatic: Learning to shop and cook for one. Balancing solitude and social life. Establishing a healthy relationship with communications media, from the relatively passive consumption of television entertainment to more active engagements through the telephone and Internet. Other challenges are more profound: Dealing with loneliness. Confronting fear that living alone is a sign of social failure. Being discriminated against in the housing market and the workplace. Relating to friends or family who are uncomfortable that someone close to them is unmarried or who presume that this makes them unhappy, too.

Although each person who develops the capacity to live alone finds it an intensely personal experience, my interviews suggest that some elements are widely shared. Today young singletons actively reframe living alone as a mark of distinction and success, not social failure. They use it as a way to invest time in their personal and, above all, professional growth. Such investments in the self are necessary, they say, because contemporary families are fragile, as are most jobs, and in the end each of us must be able to depend on ourselves. On the one hand, strengthening the self means undertaking solitary projects: acquiring domestic skills, learning to enjoy one's own company, and establishing confidence that one can set off for adventures on one's own. But on the other it means making great efforts to be social: building up a strong network of friends and work contacts, and even, as the journalist Ethan Watters argues, forming "urban tribes" that substitute for families by providing community and support.[2]

Anchoring oneself in work and a tribe can help

make going solo a rewarding experience, but it's rarely an enduring one. Most people who live alone into their thirties eventually find that their community weakens as close friends get married and have children, and that work, however rewarding, cannot satisfy their deepest needs. This puts them in a predicament. Those who have learned to enjoy their "age of independence" must choose between trying to reproduce it and seeking out a partner and a family. For men this choice is rarely urgent, but for women it's a different matter, because living alone as they enter their late thirties means spending their nights beside a biological clock that keeps ticking, and they must confront the possibility that they'll never give birth to a child of their own. It's this situation that's prompted writers like Lori Gottlieb to argue that single women should settle on not quite desirable partners. But the argument is hardly persuasive.[3] Marriage is hard enough when both parties enter it enthusiastically. Young adults who have learned to live alone doubt that marriage would be easier when it's a compromise from the start. They are open to discovering the right partner, but if they can't they think they're better off in a place of their own.[4]

MOST YOUNG ADULTS who live alone see it as a stage, not an end point, and those who try it are usually excited for the challenge. Whether or not they are actively searching for a partner, they expect to find one and eventually to get married. Today 84 percent of American women have been married by the time they reach age forty, and 95 percent have married by the time they reach sixty-five. True, the generations born in, say, 1945 and 1970 have profoundly different views on marriage—just not on the question of whether they will have one. Contemporary Americans may be skeptical of the institution, but about 90 percent of those who have never been married believe that someday they will.[5]

The major difference between marriage for those who are now sixty-five and those who are twenty-five is not whether to do it, but when. On average, American men and women born in the 1940s got married at ages twenty-three and twenty-one, respectively, and by the time they'd reached their forties fewer than 6 percent had never wed. Today the median age of first marriage is higher than it has been at any point since the census began recording it: twenty-eight for men and twenty-six for women. In Massachusetts, New York, and Washington, D.C., the median age of first marriage is now over thirty, just as it is in European nations such as Sweden and Denmark. In addition, an unprecedented number of Americans in their forties have never married: 16 percent of men and 12 percent of women.[6] They have plenty of time to live alone.

How do they use that time? In *Against Love*, Laura Kipnis argues that avoiding binding relationships will free people for more play. She even suggests, provocatively, that such liberation could threaten the status quo. "Free people might pose social dangers," she writes. "Who knows what mischief they'd get up to? What other demands would come next?"[7] Alas, in the interviews conducted for this book, the most ambitious of those who live alone offered a clear and far less barricade-scaling answer: They are spending their "free time" at work.

In modern economies most of us are free agents, competing against one another for good jobs. In this environment, it's hard to know what free time really means. Today's workers, particularly the younger ones, are well aware that there's no longer a social contract between capital and labor. Instead, each of us works more and more in hope of getting established on our own, especially during the early part of our careers. For a rising generation of aspiring professionals, the twenties and early thirties is precisely *not* the time to get married and have a family. Rather, it is the life stage when we can pour ourselves into school or work and make an impression. We surrender control of our time to those who educate and employ us, and what remains we give to the task of improving ourselves. We learn new skills. Demonstrate our versatility. Travel. Relocate. Build a network. Develop a reputation. Climb the ladder. Go on the market and find something better. Do it all over again. All of this is easier when you're not accountable to anyone, and especially when you live alone.

There is a price for prosperity in the contemporary economy. The work world makes extraordinary claims on the lives of young workers. Give yourself to business during the prime of your life, or give up your hope of achieving any real success. This is true in for-profit corporations, but also in seemingly less exploitative workplaces, including universities and nonprofit organizations that are dedicated to improving our quality of life. When I was in graduate school at Berkeley, for instance, I knew several students in their late twenties whose adviser, a pioneering female scholar, actively discouraged them from entering serious relationships before they had made their mark. Academia has become extraordinarily competitive, she argued. Tenure-track jobs are disappearing everywhere, and teaching jobs that pay the bills are scarce. Relationships are demanding and distracting. They can slow you down or, worse, compromise the quality of your work. What's more, few of them last. Don't you owe it to yourself to prioritize work?

The so-called "creative class" of those who

work in the knowledge economies share a similar ethos. True, the lucky ones can occasionally enjoy a Ping-Pong game or free food in the office, but they also face enormous demands on their time and energy. They are not only vying for market share in fiercely competitive industries, from software to cinema, advertising to art. They are also trying to break down the barriers between their personal and professional lives, making work the primary site for what Matthew Crawford calls "soulcraft," and often for their social time too. In *Free Agent Nation*, the business writer Daniel Pink reports that self-employed entrepreneurs in a wide variety of fields also experience work as completely consuming. Pink calls the tens of millions of Americans who exist this way "soloists" because their "prospects depend mostly on their own individual efforts" rather than on the "benevolence of a large institution." This change in the nature of work can be liberating, terrifying, exhausting, and exhilarating. As one of his sources puts it: "The worst part about going out on your own is that you have to work twenty-four hours a day. The best part is that you get to choose which twenty-four."[8]

There's less choice in fields such as banking, law, media, or medicine, where managers need not advise anyone to put themselves—or, really, their work—before their relationships, because the job implicitly requires it. In these and other high-power, high-paying professions, some employers demand that young workers spend most of their waking hours—seventy, eighty, ninety per week—in the office, or traveling on business, or checking in from a BlackBerry if they stray into personal time.

Today young professionals routinely cancel lunch dates, evening plans, even entire vacations, because "something's come up" at work. Take Mark, an investment banker who, when in his mid-twenties, never showed up to the apartment he'd rented with his girlfriend on the West Coast, even after she'd moved into it, because his job suddenly required him to stay back east! Needless to say, their relationship soon ended, and eventually he began to plan his life around the realities of his vocation. "I would still date," he tells me. "But I sought out much younger women who were not interested in the answer to the dreaded five-word question: 'Where is this relationship going?' I wanted to be open to meeting the right woman. But I was also avoiding it because I prioritized my career and spent my social time with coworkers. I thought I'd have time for marriage and kids later on."

Mark is not the only one who has adapted to the 24/7 work culture by making the office the hub of his social life. One attorney we interviewed says that, after two years of seventy-hour work weeks, his gay colleagues had become his primary peer group. And Justin, the journalist we met in chapter one, says that he doesn't mind the long hours because "it's a social environment, you know? I'm surrounded by a lot of people with similar interests. I do a lot of interacting, talking, e-mail, bopping down the hall to discuss a story or just shoot the shit." He, too, reports that his friends from work are now his most common companions outside the office. "We go out to lunch together. And we have sports teams from outside of work. A tennis team, a softball team. It's fun."[9]

The office is not the only place where the lines between the personal and professional lives of young adults have blurred. Now that smart phones are standard accessories in their cultural universe, and expansive social networks on sites such as Facebook generate constant chatter among "friends" from every sphere of life, the worlds of work and play swirl together in a steady stream of messages that they follow wherever they are. One woman we interviewed, an attorney in her early thirties who works in politics, tells me: "Of my nine-hour day, I'm spending seven hours responding to e-mails"— mostly job related, but many from friends and family, too. "I also have, like, three hundred fifty people in my cell phone," she explains. It buzzes often, she checks it constantly, and she always tries to respond quickly, even if she's out with friends and the call or message is from work.

This behavior is not unusual. Although we often associate living alone with social isolation, for most adults the reverse is true. In many cases, those who live alone are socially overextended, and hyperactive use of digital media keeps them even busier.[10] The young urban professionals we interviewed report that they struggle more with avoiding the distraction of always available social activity, from evenings with friends to online chatter, than with being disconnected. "Singles in the U.S.: The New Nuclear Family" confirms this. The large-scale study by the market research firm Packaged Facts reports that those who live alone are more likely than others to say that the Internet has changed the way they spend their free time, more likely to be online late at night, and more likely to say that using the Net has cut into their sleep. Not that they are homebodies. According to a Pew Foundation study of social isolation and new technology, heavy users of the Internet and social media are actually more likely than others to have large and diverse social networks, visit public places where strangers may interact, and participate in volunteer organizations.[11] Singles and people who live alone are twice as likely as married people to go to bars and dance clubs. They eat out in restaurants more often, are more likely to take art or music classes, attend public events, and go shopping with friends.[12] To be sure, many occasionally struggle with loneliness or with the feeling that they need to change something to make their lives feel more complete. But so, too, do their married friends and family members and, really, most everyone during some periods of their lives. Finding a partner or a live-in companion is not enough to solve the social pain of loneliness, which is a fundamental part of the human experience.[13]

AS THEY HIT their middle and late thirties, however, many singles who live alone begin to question why they haven't coupled up yet, and whether they would be happier if they did. It's not easy to answer. Mark, for instance, says that staying single through his thirties allowed him to experience things that his friends who married and had children could only dream about: Living in different countries. Taking adventurous vacations. Dating lots of women and figuring out what kind of partner he wants. He's also certain that he's benefitted from spending so much time and effort building a professional network early in his career, because he needed it to find a new job during the recent financial crisis.

As he approached forty, Mark began to believe he had missed out on something important: "I look at my friends who are married and have these adorable young children, and I worry that I made a mistake. My life feels pretty empty sometimes, and I'd like to be part of something more meaningful than what I do at work. I'd actually like to marry the woman I'm dating now. But she may not be interested in starting a family with someone who's spent the past several years doing the kinds of things I've been doing." Women, he knows, can be suspicious of never-married men in their late thirties and forties. "I need to convince her that I can cut down on the endless work hours and give up the big nights drinking at nightclubs full of single women. I feel like I'm done with that. She's not sure."

Of course, as a successful man in a city crowded with single women, Mark enjoys certain luxuries that women his age do not. Most important, he's in no hurry to answer the question of whether he wants to become a biological parent, and he believes that if things don't work out with his current girlfriend he can search for another without worrying that his reproductive capacities will have diminished.[14] Although some women may be suspicious of long-term bachelors, Mark has no fears about becoming stigmatized. Gentle ribbing from his mother, who's long past ready for grandchildren, and occasional jealous confessions from married friends who fantasize about being single in New

York City are the main ways that his single status comes up.

Women who live alone in their thirties and forties face far more social pressure. Whether single by choice or by chance, most of the women we interviewed report that, after their twenties, concerns about whether and how to find a partner and have children became an inescapable part of their lives. They notice that certain people—friends, family, even recent acquaintances—are always calling attention to their domestic status. These are the ones who, in nearly every conversation, quickly ask whether they are dating anyone or start suggesting eligible bachelors, and treat everything else as secondary. This experience is common among women who go solo, so much so that many question whether it's really about them or the projected anxieties of their acquaintances. But nearly all report that it makes them feel stigmatized. Regardless of their personal or professional accomplishments, they see their public identity as "spoiled," as the sociologist Erving Goffman put it—reduced from something big and complex and interesting to that of the single woman alone.[15]

Questions about dating are hardly the only source of stigma for young women who live alone. Television programs and magazine stories regularly trot out psychologists with advice on how to make yourself more attractive and find a partner, or sociologists who warn about how much you will suffer if you don't. (For instance, Linda Waite and Maggie Gallagher, authors of *The Case for Marriage*: "Science tends to confirm Grandma's wisdom: On the whole, man was not meant to live alone, and neither was woman.")[16] Politicians across the spectrum decry the decline of marriage and the culture of "selfish singles." Doctors warn their female patients about the risks of delaying childbirth until they reach "advanced maternal age." Antisingle messages even come from within, since it's hard not to internalize a lifetime's worth of messages about the importance of coupling up or having children, not to mention the horrors of spinsterhood.

Women who live alone are all too aware that delaying marriage means reducing the odds of having a biological child. They may not have read the recent study showing that, in the 1970s, only one in ten American women ended her childbearing years—at age forty-five, though for most women it is younger—without giving birth, whereas one in five women do so today.[17] But since they know many other women in their situation, they wouldn't be surprised by the trend. If living alone and being childless in one's late thirties and early forties has become more common, it hasn't gotten any easier. Even the most confident and successful solo women we interviewed openly questioned whether they had made the right choices for themselves.

Molly, a Web designer in her late thirties, defines herself as a fierce individualist. "I've always liked to have a lot of alone time," she explains, her soft brown eyes seeking out understanding and her mouth slightly open, making her appear somewhat vulnerable or exposed. "I'm not someone who intertwines that well." She and her sister grew up as latchkey kids with divorced parents, both of whom used Molly as their mediator. "I wasn't just the caretaker. I was also, like, the rodeo clown. Everybody always put their stuff on me, and I had to run interference. When I went off to college, I was so excited. I felt like enormous amounts of weight were lifted off of me. I didn't call home for months."

Molly moved to Boston after graduation and rented a place with roommates. She went out a lot and had a few relationships, but nothing serious. After six years she moved to New York City, and when she could afford it got a place of her own in Kips Bay. Now Molly's thirty-seven, and she doesn't think she's incomplete without a partner, even when she's home alone. "I really love being able to create that little vacuum of space for myself," she says. "I don't ever feel desolate. Sometimes I don't even answer the phone if it rings. It's not like I don't have good interpersonal relationships. But I think that sometimes they can be too close, and to have that with someone, and also be living together—there's just like no relief, no time when it's just me by myself, not having to think about anybody else and whatever. It's just too close for comfort for me."

Despite herself, when she was in her twenties and early thirties Molly thought she might enjoy moving in with a partner or getting married. "I did enormous amounts of dating," she says. "I was looking for *the* guy." A few of her relationships lasted a year, at which point she would ask herself, "Do I want to go the distance with this person? And I just always opted against it." By the time she turned thirty-five, Molly had tired of trying. She was working long hours, and using her hard-won free time to meet men felt wasteful, even self-destructive. She started spending more time hanging out with friends, mostly coworkers and people she'd met on snowboarding trips. "I just like that I don't have to worry about anybody else's anything," she explains. This has made her happier than dating, and so she has decided to stop searching for a man.

Yet not even Molly can escape worrying that she's making a bad decision or, worse, that her satisfaction living alone reflects a personal failure. Usually she feels fortunate to live at a moment when going solo is a viable option. "Living alone is just something that I like so much," she says. "If I were living in a different time, when you went from your father's house to your husband's house, I wonder if I would have learned as much about myself." But at low points it's different: "I just kind of wonder, like, is there something wrong with me, that I'm not with somebody? Was there something that happened many years ago that's still sort of echoing into my whole life?" No matter how much she enjoys going solo, or how well it suits her, it takes extraordinary strength to feel good about being on her own, Molly explains. When you live alone as a woman, confidence is something you have to build.

Ella, a public interest lawyer in her mid-thirties, is brazen and brilliant, with long blond hair, big blue eyes, and muscular arms. She is also particularly attuned to the challenges of learning to live alone as a woman, and her efforts to overcome them are worth exploring at length. "I see so many women of my age around me who are feeling desperation," she explains. "Like, 'I can't be alone! There's something wrong with me if I'm alone!' I don't feel that at all. I've had friends over the last four or five years—women who were hysterical about finding a man. They were lonely and they didn't know how to be in the world alone. I really don't ever want to become that way." She gets upset when she hears people urge women her age to marry undesirable partners. Ella believes that most women would be better off holding out until they find what they are looking for, and if not, learning how to live alone. After all, by the time she had reached her mid-thirties she had already seen several friends endure the trauma of divorce or separation, and she's skeptical that those who take the advice to "settle" would avoid this fate.

Perhaps Ella would view things differently if it was clear that marriage generated tangible benefits for someone in her situation. But she doesn't think that the studies documenting the benefits of marriage have much relevance to her case. Ella is a voracious reader, and she knows that men get the lion's share of the marriage dividend, especially now that a growing number of women are not just outliving, but also outearning their spouses.[18] She's also seen research showing that married women are actually more likely than singles to suffer from depression and that, as they get invested in domesticity, they become less likely to sustain their large social networks or advance in their careers. At this point, her family, close friends, and work projects are her greatest sources of meaning. The challenge, as she sees it, is to make the most of them, and to learn how to enjoy both the solitude and the companionship that her lifestyle affords.

Ella has done this deliberately. Soon after she settled into her current job, she purchased a cozy one-bedroom apartment in Brooklyn Heights, where there's vibrant street life, a wide range of services, and a lot of other singles her age. She became a regular at a local yoga studio, where she not only learned how to focus her mental energy and feel more at ease with herself, but also developed a new set of friends. "I've been going there for about four years now, so I know everybody," Ella explains. "It's a really tight-knit community, not competitive or weird." Although she had always seen herself as an outsider, not a joiner, after a few years in the neighborhood she discovered that she had become ensconced there, and she liked it. "A really nice thing about living in New York is that it's so anonymous," Ella says. "But it's nice to create your niche, especially when you're living alone. And I really love having lived in one place long enough to walk around and run into people I know every day."

Ella also likes staying home on occasion and not seeing people. With work and her busy social life to manage, sometimes it feels better to keep to herself. "I'm almost too content on my own," she acknowledges. But getting this way took some effort. Though Ella has always liked cooking, at first it wasn't easy to do it without company. The elaborate process of planning, shopping, preparing, cooking, and eating felt strange and wasteful when she did it all solo. She didn't exactly long for the idealized family dinner, but she was all too aware that many of her contemporaries view dining alone—whether at home or in public—as a sign of social failure, or just plain sad. Moreover, Ella shared the sentiment that some nay-saying singles conveyed to the food writer and editor Judith Jones: "I like to cook for others, to give my friends pleasure. Why would I want to go to all that trouble just for me?"[19] Gradually, however, Ella recognized that cooking for one required cultivating a special talent: the will and capacity to use her time, money, and creative energy to fulfill her own needs. It was a challenge worth pursuing, because the skill—as those who have mastered it attest—transcends the kitchen. Fundamentally, it is about learning to take care of yourself.

Knowing how to enjoy going solo outside the home is just as important as living well inside of it. Yet young adults who live alone often struggle to take pleasure in certain mundane, everyday activities—going to a restaurant, bar, concert, or movie, for example—because they grew up believing that these are things one shouldn't do alone. For many, traveling alone is particularly daunting. Single women are often warned about the dangers of going on the road without a companion. Even travel writing that encourages women to do so can easily convey the opposite message. The article "A Woman Traveling Alone? The World Can Be Your Oyster, Too," which appeared in the *Boston Globe* in 2009, notes that traveling alone can be quite a social experience. Yet it also warns, "Safety is the top concern for female travelers," and quotes the author of a book for female travelers who says, "The moment we step out of the door, we are aware of the footsteps behind us." The article's advice: "Consider taking a women's self-defense course . . . [and] learn how to decrease your chances of being a victim."[20] This is sage, no doubt, but not exactly emboldening.

Ella, who lived abroad as a student and now travels regularly for work, has turned herself into an intrepid traveler. She takes adventurous treks and ambitious group tours to remote countries as well as silent, weeklong yoga retreats outside the city, because her apartment does not offer a sufficient escape from the stress of urban life. Like most singles, Ella perceives that the travel industry is designed for couples. Hotel rooms and car rentals, for instance, typically cost the same for one person as for two, and advertising usually targets couples and families.

In recent years, however, she has noticed that the market is beginning to accommodate the emerging demands of independent tourists. According to the Travel Industry Association, singles and solo dwellers account for 27 percent of the domestic tourism market, and about 10 percent of leisure travelers go alone. Recently a number of hotels, spas, and cruise lines have taken notice. In February 2010, for instance, Norwegian Cruise Line announced that it would install 128 studios for solo travelers on its Caribbean tours. These guests would pay the same per-person rate as members of couples, a major change from standard industry practice, which demands that single travelers pay for two.[21]

Yet travel, no matter how welcoming the accommodations, is ultimately just a temporary escape from the challenge of crafting a meaningful life alone. And as veteran adventure seekers like Ella acknowledge, if you're not thoughtful about how you do it, the search for the new can get old. "I've heard so many people say that they love living alone because it allows them to travel whenever and wherever they want," the journalist Ethan Watters told me. "But traveling turns out to be a false god. It can't answer your deepest questions, or deliver you much more than an extended break." Eventually all solo tourists learn that home is their final destination, and that's where they have to make their lives work.

● ● ●

DISCRIMINATION–FROM EMPLOYERS, real estate agents, and housing associations—makes arranging one's everyday life more complicated, and the people we interviewed report that learning to fight it is essential for living alone. For instance, singles report that their supervisors and colleagues respect the personal time of employees with spouses and children, but not theirs. "In my office, I'm the only one living alone," Ella explains. They all work long hours. But when there's something urgent, something that might take a while to complete, Ella often gets the call because everyone knows she has no companion or children whose needs demand attention and may get in the way. This is a common complaint. Molly, the Web designer, says that in her office "single people are expected to work more, harder. If you have this claim of a child at home, it's understood that you're going to leave earlier than other people, it's understood that of course you can't work on the weekend."

Sherri Langburt, an entrepreneur in her late thirties, started a Web site that offers products, advice, and community building for singles and singletons after experiencing discrimination firsthand. She's thin and fashionable, with a heart-shaped face, long brown hair, and an edgy, slightly nervous disposition. She's concerned about the ways in which unspoken prejudices shape people's personal and professional experiences, and when I first meet her she complains that differential treatment in the workplace runs deeper than most people think: "When I worked in corporate America, I was in a situation where everyone in my office got pregnant around the same time. So I'm coming in at eight and they're coming in at ten thirty, and then they're going to doctors' appointments at two. And I get it, but there's no balance. I mean, they're leaving at five once they have the kids, because they need to get home. That's fine, but then I'm sitting there working until seven. There was just a very big difference in the workloads." What really irked her, however, was the time she was denied a bonus that her married colleagues in an underperforming division received. When she complained, her boss, who was friendly but always treated her as if she were "some kind of party girl," told her that the managers believed that, as a single woman who dressed well and appeared to have an active social life, she was doing fine as is. "People make assumptions. He said, 'You wear all these clothes, and you're always out, and we figured you don't need it.'" Sherri left the job soon after to start SingleEdition.com, and one of the Web site's most popular features is a forum in which participants discuss how to handle discrimination in the workplace.

Another popular feature is a forum for singles to discuss discrimination in the real estate market. This is a particular problem in cities with a lot of cooperative apartments, because in these buildings prospective buyers have to be approved by private boards whose members may not believe that those living a "singles lifestyle" make appropriate neighbors. Sherri experienced this personally when she moved to New York City and started working with a real estate agent. She found several co-op apartments appealing, yet the agent steered her away from them: " 'You're a woman, you're single, and you're Canadian,' " he told her. " 'No board is ever going to approve you.' He kept saying that. But I had this great job. I had money in the bank. And this guy was, like, no." Exasperated, Sherri decided to switch brokers. "Everyone was sending me names for the best broker in the city, and they would all just say the same thing: 'You clearly have the financial backing and the secure job. But you're single, you're a woman, and you're from Canada. Three strikes. You're going to get rejected.' It kept happening over and over. It was ridiculous! I was thirty-two years old and I'd call my friends crying." Eventually Sherri stopped trying, and didn't start again until she got married. "With my husband," she says, "it was easy-peasy."

Those who do not need approval from co-op

boards have an easier time finding a home. In fact, the spike in housing purchases by singles is one of the most remarkable changes related to the fast rise of living alone. This was also inspired by an important legal reform. The Equal Credit Opportunity Act, which Congress passed in 1975, prohibited lenders from rejecting applicants on the basis of sex or marital status and from asking women what kind of birth control they used or whether they planned to have children. Singles, particularly women, were suddenly able to enter the housing market. According to the National Association of Realtors, in 1981 single women represented 10 percent of all U.S. home buyers; at the time this practice was so novel that the *New York Times* reported, "Invariably, when single women talk about having purchased a home, the sentiment expressed is: 'I never would have considered this ten years ago.' "[22] By 2009, single men and women accounted for 10 and 21 percent of all home buyers, respectively, and together they represented nearly one-third of the market. Single men and women also made up 12 and 24 percent of first-time home buyers, respectively, or more than one-third of the market. In the 1950s, real estate agents would have been surprised to see a single female client in their office; now it's surprising if they don't. "I've been in realty for about fifteen years now and the trend has increased throughout the years," the president of the Chicago Association of Realtors told a local newspaper. "It's not a trend, it's a norm."[23]

The increase in home buying by single women under age forty-five is especially striking. From an economic perspective, the cause of the change looks obvious. Today more women have received advanced education and established themselves in successful careers than ever before. In 1970, for instance, 36 percent of all college graduates were women, compared to 54 percent today. Women's income still lags behind men's, and there's not yet equal pay for equal work, but the pay gap is narrowing. In the 1970s, the median income of full-time female workers was about 52 percent of what full-time male workers earned. By 2007, it was up to 71 percent. Single women have made even greater gains, particularly compared to single men. According to the Pew Research Center, "Among U.S.-born unmarried adults ages thirty to forty-four at every level of education, women's median household incomes rose more than men's from 1970 to 2007," and "Unmarried women in 2007 had higher household incomes than their 1970 counterparts at each level of education."[24]

Single women's relative economic success is only part of the reason that they have become the fastest-growing participants in the housing market. After all, on average single men continue to earn more than single women, yet they are much less likely to purchase places of their own. My interviews suggest that the spike in women's home buying is due not only to their economic success, but also to dramatic changes in the social psychology of living alone. Whereas not long ago most women viewed getting married as the key moment in the transition to adulthood, today there are other ways to make the change. Men who live alone in their thirties and forties show little interest in committing to a home or a neighborhood, and they rarely feel the need to settle down. But for a growing number of single women in early adulthood, buying a home has become a powerful way to pivot from one life stage into another. It's a signal, to themselves and to those who know them, that they are ready to invest in themselves.

Kimberly lives in New York City and works in the film industry; her shoulder-length brown hair frames a pale complexion and a sweet but somewhat sinister smile that conveys her confident and mischievous side. She's enjoyed great success in a competitive field, but she admits that she experienced an emotional crash when she found herself alone in her early thirties. It took several years to address the pain related to her own unmet expectations. "I was sad and depressed and lonely," she recounts. "It wasn't really where I wanted to be." But work kept her busy, and that helped her avoid despair. "I could ignore it during the week because I had somewhere to be all day and into the night, but those weekends got hard. Like, you know, you wake up on a Sunday and you just have nothing. You plan nothing and you're on your own." Kimberly used television to distract herself from nagging questions about why she didn't have a partner or a tighter friendship network, only to find that it left her feeling empty. "I used to watch a lot of TV, but that was a real fast way to get depressed and lonely."[25] Although she realized that she needed to get off her couch and out into the world, she had trouble getting motivated. She would wait for the phone or doorbell to ring, but they didn't. "It took me a long time to figure out that it wasn't gonna happen the way it happened in college. People didn't just drop by, and it was just harder to make friends. Everybody's busy and nobody really has any time. And I was scared, scared to put myself out there. For three years I would call my brother every weekend [to complain]. I'd have nothing to do."

When Kimberly reached her mid-thirties, something snapped. "I got sick of being lonely," she says. "It took a long time, but something happened and I grew up and transformed." Kimberly insists that the decisive moment came when she opted to move out of her apartment and buy a place of her own. It was a stretch, financially and psychologically, but it was important, because it signaled that she was no longer waiting for a man to help her jump into a new life stage. She was doing it independently, on her own terms. "I hadn't settled down with anyone. I hadn't fallen in love. And I had to stop and take a look at that. I never thought I'd buy an apartment alone. I sort of resisted it the whole way through. I didn't want to hang curtains by myself. I'd always thought I would do it with a partner and a lover, and so that was hard."

Immediately, the change felt good. So good, in fact, that Kimberly kept changing things. She decided to remake her body, got a personal trainer, began biking on weekends with a group, and lost thirty pounds. She renovated her apartment, opening up space so that she could throw dinner parties. She reached out to people, inviting friends out, putting herself on the line. Her big breakthrough was placing a profile on an online dating site, something she'd been "terrified" to do before. She worried someone she knew would recognize her and that they would confirm her fear "that I was a loser because I wasn't already in love." That fear diminished as Kimberly settled into her new life. "I got more confident in who I was, so I was less afraid to talk to people, less afraid to make friends, and less afraid to go out and be adventurous."

She was dating, but she stopped going out on second and third dates with men who didn't really interest her, because she no longer felt as insecure and she didn't need everyone to like her. She cut back on her TV viewing and kept herself from falling into a vicious cycle of depression, social withdrawal, and loneliness. She quit her job and started freelancing, which she'd wanted to do for years. Then Kimberly made an even bolder move. She reached out to Single Mothers by Choice, an organization that supports women who want to become parents but refuse to settle for an unsatisfying partner, and began to consider having a child on her own.[26] Like so many single women in their late thirties, Kimberly couldn't avoid hearing the "booming alarm bells" on her biological clock, and she decided to confront the issue head-on. As Kimberly saw it, she had become so strong and self-sufficient while living alone that she could now handle the responsibility of caring for another. To be sure, it wouldn't be the kind of domestic partner she had imagined when she turned thirty, and she was hardly certain that she would go through with the process, since having a child would make finding a man even more difficult. But Kimberly no longer felt sorry for herself. "I'm lucky," she says. "I have some money and I have family support. I think I'm gonna figure it out."

PEOPLE WHO LIVE ALONE are well aware that, however enriching it may be, becoming a single parent is also the most challenging way to get domestic companionship. There is another, more popular alternative for people who want to live alone but also need someone to care for or something to help stave off loneliness: getting a pet.

Animal companions are a common feature of Western cultures. "In 2004," writes the historian Katherine Grier, "more than 60 percent of American households contained pet animals; 36 percent included children." An essay in a public health journal reports that U.S. pet ownership rates "are typical of developed countries around the world . . . Examples of dog, cat, and/or bird ownership in European households include Belgium (71 percent), France (63 percent), Netherlands (60 percent), Britain (55 percent), Italy (61 percent) . . . and for all seventeen European countries surveyed (52 percent)."[27]

There is a long-standing myth that people who live alone are more likely than others to own pets because they use them as substitutes for human relationships, but the evidence doesn't support this. Pets, as dog owners know, often serve to promote interpersonal interaction rather than to prevent it. Moreover, people who live alone are far less likely to own a dog or a cat than people who live in couples or in multiperson families. In 2006, for instance, roughly one out of five solo dwellers had a dog and one out of four had a cat, while for families of four about one in two had dogs and more than one in three had cats.[28]

The number of solo dwellers with pets is not insignificant, however, and in our interviews those who lived with a dog or a cat left little doubt about how much they value their relationships with animals. One woman we spoke to, for instance, wondered whether having a pet meant that she shouldn't count as living alone. Another said that owning a dog has been transformative, but mostly because taking care of it has made her leave the house and engage with other people more often. She takes her dog on errands, ties him up on a long leash when she's hanging out in her front yard, even brings him to the neighborhood bar. "I'm chatting with more people on a daily basis now," she reports. "I was more holed up before. The dog really did open up my world."[29]

Angelina, who's in her late twenties and works at a labor union, spent years living with allergic roommates. Getting a cat, she says, "was, like, one of the reasons I decided to live alone. I got her right away. My relationship with the cat is pretty huge. She greets me when I come home and she keeps me company all the time." Angelina likes the fact that caring for her cat is not especially demanding. "It's hard to clip her claws alone, and it's really hard to get her in and out of her carrier," she explains, but otherwise it's easy. She can leave the cat alone with a big bowl of food and water if she goes away for a few days. She can shut her out of her room if she brings someone home. "Having a one-bedroom apartment has made it perfect, though. She has her own room to play at night."

There's a price to pay for maintaining this arrangement with a pet, however. As Donna Haraway, social critic and author of *The Companion Species Manifesto*, acknowledges, "The relationship is not especially nice; it is full of waste, cruelty, indifference, ignorance, and loss, as well as of joy, invention, labor, intelligence, and play."[30] Then there's the financial toll. Renting the big apartment that makes cat ownership so pleasant has drained Angelina's pocketbook. "If I had gotten a studio, I would have thought twice about having a cat, because I like the idea that I can shut her out if I need to," she explains. "But I'm paying $1,100 a month for this one-bedroom, about 45 percent of my take-home pay. Then there's gas and electric and now phone and Internet—all things I would have divided by three if I had roommates. So my finances have spun out of control." Ultimately, the big apartment proved unsustainable, as did the lifestyle Angelina had built around it. She decided to leave her job, enroll in graduate school, and move to a cheaper city. That the cat would accompany her was never in doubt.

Like Angelina, most pet owners are convinced that they get tangible physical and psychological benefits from their relationships with animal companions, and a good deal of research (though not all) supports this belief. In a survey of the scientific literature published in the *Annual Review of Public Health*, animal experts Alan Beck and N. Marshall Meyers write, "All indications are that companion animals play the role of a family member, often a member with the most desired attributes . . . For some, pets increase the opportunities to meet people, while for others pets permit them to be alone without being lonely." The rewards of pet ownership vary depending on the circumstances, but the list of documented effects reported by Beck and Meyers includes: prolonged lifespan, reduced anxiety and isolation, decreased risk of high blood pressure and heart disease, perceived security, even increased laughter. "Animals can also play a role in improving the well-being of people of all ages who are stigmatized," they conclude. In public, some who live alone may feel stigmatized or stereotyped. But when they're home, playing with their pet companion, they can hardly feel the bite.[31]

THE TRUTH IS, eliminating the pain related to living alone is no more possible than eliminating the pain related to living. Some feelings—loneliness, regret, fear of failure, anxiety about what lies ahead—are said to be common among singles. Lori Gottlieb, for instance, depicts single women in their thirties and forties as "miserable," while Linda Waite describes the unmarried as emotionally unhealthy compared to their married peers. As people who live alone are quick to point out, however, people who are coupled up, or have children, or live with friends and family experience no shortage of difficulties—loneliness included.

The young adults we interviewed were not shy about discussing the hardships of going solo. But their thoughtful attempts to meet the challenges generated by living alone were productive, and often successful. Young adults can and do learn how to live well without a domestic partner, and they benefit from this knowledge when they move in with someone, as the great majority ultimately do. Some, including those who've always thought they would get married, come to enjoy living alone so much that they question whether they could give it up. Perhaps this explains the results of a recent Pew Research Center study, "Not Looking for Love": "Most young singles in America do not describe themselves as actively looking for romantic partners. Even those who are seeking relationships are not dating frequently. About half (49 percent) had been on no more than one date in the previous three months."[32]

Hoang, a professor in his early thirties, recently broke up with a long-term girlfriend and is wondering how to take care of himself. "I have anxieties about living with someone, like a girlfriend or something," he says, from behind thick-framed glasses that cannot hide the fatigue in his eyes, "because I'm cool living by myself—all that self-awareness, comfortable-in-your-own-skin stuff." Not that living alone is perfect. Hoang does a lot of writing in his apartment, and he often loses himself in a "floating-through-space-type existence" that can feel isolating and lonely. But the rewards more than compensate for the difficulties. "I've learned to enjoy things that I know I've always liked but didn't really have the time or patience to truly delve into," Hoang explains. "Like, I've always had a lot of music and records, but before I wouldn't just sit at home and listen to a record because I would always have another person around. I fear not being able to relinquish what I get out of being single."

At times, those who find themselves growing attached to their solo lifestyle sound a cynical note about relationships in general, and their words reveal how far the cult of the individual has advanced. "All you have ultimately is yourself," Hoang says. "Something could happen to everyone else in your life and you would end up being alone, so I like the idea of being used to it when I'm still young. I like my friends, but something could happen, something tragic, or our relationships could change. So I try to grow less reliant on my friends and more reliant on myself. Living alone is an embodiment of that." Hoang observes a world of divorce, broken families, and failed friendship, and anticipates that the people he loves most will someday disappear. "It's less complicated for me to just live by myself," he explains, with a voice full of sadness and resignation. Others who share Hoang's view make light of their condition. In *Single*, a documentary based on the premise that "finding and maintaining a lasting relationship has never been more challenging," several men and women are asked to name the best thing about being single. "Not worrying about being broken up with," one person responds. "I will not be rejected today," says another.

It's easy to understand why some people who have been injured by rejection and separation become cautious about putting themselves on the line in another serious relationship. But when caution turns to cynicism and leads those who live alone to shield themselves in safe houses, the situation can be perilous, too. For no matter how socially active, professionally successful, or adept at going solo one makes oneself, there is something uniquely powerful about the intimate connection forged through sharing one's home with another person. Then again, there is also something uniquely painful about sharing one's home with someone who has squandered or abused this intimacy and trust. As we see in the next chapter, one reason so many people separate is that they are lonely with each other.

3.
SEPARATING

I GREW UP in a generation that yearned for romantic passion, yearned as if that was the key to all salvation, to all self-discovery, to everything." Helen, who's in her early sixties and twice divorced, sounds incredulous, if not a bit self-mocking, as she tells me this. We're sitting in the spacious Greenwich Village apartment where she has lived alone for decades, and Helen, a writer and teacher with piercing eyes and a sharper mind, seems completely at ease applying it to her own life. Since childhood, she has seen herself as fiercely independent, but this did not prevent her from subscribing to her generation's belief in the redemptive power of true love, and it shaped her early adult experiences. The yearning for the perfect marriage was odd, she says, because as children in a time when "divorce was unheard of," she and her female friends were exposed to the brutal consequences of the vow "till death do us part": "I remember sitting around my mother's kitchen table when I was a child, and I was surrounded by a world full of internal drama, the drama of unhappy domestic arrangements that didn't have a chance of being resolved. Women were talking about abortions that their husbands were never going to know about. Women were having affairs. They were miserable, and they were alone inside their situations."

The 1950s and early 1960s were confusing times to become a woman, Helen says. On the one hand, she and her middle-class peers were finding new opportunities in their professions and breaking through old barriers that confined them to the domestic sphere. On the other, they still faced overwhelming pressure to find the right man and organize their lives around marriage. "I was in Europe when I was twenty-three," Helen recalls, "and I wrote these letters to my mother saying, 'I know I have a great work in me to do, and I want to do it. But I also know that I need, above all else, a loving partner in order to do the work.' I was waiting, like every girl in the world, for a man to make a life for me."

She didn't wait long. Helen returned to New York and got a teaching job. At twenty-five, in a ceremony at her mother's house, she married a Dutch Catholic artist who, she hoped, "would bring out the bohemian in me." He didn't, and the marriage, which Helen calls "instrumental," didn't work. "It wasn't bad faith," she explains. "But I married a fantasy, an image. I got married because I knew I needed to have a husband in order to do the work." It didn't take long to learn that her husband could not help her become the person she had projected, nor could she fundamentally change him. "We became real to each other," she says, and together they realized that what they made each other was unhappy. After two and a half years together, they divorced.

Helen held on to her faith in the importance of marriage. She continued dating, and within a few years she had fallen for a Jewish psychologist, "the son of communists," someone "as different as he could be" from her first husband. They were married, again at her mother's house, when she was thirty-two. But despite the different particulars, the result was the same. Helen felt lonely and unsatisfied, and they couldn't make things better. Two and a half years later, she asked for a divorce. "My mother couldn't stand him," she says. "And when I left him, I called her and said, 'Mom, it's over.' " She was totally supportive, but she did say, "Helen, the next one's on you!"

There hasn't been a next one. Some thirty years later, Helen now believes that "marriage is fucking boring" and tells me that "I was never more miserable in my life than when I was married." In her view, living alone stands in opposition to living falsely in a conventional but unhappy marriage, just because society tells you to. After Helen's second divorce she made "a tremendous realization"—two, actually. First, she recognized that "without these men, I was gonna make my own life. Nobody was gonna take care of me." Second, and more important, she noticed that a growing number of women in her generation had also been let down by marriage. They were discovering that falling in love and living with a husband didn't fulfill them, didn't allow them to become who they wanted to be. "We fell in love once, and it didn't work. We fell in love twice, and it didn't work. Once that happened, you had experience. And once you had experience, the whole myth of romantic love as salvation came to an end."

The men and women of Helen's generation divorced in unprecedented numbers. "We'd seen people mismatched, living together in dead marriages for years and years because they dreaded being alone or they didn't know what to do with themselves," she remembers. "They didn't know how to think about their lives." The cultural change that made divorce acceptable was genuinely liberating, because it freed unhappy people to search for something better. But it also cast millions of people into an ocean of uncertainty. "It's like anarchy," Helen explains. "After you blow up the family and break up society, what do you do?"

Helen and her contemporaries didn't have the answers, and neither did the generations that followed them into the throes of the divorce revolution. But uncertainty about how to remake one's life after separating from a spouse or long-term partner has hardly prevented dissatisfied couples from breaking up their relationships. According to the federal census, today about one out of every five adults has divorced.[1] And although divorce rates in the United States have dropped somewhat since their peak in the early 1980s, Americans are still far more likely to split up than are couples in all other Western nations. "At current rates," writes sociologist Andrew Cherlin, "nearly half of all American marriages would end in divorce."[2] As a consequence, millions of people who never planned to live alone now find themselves going solo, challenged to adjust their expectations and remake their lives.

For many, the solution is to remarry. Americans, ever hopeful, are more likely than people in other nations to give marriage a second chance—and quickly! In the United States, the median time between a divorce and a second marriage is a mere 3.5 years. But a close look at the numbers shows that not everyone is in a hurry to tie the knot a second time. Young divorcees remarry far more often, and more swiftly, than the middle-aged and the elderly, as do those who live in the South and in rural areas, where cultural conservatism, fewer professional opportunities for women, and a less vibrant singles scene make marriage a compelling choice.

Overall, remarriage rates dropped precipitously during the second half of the twentieth century, even in the United States. In 1950, for instance, two out of three divorcees remarried within five years, whereas in 1989 only one of two did. And although 80 percent of women who divorce before age twenty-five marry for a second time before turning thirty-five, those who divorce when they're older are far more cautious.[3] According to national statistics, only 44 percent of women and 55 percent of men who divorced over age twenty-five have remarried, and a recent American Association of Retired Persons (AARP) survey of people who divorced between the ages of forty and sixty-nine found that just one in three had wed again.

Why have so many of us given up the supposed benefits of wedlock for the tumult of being single and the possibility that we will spend the rest of our days living alone? One reason is that modern women, untethered from traditional economic and sexual constraints, have discovered that going solo can liberate them from the many unrecognized, unappreciated, and unrewarded responsibilities they (still) take on as homemakers and caretakers, and allows them to attend to their own needs. (The burden of the "women's role" in marriage helps explain why two out of three women surveyed in the AARP study claimed that they had demanded a divorce from their spouse.) Another reason is that men who are unhappy in their marriages develop fantasies about having a more adventurous sex life as singletons, though the evidence shows that the reality rarely meets their expectations. The booming singles culture of contemporary cities does, however, allow those who separate from a spouse to be socially engaged and personally stimulated rather than isolated and withdrawn. We also opt out of unsatisfying marriages because we cherish freedom, personal control, and our search for self-realization. For both men and women, living alone is a tempting way to achieve these goals.

NONE OF THIS IS TO SAY that divorced city dwellers have abandoned their interest in finding another spouse or domestic partner. The great majority of those we interviewed say that they recognize the benefits of being married or cohabiting, at least when things are going well. Separated women tend to emphasize the value of small, everyday intimacies. "I liked the feeling that someone knew me on a day-to-day basis," says Kaela, who's forty-one and has been on her own for five years following a divorce. "He knew the stuff that you generally hide from others. It's nice to feel the comfort of being who you are around someone else, sharing the things that come out in that unstructured time that just kind of happens, the no-pressure casual time that is so sweet." Dina, who's in her thirties and was married for four years, says, "I knew the sound of him coming up the stairs and this particular way that the door outside our door opens. I miss the rhythm of his steps. It's a physical absence in my life." Madeline, a sixty-one-year-old technical writer from San Francisco, has been happy living alone for two decades. Yet she valued "the company, the conversation, the sharing, the communication, the knowledge that someone is there. It must be psychological," she concludes, "because life seems easier if you have someone going through it with you."

The benefits are also economic. Both men and women affirm what the statistics tell us: that there are tremendous financial advantages to being married or living with a partner. The ability to afford a larger home or a better neighborhood and to split expenses that are the same no matter how many people use them, like cable, Internet, and utilities. The security of having someone else's income and benefits in case you get sick, lose your job, go back to school, or decide to try something different. The luxury of pooling income for savings, or blowing it on things that are better when shared.

Moreover, decades worth of careful research confirms that most divorces result in a substantial decline in the standard of living for both parties, with women suffering far greater losses than men.[4]

Divorced men who are asked about the benefits of marriage tend to bring up other luxuries. Sam, a large and jocular man who, at sixty, has allowed his waist to expand and his health to deteriorate, has been single for nearly three decades. It's not surprising to hear him say that he now appreciates the way his wife took care of him and their apartment. Like most wives of her generation, she did most of the domestic work. But Sam says he reciprocated by taking over other household tasks, and this, he insists, not only made his home life pleasurable, but also made him a better man. "It's good to have responsibilities," Sam explains. "It makes you perform better. When I was married, I would make sure that the clothes were always washed and there was not a big pile in the corner, that I put away my shoes and washed my dishes. Sometimes when you're on your own you become lackadaisical on cleaning and taking care of yourself. When I'm by myself, I tend to work, go home, watch TV or sporting events. I become a couch potato. I have a hard time finding somebody to date."

Sam is but one of the many divorced men we

interviewed who say that living alone has hurt their sex lives. Ray, who's been single since moving from Taiwan to California eight years ago, says that "sex, guaranteed sex," is what he misses most about living with a woman. "You don't have to go out there and hunt for it. You're not spending all your energy trying to be a playboy, so you can relax and do other things." (I should acknowledge that Ray, who's short and pudgy with neatly combed straight black hair and slightly yellowed teeth, is the only man who used the phrase "guaranteed sex" to describe the virtues of cohabitation. Others reported that while living with a partner made sex more accessible, it was hardly guaranteed.) But in fact middle-age men who have remarried are more likely to have sex regularly than those who have divorced and gone solo. According to the AARP survey of divorcees between the ages of forty and sixty-nine, 57 percent of men with a domestic partner (married or not) said that they'd had intercourse once a week or more during the previous six months, compared to 43 percent of men without a partner. Men with a domestic partner were also three times less likely to experience long periods of celibacy—16 percent said that they had sex "not at all" during the previous six months, compared to 49 percent of divorced singles. It's not surprising, then, that single men were twice as likely as their partnered peers to report masturbating at least once a week.[5]

For women, the sexual benefits of living with a partner are even greater. Consider how those who have remarried or moved in with a lover answered the AARP survey about their sexual activity during the previous six months: 88 percent said that they had kissed and 54 percent said that they had intercourse once a week or more. Compare these figures to the responses from divorced women who had remained single: 18 percent said they had kissed and 9 percent said that they had intercourse once a week or more during the previous six months. Their responses to the celibacy question were similarly disparate: 17 percent of remarried women and 77 percent of unmarried divorced women said that they had not had sexual intercourse, while 42 percent of remarried women and 81 percent of unmarried divorced women said that they had not had oral sex, either. But they self-report the same frequency of masturbation: Whether coupled up or single, 7 percent of divorced women over forty do it once a week or more.

Admittedly, the AARP survey does not tell us everything we might want to know about the sex lives of middle-age divorcees. For instance, many of the divorced women we interviewed insisted that they weren't suffering from their sexual inactivity, because their libidinal energy had diminished as they got older and adjusted to being on their own. "I don't want to be going around in a perpetual state of disappointment and heartbreak," says Sandy, a fifty-seven-year-old in the San Francisco Bay Area, when asked about having a sexual partner. "It's not in my life, it's not happening for me. And I suppose if I really wanted that I could go out and get it, but I don't want it just to have it. I don't feel the necessity of having it."[6] Moreover, the AARP study measures the quantity of sex, not the quality, and some would surely prefer to have less sex with more partners than more sex with the same partner. Overall, however, the sexual benefits of getting remarried appear just as significant as the economic ones. But if the historical trends in remarriage tell us anything, it's that a growing number of divorced and separated people believe that living with another partner also carries substantial costs—great enough to make going solo a more attractive option.

THERE'S NO DOUBT that many of these singles are still looking for a spouse or domestic partner, and many single women complain that good candidates—namely, men who are looking to pair off with a woman in their age range rather than one much younger—are hard to find. There's more to the story than this, however. In the AARP survey, 43 percent of women and 33 percent of men who divorced between the ages of forty and sixty-nine said that they are now "against marriage" and unwilling (in the abstract, at least) to do it again. Their own negative experiences are one key source of this skepticism, but so are the experiences of others. Between 1950 and 1989 the rate of second marriages that resulted in divorce nearly doubled, a trend that means even those who believe in the institution's virtues have a hard time believing that they can learn from their own mistakes.[7]

Kaela, the forty-one-year-old who lives in Berkeley, is petite and professional, dressed in a sleeveless green shirt and a long patterned skirt that fits with the local style. Although she is open when discussing intimate details of her personal life, Kaela keeps her face turned to the street until the end of our interview, when she gets comfortable enough to show her expressive amber eyes. In her view, the best thing about living alone is "knowing that I don't have to consider anyone else. I can indulge my weird little habits"—from eating the same thing for four days in a row to watching cheesy TV shows and waking up to read in the middle of the night—"and do what I want to do." The other thing she loves about living alone is that she's no longer frustrated by a man who has selectively deskilled himself out of cooking and cleaning and uses this as an excuse to dump domestic work on her. "A lot of men have this fake helplessness when it comes to household stuff," Kaela explains. "My partner and I just had different standards, so we'd have the kinds of disagreements that many, many couples have."

Charlotte, who at fifty-two carries her big-boned body with grace and confidence, is an office manager in Manhattan. She married young and had two children before divorcing four years later, and in her view the kids are the only good things that resulted from the relationship. She raised them as a single mother and has been living alone since the youngest one moved out a dozen years ago. Initially, it was difficult: "I had a little bit of the empty-nest syndrome going on. It was extremely lonely. And it was scary. I mean *scary*—like the killer is under the bed or in the closet downstairs." But within a few years she had overcome these fears. Charlotte moved into a smaller home that suited her downsized domestic responsibilities and turned it into an oasis from the city and her office, where she spends most days dealing with other people's needs. "I paint, I write, I read. When I feel like being bothered with somebody, I am."

Charlotte has learned to love her domestic autonomy. "When you live alone, there's no compromising," she explains. "I do everything I feel like doing, when I feel like doing it. And it is totally self-indulgent. It's just all about you." It's not that she's a narcissist or an introvert. But after a bad marriage and two decades as a single mother, Charlotte feels entitled to put her own needs and desires before those of others. "I don't think I want to tend to a living thing ever again," she says. When her children left home, Charlotte plunged herself into the local art scene, and she spends many evenings and weekends going to galleries or painting in a shared studio. Yet she keeps her contacts at a distance. While Charlotte once enjoyed entertaining, these days she rarely invites anyone into her home. "I can't manage to have any fun at the party," she admits. "It's a lot of work. And I always ask myself, like an hour before people come, 'Why are you doing this? *Why?*' I spend the whole evening being their slave. It costs me an arm and a leg, and now my house is all messed up, and people want to know when I'm gonna invite them back!"

Charlotte still enjoys companionship. She's close to her family members, and occasionally she dates. The most intense relationship she had after her divorce was about twenty years ago. She wound up living with a man, but she calls the experience "awful" and "disastrous"—so bad that it "put the nail in the coffin" and led her to shut out suitors for years. As she approached fifty, however, some of Charlotte's relatives worried that she would never find a partner. "My

mother was warning me, 'You need to get out,'"
Charlotte recalls. "People start to tell you things
like 'You're gonna grow old alone' and 'You
better lock down something now while you
can.'" Charlotte took their concerns to heart. She
feared that she'd become reclusive. She
wondered what would happen to her if she lost
her job or got a serious illness. She questioned
whether her self-indulgence had gone too far.

One of her cousins always tried to set her up on
blind dates, and although Charlotte was usually
skeptical, recently she agreed to give it a try. It
worked. "I like him," she confesses, as if she's
still surprised. "I mean, I don't like *everything*
about him . . ." Charlotte is cautious about the
new relationship, but not too cautious. At the
time of her first interview, she was spending two
nights a week with her boyfriend and things were
heating up fast. Recently, he even brought up the
possibility of marriage.

Charlotte is struggling to make a decision. She
enjoys her uncompromising lifestyle, the freedom
to do what she pleases whatever the hour. But
she's "afraid of being alone down the road," as
she puts it, and she worries about the frightening
prospect of aging alone if she doesn't move in
with someone soon. Her daughter, she says, "is
worried that I'm going to be old, broke, possibly
sick, and maybe unhappy that I've made this
choice. Every now and then I get afraid that she's

142

right." Charlotte's predicament is stressful, and she complains about the dearth of wisdom to help guide her decision. She's aware of all the pundits and professors who espouse the value of marriage, and although she hasn't read the studies personally, she knows about the social science literature that claims married people have more economic security and even longer lives. But like many veteran single women, especially those who have been through a divorce, Charlotte doubts that a husband would protect her from the ravages of aging or dying alone. She knows that the odds suggest she will outlive a male partner, and if they are right then getting married would eventually place her in the stressful and unhealthy position of becoming a dying man's primary caregiver—not exactly a responsibility she wants.[8] During the interview, she shifts back and forth on her options, landing on a note of puzzlement: "I don't know what I'm gonna do."

CHARLOTTE'S CONCERNS about marriage are not unusual among divorced women in her situation. After all, the AARP study reports that usually "women do the walking," and in many cases it's because they believe they'll be better off going solo and establishing their own identity than living with a man who might crowd them out. The survey also shows that middle-age divorcees are more afraid of failing in another marriage than of not finding someone else. Most of the divorced women we interviewed reported that they were open to moving in with another man someday, but only under the best of circumstances. Some insisted that he would have to be self-sufficient, so that they wouldn't have to do all the domestic work. Others said he would have to respect their hard-won autonomy and understand that they already had lives of their own. "You become a lot pickier when you're older," explains Madeline, the sixty-one-year-old San Franciscan. "You're just not willing to live with a whole lot of stuff you lived with when you were younger and you've got that primal urge to mate. You sort of self-select."

There is a cost to this pickiness. Madeline, who's slim and dressed stylishly in black from head to toe, acknowledges, "I'm not having any sex." But she insists that "at my age it ceases to nag at you." In fact, her experience going solo has changed the way she sees her generation: "I always thought that the reason women were alone when they were older was that they were simply rejected. I don't think that anymore. I think they just say, 'I've been there, done that,' and unless you're really something special, you're fine as a friend."

FRIENDS PLAY A SPECIAL ROLE in the lives of women who move into a place of their own after divorce or separation, and the sheer number of people who live alone in contemporary cities means that finding other people who can bond over this shared situation is easier than ever. Although divorcees often fear the specter of social isolation, the General Social Survey (GSS), which is the largest study of American social behavior, shows that single women above age thirty-five (divorced as well as never married) are more likely than their married contemporaries to do the following activities: see or visit a best friend at least weekly, have a "non-visit" contact (such as a call or an e-mail exchange) with a best friend at least weekly, spend a social evening with neighbors, regularly participate in informal group activities, and be a member of a secular social group.[9] In my interviews, divorced women often said that their friends aren't just companions, but also "chosen family," their most reliable sources of social and emotional support.

Fifty years ago, single women who lived alone stood out in their families and communities. They were odd and unusual, and this made them objects of pity if not scorn. Today, however, the population of middle-age adult women who live alone and are likely to stay that way for years or longer is so large that we take it for granted. Helen, for instance, says that when she first lived alone she felt lucky to be in Greenwich Village, which was full of women in her position. Over the past forty years she has watched this scene make its way into the cultural mainstream, and now she believes that "living alone is easier than ever because there are more people to keep you company." It's not hard to find them. On the Internet, people who live alone—including a surprising number of middle-age divorcees—use social networking sites to find new friends, romantic partners, and groups of people who share their interests. Contemporary cities are full of singletons who are remaking their own societies, creating environments in which, as Helen puts it, "you don't have to feel marginalized, or even alone."

Feeling lonely is another issue. For no matter how much time divorced and separated women spend with friends and neighbors, they find it hard to escape at least an occasional pang of loneliness, and in some cases the pain lasts longer. Compared to women who live with a romantic partner, women over thirty-five who live alone are twice as likely to report feeling lonely four times a week or more and about half more likely to report feeling lonely at least once a week.[10] (But keep in mind that this does not mean living alone causes loneliness. It's possible, for example, that people who feel lonely more often wind up living alone because they have trouble sustaining intimate relationships of all kinds.) "Many people—and I'm one of them—absolutely live with loneliness all the time," Helen says. "It's like an illness. Ten thousand mornings I wake up and just go through the day, and the aloneness is like a cubic force in me in a way. It's dark." Helen has developed techniques for taming these feelings. She spent decades in therapy, and she has trained herself to think and write about her feelings rather than running from them in the predictable ways— whether sleeping around, drinking, or filling time with TV. It's a luxury to spend so much time on herself, she acknowledges. But to Helen it seems necessary, because the challenge of making herself feel right is so great.

In Helen's view, for most of us loneliness is inevitable. It's part of the human condition, and she rejects the belief that living alone is its source. Like many divorced women we interviewed, Helen copes with her own feelings of social failure, in part, by dismissing the notion that another marriage or romantic relationship would alleviate them. "People are in this incredible panic to avoid being alone in the room with themselves," she explains, but their desperation can lead to disaster, because "there's nothing more lonely than being with the wrong person." Madeline has a theory about why so many divorced people feel this way: "When a relationship doesn't go well, it's a very lonely situation. You can't go to the person that you're with for help with this problem because, in your eyes, *they are* the problem. So you become a little island all to yourself within that relation-ship, and it's very lonely."

The divorced women we interviewed don't deny that, viewed historically, the institution of marriage has helped to nurture children, create communities, and establish powerful social bonds. But they often insist that these common goods generally came at women's expense, and that at this point in their lives they need not worry about them. Moreover, they refuse to romanticize marriage or "the good old days" when couples stayed together no matter how much they suffered and women were locked out of jobs that would allow them to make it on their own. It's one thing to debate the issue sociologically. At a personal level, the real question is: When does life feel better? Living alone is hardly painless, but for many who have endured a failed marriage, it hurts less.

WOMEN WHO LIVE ALONE are not the only ones who suffer from loneliness after divorce or separation. In fact, women's tendency to make and sustain social connections makes them less vulnerable to isolation than men. According to the General Social Survey findings, men above age thirty-five who live alone (both divorced and never married) are more likely than men who live with a romantic partner to see or visit a best friend at least weekly, spend a social evening with neighbors or friends, and belong to a social group. But the only one of these activities they do as much as women who live alone is socialize with friends—in every other area single women are more socially engaged. Men who live alone also have relatively high rates of loneliness. (As with women, this loneliness might be the cause rather than the consequence of living alone.) They are twice as likely as men who live with a partner to self-report feeling lonely at least one day a week and about three times more likely to feel lonely four or more days a week.[11]

Yet they are rarely miserable. Lou, a fifty-seven-year-old attorney and part-time musician who lives in a small, ground-level apartment in West Berkeley, has had his own place since his second marriage collapsed fifteen years ago and he relishes the autonomy it affords him. "When you're married, you don't have your freedom," he explains. "You have to think about everybody else and not just yourself. Now I can sit here and watch TV all day long and nobody's going to say 'boo' to me. I can practice my trumpet whenever I want. I have my own space and I feel com-fortable in it. Everything about it is how I want it to be." Between work and his jazz gigs, Lou keeps himself busy, and he enjoys having downtime in peace. "There's enough in my life that it doesn't bother me to be alone and not going to parties every week. It used to be that I didn't ever want to go out by myself. But now I'll go to movies on my own, go to a Chinese restaurant. I don't have to make plans or think about it. I just go."

Occasionally, however, this freedom can be oppressive. "I feel lonely sometimes," Lou confesses, but whereas many divorced women his age devote themselves to planning lunches and nights out with friends or coworkers, Lou has adopted a more passive approach. "I don't spend a lot of time trying to fill up my social calendar. I just take it as it comes." Recently, he's begun to worry that this lifestyle isn't good for him. He has filled his days and nights with work, music, commuting, and television, and the absence of more intimate human companionship—sex, but also simple, everyday contact and the rhythms of being in a shared space—is haunting him. "Maybe it's just my doing," he says, "but the fact that I have been alone for so long is probably the biggest failure in my life." Like many men in his generation, Lou believes that he lacks the social skills that he sees in women. He struggles to sustain his relationships with friends and family, and has even more trouble meeting new people or finding dates. When he gets down or lonely, he spends even more time on work and music. "I don't dwell on it," Lou explains. "That's just the way it is."

Sam, the sixty-year-old who admitted to neglecting his home after he separated, explains, "I tend to not have a social life. I become a work-aholic, working way too much, like a hundred forty hours every two weeks. And it leaves me very little time for fun." He's a counselor for men in the criminal justice system, and his work is fulfilling because he gets so deeply involved with men whose lives he can help to change. It's also exhausting, emotionally and physically, and at the end of most days he doesn't have much to give. Sam loves music, so occasionally he'll go to a club by himself and just listen. On most nights, however, he's fine being home alone.

Still, Sam says that he feels good about his situation. He wishes he lived closer to his three children and his siblings, and holidays can be hard when he can't travel to be with them. He'd like to date more often and would prefer to have more sex as well. But he wouldn't trade places with most married men he knows, and he certainly has no interest in a relationship like the one he had before. In Sam's account of his marriage, things fell apart because his ex-wife insisted on doing things that she knew he disliked but she wouldn't accompany him to things he wanted to do, either. He found himself married to someone who wasn't with him.

"That was lonely, to be with somebody and not to be. I was all by myself, and I didn't know how to do things on my own." Sam had always enjoyed drinking, but he did more and more of it as his lonely marriage drove him to despair. "I didn't have happiness," he recalls. "And everything I did was for the pursuit of alcohol. It was my companion and my first love. And when I did sober up, I didn't know the person that I had married. I wasn't connected to that person." Divorce not only liberated him, it allowed him to reconnect with himself.

Sam has been sober for several decades now. He attends Alcoholics Anonymous meetings regularly and says that, although he lives alone, "I seldom feel lonely because I'm closer to God." This, too, is not an unusual sentiment. As the Stanford anthropologist Tanya Luhrmann has shown, a growing number of contemporary Christians (including the nearly 40 percent of all U.S. citizens who identify as evangelical or "born-again") say that having an intimate relationship with God is a central feature of their personal life.[12] Among all singles age thirty-five and above, half of women and a third of men report that they attend a religious service at least once a month, and churches have taken notice. Today, clergymen and -women frequently offer special ministries for people who live alone. In their book about living alone after the end of a marriage, the Christian educators Herbert Anderson and Freda Gardner argue that people can enjoy rich and spiritually fulfilling lives if they maintain close connections to God. "What is finally distinctive about Christian anthropology," they write, is that "the ultimate aim of human life is to be in relation with God . . . God comes to each one as a friend and, in accepting that gracious offer from God, no one need feel that she or he is all alone."[13]

Many divorced men we interviewed feel socially integrated even without a strong connection to God. They may not have as much contact with their friends as women do, but they are far more likely to date and be sexually active, and often they take so much pleasure in the liberties born of going solo that they lose interest in commitment altogether. Steven, a policy analyst in his late forties who lives in New York City, divorced his wife six years ago and says that he never anticipated that living alone would be so compelling. He has a flexible work schedule, and on most evenings he stays up late exercising at the gym, watching sports and movies, or socializing in restaurants and bars. He dates often, and remarks on how easy it is for a successful man his age to find smart, attractive, and available women in the city. It's a single man's luxury, he acknowledges, but it's not one he enjoyed when he was young.

Steven got married in his early twenties, before he had much experience with other women, and became a father soon after. He adores his children, but he grew estranged from his wife as their interests veered in different directions. His career took off and the world opened up to him just as his home life began to be constraining. Steven spent years pouring himself into work —partly because he liked it and partly, he now believes, to avoid confronting his family situation. Eventually the problems grew impossible to ignore. Counseling didn't help much, because he and his wife were fundamentally incompatible. The marriage could be justified only for the sake of their children, and who could say that they were better off living in an unhappy home?

Two years after the separation, Steven got involved with a younger woman who wanted something serious, and he was drawn to the idea. She might not have been a perfect match for him, but she seemed pretty close. They had a great sex life, liked each other's friends, traveled well together, and shared taste in movies as well as work interests. They started spending several nights a week in each other's apartment, and eventually, like so many other couples living in expensive cities, they found it hard to justify the costs. She moved into his place, and Steven enjoyed sharing a home with her . . .

until he didn't. The problem, he realized, was that living with someone—even a women he loved—meant denying himself the chance to enjoy an unfettered existence: Dating new women. Staying out as long as he wanted and not worrying about anyone else. Watching sports. Seeing movies. Meeting friends.

Steven had grown to appreciate the virtues of living lightly, without obligations. He was willing to give up some of this, but after his girlfriend had moved in, the relationship took on more weight than he could handle. When she started bringing up marriage, perhaps even children, everything snapped. "I feel awful about it, because I really do love her," Steven tells me. "But there's something in me that just cannot commit to another relationship. And part of it is that I really like living alone right now. There's just too much to give up."

Charlotte, who was mulling over a marriage proposal during our first interview, has also decided that she'd lose too much if she accepted. In our follow-up interview, she explains that, after fourteen years of going solo, she's not willing to give up her independent lifestyle. She has grown anxious about intimacy, and particularly about letting someone see how she acts and who she is when she's in her own space. As she enumerates some of her domestic quirks—eating what she wants, when she wants to; spending full days in her pajamas; keeping the TV and radio on at the same time—she says that her suitor "doesn't have a clue who I am" and predicts that "it would slide downhill once he found out." Right now, Charlotte says, things are simply too good to risk giving up everything for a live-in companion who may not love her when he really gets to know her.[14] She is hardly certain that she has made the right decision. "You'll have to interview me again in twenty years," she jokes, and if things turn out badly, she promises to complain, "Why didn't you stop me then, when I had a chance?"

CHARLOTTE HAS A GOOD SENSE of humor about her predicament, but divorcees who live alone in their fifties and early sixties often have a hard time confronting their concerns about growing older on their own. Some get previews of how challenging it might be during episodes of severe illness or injury. Sam, who once struggled with alcoholism, suffered a heart attack, had major surgery, and then developed a severe lung infection about a year ago. "I didn't know if I was going to live or not," he recalls. "I stayed in the hospital from August to November, and I don't even remember August and September." What was certain, however, was that he would be unable to take care of himself after the hospital released him, and that meant calling on family members to help. His mother, who's in her late eighties, had visited him after the operation, but she was unfit for the responsibility of managing his care at home. Fortunately, Sam has always been close to his sister in Washington, and she offered to look after him if he could move in with her. Though it was far from California, his boss was willing to give him extra time to recover, and Sam spent two months recuperating in his sister's house before he was well enough to return. Now he says, "Everybody thinks I need to get married and have a wife" to take care of him. But Sam took away a different lesson: His family would be there for him when he needed them most.

Not everyone shares this confidence. Lou, the fifty-seven-year-old attorney and musician in Berkeley, has a back condition that occasionally leaves him "hurting like hell" and "hardly able to walk." When he lived in San Francisco, he could call on his son to help him move around his apartment or get food and medicine. Now his son has moved elsewhere and he doesn't have any family nearby. So what would he do if he were bedridden, or worse? "Maybe somebody could . . ." He takes a long pause and thinks about it. "I could call somebody . . . I don't know." The issue gnaws at him during the interview, and by the end he is adamant that he needs to find a partner before he gets much older.

"I'd really like to have some companionship," he acknowledges. "Is it too much to ask?"

The divorced women we interviewed had more faith in their support system of friends and family, in part because they had worked so hard to build and sustain it. This isn't surprising, since, as psychologists such as Carol Gilligan have argued, from an early age girls are encouraged to develop intimate relationships and to value mutual support, while boys are pushed into larger group settings (such as sports teams) where competitive, rule-based activities prevail. According to one review of the literature on gender and social networks, "From childhood to adolescence, girls appear to seek more help and support from others than do boys." The result is that, compared to men, adult women tend to be more empathic and sensitive to the needs of others. They also tend to be more active social planners, which helps them stay connected even after their marriages fall apart.[15]

As for Madeline, she would be thrilled to find the right romantic partner to accompany her on the next part of her life. But she would also be shocked, since every story she knows or statistic she hears suggests that it's not going to happen. Most of her closest friends are single women who live alone too, and they all expect to stay that way. "By any objective measure we should be depressed as hell," Madeline says. What's surprising is that "I'm not, and none of the women I know are. It's almost one of the best times of my life. I have more friends now than I've ever had. And I'm making a concerted effort to enlarge my social circle."

Madeline reads a lot of science, and she has come to believe that expanding her social network could help protect her from the dangers of growing isolated as she ages. She's been reaching out to new people in hope of enriching her life with the kinds of "social capital" that the Harvard political scientist Robert Putnam made famous. She's determined not to be alone. Madeline sees her behavior as more than simply strategic, however, because she enjoys the experience of putting herself out there and seeing what happens. She's over sixty, after all, and if she doesn't try things now, when will she?

In recent years Madeline has started using social networking sites quite often. A site like Meetup.com helps her find discussion partners who speak Italian or share her interest in politics, and she finds an occasional date on Craigslist. She connected with her neighbor a few years ago, and now the two of them often knock on each other's door and take spontaneous walks to local cafés and parks. She also decided to get to know some of the gay men in her neighborhood whose social world had always seemed closed to her. Now she says, "I am the fag hag of the

Western world, if you'll excuse that expression. I can go out every night with another young gay man and they are wonderful to me—wonderful company."

She hasn't yet had to activate her support system for anything more than the occasional emotional boost that everyone needs. But she trusts that her friends will be there for her when she needs them, and after one failed marriage and then a twelve-year relationship that dissolved, she can't say that about a romantic partner. Now, Madeline insists, she's not going to do anything to jeopardize the strength of her network. "There's such a thing as too much togetherness. If I were to find a relationship, we wouldn't have to do everything together, we wouldn't have to share friends. And I never again want anybody living with me, nor do I ever want to live with someone else."

4.
PROTECTING
THE SELF

NO ONE REALLY BOWLS ALONE.
The provocative phrase, from Robert Putnam's sweeping account of the decline of civic participation in the United States, is a metaphor, not a finding (as he acknowledged). Putnam used it with great effect to dramatize the fact that participation in bowling leagues had fallen during the second half of the twentieth century, as had participation in a number of historically significant civic associations and membership groups, from the Boy Scouts to the Elks clubs and the League of Women Voters. The truth is, Americans continue bowling together, but with friends (and friends of friends) in their social network, not in formal teams or organized groups.

The distinction is important. When *Bowling Alone* was published in 2000, pundits and policy makers worried that families were watching TV together in their living rooms rather than interacting with each other in the public sphere. Today, our most pressing social concerns are different—and not just because we're nostalgic about the days when family members watched TV together rather than on their own mini-screens! In the first years of the twenty-first century we've witnessed the rise of new forms of interpersonal engagement and civic participation, from MoveOn to MySpace, e-government programs to microlending initiatives such as Kiva. We are, as headlines tell us: "Addicted to Social Media," "Trapped in a World Wide Web," "Caught in the Net." Our most burning questions about the nature of contemporary society are not about isolation, but the problem of being hyperconnected, or of living with what the technology guru Linda Stone calls "continuous partial attention," because we are so deeply embedded in the personal, professional, and social activities we perform online.

All of this should affect the way we understand how and why we live alone today. Whether or not we go solo, most of us are immersed in one or more social worlds, and today a growing number of critics have begun to worry that we are in too deep. We are experiencing "the end of solitude," writes the essayist William Deresiewicz, who claims that in contemporary culture "we live exclusively in relation to others" and that too many of us find it "impossible to be alone." The sociologist Dalton Conley goes further, arguing that we are witnessing the death of the individual and the birth of "intraviduals": busy professionals whose lives are dedicated to "managing the myriad data streams, impulses, desires, and even consciousness that we experience in our heads as we navigate multiple worlds."[1]

Arguments like these are intriguing but not quite persuasive. Granted, there's good reason to worry about the cognitive development of young people who spend their days steeping in text messages, TV, and the Internet; about the rise of knowledge-based service-sector jobs that require professionals to spend their days and nights e-mailing and doing relationship management with clients or colleagues; about the psychological well-being of "crack-berry" junkies who cannot focus on the world beyond their smart phone. But does this really signal the end of solitude or individualism? After all, the "network society" emerged only after massive numbers of young adults began living alone for the first time in history and unprecedented numbers of children started growing up in rooms of their own. It's hard not to see a relationship between the demand for constant connection, whether online or on the job, and the enormous increase in the amount of time we spend on our own. And it's important to note that not everyone— indeed, most of us—*aren't* always elsewhere, seeking out contact or a new Facebook friend.

In fact, we interviewed a number of people

who said living alone was a way to buffer themselves against the intense pressures of social and, especially, vocational life. To be sure, this strategy for protecting the self means something different for affluent and middle-class people than it does for the poor, the mentally ill, or the physically frail. For successful professionals, living alone as a form of self-protection typically means establishing one's home as a sanctuary in the city, one that facilitates the very pursuit of solitude and self-discovery that Deresiewicz and Conley fear we've abandoned. It doesn't always work this way, however. Some of the affluent and middle-class people we interviewed acknowledged that they'd sought out a place of their own to avoid toxic relationships, or to escape from a community that took more than it gave. The disadvantaged men we interviewed were even more likely to report motivations like this. For them, living alone can easily lead to a dangerous extreme, resulting not only in domestic autonomy but also in reclusiveness, hoarding, and other antisocial behaviors that turn one's safe house into a tomb. Even more judicious forms of social withdrawal may lead to a kind of miserable security, as in the case of many of the ex-convicts, substance abusers, and unemployed men who take refuge in single-room occupancy hotels (SROs) and cheap efficiency apartments to avoid friends and family whose company brings more trouble than it's worth.

Living alone is a way to protect the self, yet it also risks imperiling it, and it's no surprise that people in good physical, emotional, and financial health are better able to find the right balance than those who are sick or poor. For those with financial security, a busy schedule, and a dense social network, living alone can be productive because it offers access to privacy, restoration, and personal development. But for the vulnerable it more often leads to what Berkeley sociologist Sandra Smith calls "defensive individualism," a dangerous state that fosters distrust toward other people and institutions, and ultimately toward the self as well.[2]

MOST PEOPLE WHO LIVE ALONE are financially secure, not poor, and those who purposely use their domestic space as an oasis from their busy, stressful work lives report that it is a regenerative, not an isolating experience. Phil is a successful journalist in his late forties, and he says that working and living in Manhattan requires giving so much of himself that at the end of the day he needs to shut things out. "I wouldn't say I'm a solitary person," he explains. "But I like privacy. I need time to recharge."

Unmistakably outgoing, with a warm smile and a kind demeanor, Phil has spent most of the past two decades living independently, and he's learned how to organize his home so that it accommodates the particular kind of solitude he seeks. "I like having control of my own space, making it like my childhood room at large, but calm, like how it feels in church. I not only live alone. I've mostly lived without a television, without a pet." Phil sees domestic tranquillity as a means of deepening his self-knowledge and, in turn, enhancing his creativity. He believes that the time he spends alone helps him to be a better writer, a better thinker, and a more engaging person. Like the late psychologist Anthony Storr, Phil argues that solitude can bring us closer to ourselves, and he can rattle off a long list of great artists and authors who spent most of their lives in a place of their own.[3]

Although his life has never been busier, living alone gives Phil ample time to confront his feelings, and he says that now, instead of getting bogged down by questions about how he got here, he uses his hours at home to think about where he's heading and whether he's living the way he wants. As he approaches fifty, he realizes that if he stays single there will be new challenges ahead. "The frailty of aging and the growing awareness of one's own fatality start to factor in. You think, you know, what's gonna happen?" What's scary, Phil says, is the prospect of dying without loved ones nearby. "The big thing that changes with age in terms of living alone is that the words 'dying' and 'alone' start to become associated with each other," he explains. "Nobody worries about dying married."

AMY, who works for a food magazine, is too busy to worry about what will happen to her as she ages. She's a youthful thirty-eight, with long brown hair and sharply defined features. Like Phil, she says that her job requires "a lot of social interaction. I'm dealing with creative people. There are divas, and egos that you have to manage. I have to cuddle, cajole, threaten, be passive-aggressive." Added to her formal work responsibilities, this relationship management takes a toll on her, especially during the busy periods. "Two weeks out of every month we're working twelve-, fourteen-, sixteen-hour days. I can't plan anything." Usually, she doesn't want to. "Work is very social," she reports, "and I like the peace of coming home and not having to interact anymore, having a chance to decompress."

At the beginning of our interview she tells me that she moved into a place of her own once she could afford it, but once she gets more comfortable she reveals another layer of her story. She has moved from a shared apartment into a place of her own twice during the past ten years, and while having money to pay the rent was necessary, in both cases she made the change to escape domestic relationships that were dragging her down. The first time was in Los Angeles, where she had been living with her brother after graduating from college and cycling through a series of bad roommates. "I just couldn't live with him anymore," Amy explains. "He was driving me nuts and I had to get away." Getting her own place proved liberating. Not only did it make her feel like a real adult, it also restored her sense of autonomy and self-control.

The second time was more painful. She was in New York, where she had moved in with her boyfriend and begun to imagine their life together. "It was far more intimate and intense than living with roommates," Amy reports. But she poured herself into it because she was in love, and she knew they could make things work. Only they couldn't. As she later learned, her boyfriend was secretly dating a woman in her early twenties. "He was a jerk," Amy says, with well-earned hostility. "I found out that he had been cheating on me since the first month we moved in together. He had been lying to me the whole time, and I didn't know." Scarred from the experience, Amy ruled out any kind of shared housing situation and has vowed that she will live alone, safely removed from a potentially harmful roommate or partner, until she finds someone who earns her trust and affection. She's not shy about looking, but she does so slowly and cautiously, ever mindful of what she has to lose.

AMY MAY BE CAUTIOUS, but, as a relatively comfortable and secure young professional, she is far less self-protective than the many disadvantaged city dwellers who choose to live alone to avoid friends and family who have previously contributed to their problems and may still threaten to put them in harm's way. Within a few miles of Amy's spacious apartment, there are thousands of solitary men clustered in New York City's remaining stock of single-room occupancy dwellings and studios. These men are struggling to shake off a heavy load of burdens: substance abuse, a criminal record, poverty, unemployment, and disease are common, and often overlapping.

The ranks of men in this situation have grown steadily since the 1970s, due not only to the collapse of the industrial labor market and the fact that employers in the service sector are reluctant to hire them, but also to the rise of women in the paid workforce, the vast expansion of the penal system, and the retrenchment of social services for the poor.[4] In 2006 the *New York Times* reported, "About 18 percent of men ages forty to forty-four with less than four years of college have never married, according to census estimates. That is up from about 6 percent a quarter century ago. Among similar men ages thirty-five to thirty-nine, the portion jumped to 22 percent from 8 percent in that time." The economic crisis of the late 2000s made things even worse, and in 2010, as a Pew Research Center study of the "New Economics of Marriage" showed, single men without a college degree had even less income and fewer prospects than they did in 1970—making them more "unmarriageable" than they were then.[5]

Many of these men see living alone as a necessary evil, since it gives them the time and space to regain their footing, but it deprives them of much needed care and social support. Greg, who's unemployed, is in his early fifties and suffers from severe heart disease. During the past ten years he's lived alone, mostly in shelters and SROs around Manhattan. When he recounts his life story, it's clear that, for men in his situation, close ties with friends and family members can be helpful or harmful, depending on the circumstance.[6] Communities, in this way, are a lot like marriages: When they're good, they're very good, but when they're bad, they're dangerous.

Not long ago Greg was hospitalized after a heart attack, and he worries about a recurrence. "I think about that sometimes, me being in a house alone. It could be a disadvantage. It might be good if I have somebody around me." But who? Greg used to be a drug addict, and for roughly twenty years he lived between jail cells, abandoned buildings, and the streets. "I went in and out of jail, in and out of jail, in and out of jail, until around '97 or '98. I hadn't had a job in over twenty years because I stayed on drugs a long time." Greg had two children with a common-law wife. He says the state wouldn't let them stay together because they couldn't afford an apartment together, and he's never spent a night with the kids. Their mother died recently, and these days he rarely sees his other family members. Eventually, Greg would like to spend more time with his children, and maybe with other family, too. Although he has been off drugs for nearly a decade, he knows that day is a long time off.

For now, Greg has devised an alternative strategy for soliciting care and attention after a heart attack. "No matter where I'm at, nobody with me or nothing like that, if it did come down on me, I make sure I get out in the hallway. I'll get to my door real quick. You don't last that long after it hits you because it cuts your wind. You can't breathe, so you're gonna pass out. If I got in the hallway and fell, somebody coming down the next floor probably see me. It might take a little time, though—might be too late 'cause wasn't nobody on my floor. But if I got out in the hallway somewhere down the line, somebody coming in gonna see me."

The shelters and SROs where Greg has lived pack a lot of people into small spaces, and there's considerable human traffic in the common areas and hallways. Greg could try to develop some relationships in the buildings and use them for social support, but he's wary of his coresidents. He's even more cautious around his older friends: "I had a lot of headaches in my days by knowing people, the type of friends that I've had. You know, it's like, 'Oh man, let me have this, let me have that.' And, you know, when you got a friend, if he got a problem, you got a problem, because they gonna bring it to you. Back in those years, we just thick and thin, everything was us together. We do our drugs together, go to homes, abandoned buildings together."

Occasionally Greg gets lonely and longs for good company, but he fears that spending time with the people in his network will lead him down the wrong path. "Most of those guys, I hardly see them anymore. I kind of avoid things like that nowadays. I guess it's kind of on me. I don't be trying to make friends to talk to. 'Hi' and 'Bye.' 'How you doing?' Almost every day I go outside, but, you know, most of the time I just go to the park, read my book. I'm not real conversational here lately. I've been so much into myself."

Tim, who's in his fifties, has also decided that he's better off keeping to himself in a small room rather than trying to live with a partner or roommates. "Whenever I lived with roommates, well, those people were always on drugs and stuff. I like being alone right now because I can't blame anybody except myself if I fuck up. It's like, I'm not antisocial, but I have a hard enough time with my own problems without other people's problems."

Recently, Tim moved into an SRO with a staff offering social services and decent security, because he wanted a place that felt safer and more anonymous than his previous building. "There's other hotels like this, with people doing drugs and stuff, saying, 'Hey, you wanna get high or anything?' But here, there's no pressure to do anything. You can just go to your room every day, you know, come home and close your door and nobody's here to bother you. There's nobody knocking at your door."

POOR MEN WHO LIVE IN SROs and low-cost efficiency apartments build interpersonal barriers to defend themselves from the potentially corrupting social influence of their peers. Others, particularly those who have fallen down the class ladder and hope to climb up again, distance themselves from coresidents to evade the stigma of poverty and failure. Some of them avoid family, former partners, and old friends because they're ashamed of their status, or because they believe they've been abandoned by those who are fed up with or ashamed of them.

Although poor men who live alone often express an abstract interest in finding a partner or reconnecting with another community, in practice the obstacles to doing either are so daunting that maintaining independence takes precedence. The result is a vicious circle: Self-imposed social isolation removes impoverished singles from job networks and potential sources of support, increases stress, and compromises health, placing them at risk for even greater detachment and suffering.

A striking number of the SRO and shelter residents we interviewed reported that they had kept to themselves because they were overwhelmed by the illnesses and deaths among people close to them. For men who, like Greg, come from poor or unhealthy environments, staying close to old friends and family members carries a risk of being exposed to trauma as well as trouble. Rick, who's fifty and gay, was at a loss when asked about his close relationships: "Everybody's dead. Everybody. It was like a swipe. I lost, like, eight to nine people within a period of, like, five or six years. Along with family members. I was close to my older brother, very close. And he was talking to me about my friend [Rick's recently deceased partner] and helping me and everything. And last October, I was getting ready to meet him for lunch and I was leaving here and the phone rang and he was getting dressed to meet me and died, so . . . So, you see. There was just a pattern to everything."

Rick's response was to hunker down in his room. He keeps his television on around the clock, using it as a diversion when he's awake and as background noise when he sleeps, turning it off only when he leaves the room. It's not an exciting life, he says, but it protects him from future pain. "Right now I have absolutely no friends. And I guess it's my choice to be just on my own. I used to be a very outgoing person, and now I'm not really a people person. I just come in my place, go in and out—that's it."

Miguel has recently been through a similarly brutal stretch, and he's responded by retreating into solitude. He says that his goal is to achieve greater autonomy, so he won't need to depend on others who, he fears, will disappoint him or disappear: "I can't really say right now that I have a close friend, or that I'm even looking to get a close friend. This particular experience that I'm involved with now is giving me a chance to grow more as a man, to allow the man in me to mature more, in the total sense, and to become self-sufficient and of self-worth in my own right.

What I need to do is to learn to become my own close friend and best friend, and to love myself, and feel self-worth and validation."

WHILE SOME MEN IN THE SROs stay close to their buildings to avoid friends and family, others worry more about the company inside. Nick, who's in his mid-thirties, reports that "most of my old friends are either dead or incarcerated." He contracted HIV from a blood transfusion when he was a teenager, spent years fighting a drug addiction, got married, had a child, got a GED, then a divorce, and soon after his life fell apart. He's been unemployed for six years, living off disability insurance and spending most of his nights in SROs that were "heavily drug-infested, mouse-ridden, cockroach-ridden" places where there were "blatant sales, prostitution, and junkies from every drug that you could think of, dopeheads to crackheads to alcoholics." Nick says that "when you've lived in a place where everything is rotten, you seem to be rotten." He had friends in the building, and he was reluctant to leave them because he liked to party. But when things got bad, he'd try to avoid them. "I became very, very, very reclusive. If I didn't have to go out, I didn't go out." His friends didn't appreciate this treatment, however, and Nick's life got even rougher. "You got people knocking on your door at three in the morning, you know. It was nuts. I was getting into fights, verbally and physically." Nick became desperate to distance himself from his neighbors and started looking for a safer, cleaner place to live. Eventually he found one, and when he moved he brought along an important lesson: Keep to yourself.

His new SRO has a comfortable common area, and residents gather there daily to pass the time, talking, reading the paper, and watching TV. Occasionally the staff offers a meal, or a movie, or classes for the residents. Nick avoids all of this. "I don't partake in the social life of this building. I kind of stick to myself. I really don't like people to know my business." He's cautious about the men in his situation, because they remind him of the man he used to be, as well as the people he's been trying to avoid. "Everybody wants to know something, and once they do they think they've got your number," he says. They start issuing invitations. They harass you. They pull you down. Like Rick and several other SRO residents, Nick spends a great deal of time locked in his room with the television on. "The less I have to interact, the better it is for me," Nick says. "I don't even know one person's name in this whole building."

Nick hopes that the new, nicer SRO will help him with the transition out of poverty, joblessness, and addiction. He wants his stay to be temporary, though he admits that, if he comes to like it there, it might beat his other options. His ex-wife is remarried and he doesn't see her anymore. But he has family in Brooklyn, and he'd like to spend more time with his children. Nick also misses the warmth of a companion sleeping beside him, and he could imagine living with a partner after he cleans up. "For right now," he says, "I'm not going nowhere. Hopefully, once I can start to get back on my feet a little better—you know, as my health continues, hopefully I'll go back to work. And possibly one day, you know, move out of here, or, you know, stay here. For now, I'm here. I'm in a good place, so I'm not gonna screw that up."

For some men in the building, however, it's hard to appreciate being in a good place when other residents are in such noticeably bad shape. Downwardly mobile residents, men who once had stable jobs and a decent income, are often embarrassed to have landed in the stigmatized world of SROs, and they distance themselves from their neighbors as a way of maintaining self-esteem. John, for instance, wound up in his SRO because he couldn't find any other housing that he could afford with his disability check. He's been in his current place for four years, during which he's made only one friend. "The majority of people I try to keep away from," he says. The substance abusers and mentally ill residents who congregate in public spaces "give you a clue there's something wrong here, know what I mean? I'm not gonna socialize with these people."

Bob, who's in his early sixties and has lived on his own for most of his life, ran a small business out of the house he owned until "the state came and condemned my whole block through the wonders of the eminent domain laws." He had a hard time adjusting to the new building. "When I was first brought in here, I mean, I was practically in tears. I wouldn't even sleep in here. I slept in a basement on Fifty-fifth Street for the first week. I didn't want nothing to do with this."

Bob eventually grew more comfortable in his building. He has gotten to know and respect the social workers, whom he sees as remarkably caring. He's pleased about the security, and he appreciates how well the staff maintains the common spaces. But no matter how much the environment satisfies him, it's still an SRO, not the apartment with a garden in which he once took so much pride. No matter how professional the staff is, the other tenants bear the marks of poverty, illness, and hardship, and for outsiders they can be an unsightly bunch. Knowing this, residents like Bob acknowledge that they feel some shame about their situation, and many try to save face by turning away from family and friends who might otherwise be close to them.

They go solo because they don't want anyone to see how far they have fallen, or because they fear that others want nothing to do with them.

Nick, for instance, explains that he pulled away from his children and their mother after he started living in SROs. "I wasn't around much for them. I didn't like where I was living. I didn't like the way I was living, so a lot of times I wouldn't show my face. The environment I was living in was taking a toll on me. And it's more embarrassment, I guess you'd say, than anything. I just didn't want people to know and see how I was." Tim, who says that living alone can be "horrible and lonely," has lost touch with his ex-wife and children, whom he tried to protect from his downtrodden environment. Now he's reluctant to reach out to family or search for a new partner, because "at this time in my life, you know, I have nothing to offer anyone." Some men believe that their family members devalued them when they moved into the world of poor single men, and complain that they've been abandoned. "I'm treated different since I'm alone," Rick says. "It seems like now nobody cares."

MARY ANN WOULD HAVE UNDERSTOOD that feeling. She lived alone for decades, and in the fall of 2007 she died that way, too. She was seventy-nine years old when she called herself an ambulance and went into a hospital near her home in Los Angeles. Her life ended there two weeks later, after a full cardiac arrest. When it happened, Mary Ann didn't have a friend or relative at her side. In fact, the only person she'd even listed as an emergency contact was Sue, who delivered drugs for her pharmacy.

"I was really surprised when they called me and said my name was on there as the person to contact," Sue tells me when I visit her home in a working-class neighbourhood in Huffington Park. "I went, 'Oh really, okay . . .'" She laughs nervously, looks toward the Christmas decorations that saturate her living room, and continues. "I didn't even know if she had a brother or family."

Sue had last heard from Mary Ann on a phone call from the hospital. She'd left an urgent message, pleading with Sue to feed and look after her two dogs, who were chained up outside the house. "When she called, she was just crying. She said that if somebody doesn't pick up the mail, they'll take her dogs away. 'They're all I have,' she said. She goes, 'I promise I won't cheat you. I'll pay you.' I wasn't worried about that. It just broke my heart a little that she'd think, 'They're all I have.'"

I visited the hospital two weeks after Mary Ann's death, because her body and belongings were still there. No one had planned a funeral, or even picked up her things. I wasn't there alone. Emily Issa, a deputy investigator for the Los Angeles County Public Administrator, was letting me shadow her. Emily is one of a hundred full-time employees at the county public administrator's office, which investigates cases in which someone dies and no one claims the body or the estate. She is sort of like a detective for people who die alone. Her job is to comb through the remains of their lives, searching for next of kin, trying to figure out what they've left behind and who should get it. Emily and her colleagues get about three thousand cases like this one each year.

Mary Ann was single, with no known siblings or children. But she owned her house, she had a bank account, and who knows what other valuables she left behind in her home. Now someone stands to inherit it, and Emily's job is to find out who. She's looking for someone who knew Mary Ann to lead her to a relative. There's also the question of who's going to bury her; before Emily's finished, she'll have to resolve that, too.

We start our search in the hospital's patient services office. There's a nun working there, and at first we think she might know something helpful, because when she sees Mary Ann's name on the case file, her face lights up. But it turns out she spoke to her only a few times, and she has little to offer besides the assurance that Mary Ann got good care until the end.

The nun hands Emily a big plastic bag. Inside is everything Mary Ann brought with her to the hospital, and Emily starts digging through it, looking for clues. There's a fluffy blue robe. A small black purse. Prescription drugs. Baby powder. Glasses. Coupons. Typical things you would find in a woman's purse.

None of this is of much use to Emily. She needs contact information. An address book. A cell phone with some names on the speed dial. There's nothing like that in the purse. She finds a notebook, and she flips through it in search of a personal note, maybe a list of last wishes. But every page is blank.

What she does get is a set of keys to Mary Ann's house. The best-case scenario, Emily tells me, is that once we get there we'll find a will or some instructions. But that happens only rarely; in her line of work, it's like hitting the jackpot: "I've been out to a case where I walk in and on the nightstand next to the bed it says, 'In case of emergency . . .' Five minutes and I'm done."

MARY ANN'S CASE ISN'T THAT EASY. When we get to her house, her two dogs are still chained up in the yard, so Emily calls animal control to take them away. The outside of Mary Ann's house is a mess. The wood panels are rotting. There's powdery gray dirt where grass once lived. An old VW minibus with flat tires sits in the dusty driveway. Mary Ann used it for storage; it looks like it hasn't been driven for years.

The inside of the house is even worse. It's dark and dusty, cluttered with stacks of video cassettes, empty juice cans, boxes from the Home Shopping Network—many never even opened. Emily, who seems completely unfazed by the scene, declares it "mildly pack rat." I tell her it seems really pack rat to me, so she explains her classification: "You can still see the ground. We see plenty of cases where you can't even walk on the ground because it's packed with stuff. You're climbing over everything."

Emily is so used to places like this that she never goes on a search without gloves and tennis shoes—and a mask, in case the person died at home and wasn't found for a while. Usually, she has to dig around. Emily doesn't just open drawers and medicine cabinets. If she has to, she climbs to the attic. She breaks down locked doors. She once found someone's business records in a refrigerator—in the vegetable bin.

Emily searches through Mary Ann's living room. You can tell she had basically condensed her life into this one area. There's an unmade makeshift daybed in front of the dusty television. Emily lifts up layers of the bed, searching for money, letters, anything that might connect her to the world outside. But there's nothing under there, just stacks of egg crates and musty blankets.

A few feet beyond the bed, we find an entire dining room set hidden under the clutter. Emily seizes on a stack of mail and canceled checks and starts rifling through it. She still doesn't find what she's looking for: No business card from an attorney or an accountant. No photos of friends or relatives. Not even a personal check—just payments, to AARP, *Ladies' Home Journal*, *TV Guide*. In fact, there's not a single sign that there was another person in Mary Ann's life. And I find that much stranger than the mess.

AFTER EMILY AND I have been there forty-five minutes without finding even one personal item, I ask her if this is unusual. "Not at all," she replies. "It's just like this. People surrounding themselves with things. Things rather than people. She almost built herself into a little cubby, like a cave here, behind all her stuff. You can tell this is where she spent most of her time."[7]

Emily's just looking for contact information, not to piece together someone's life story. But sometimes she gets those stories anyway. She tells me about two cases that she hasn't been able to stop thinking about. One involves a woman whose husband died in World War II. She survived another sixty years, but her personal correspondence was a record of how she'd tried to keep her mind in the 1940s. The other concerns a man who killed himself by smoking up his room with a portable barbecue grill, which he'd placed on his bed. When she arrived, Emily tells me, the whole apartment was black from the smoke, and the only white spaces were the ones she and the dead man had left with their footprints. It was disturbing not only because of the nature of the suicide, but also because of the way that the footprints connected her to the case. Emily doesn't have time to dwell on these stories, though. There's too much work to do at Mary Ann's.

More than ninety minutes into the search, Emily finally finds something personal. Buried in a pile on one of the dressers is a sign of a family history: a picture book, with photographs of a little girl dancing, and some others from a studio, the kind used as head shots in Hollywood. The child is pretty, with Shirley Temple curls and deep dimples, but we don't actually know that it's Mary Ann, because the label says only "1933." There's not a name in sight.

It's remarkable how little we find out about Mary Ann. We learn that her mother once lived with her at this address, because there's lots of mail to her. Mary Ann was into herbal medicine and natural remedies. Her father married four times, and her mom was his third wife. She'd microchipped her dogs.

Emily tells me she doesn't want to make a personal connection with the people she's investigating. She doesn't usually try to figure them out, because there are so many of them that it would be emotionally draining.

I ask Emily if she ever wonders who Mary Ann thought would clean up her stuff. "No," she replies. "It's never even crossed my mind. Most of the time you see these people don't want anyone in here. People who knew them never knew this part of their lives existed."

"She must have known that someday she would die and someone would find all these things," I insist.

Emily speculates: "Maybe it's because she didn't think she had anyone to leave it to. 'Who cares about my mess, because I have no one to leave it to anyway.'"

AFTER NEARLY TWO HOURS, the only thing we've found that might help Emily track down a relative is a thirty-year-old Christmas card addressed to Mary Ann and her mother. It's from a family in Virginia, and they must be related, because in the card they ask for help with a family tree for their kids. Emily deposits it in the clear plastic bag she'll bring back to the office. By now it is getting late in the afternoon, and Emily has to return to her office, because there's a five p.m. deadline for bringing valuable items that belong in the estate to storage.

Emily seals the front door and we walk outside. A few neighbors are looking at us, curiously, and we approach them. She asks Luis, who owns the house next door, if Mary Ann's family ever came by. "She had no visitors," he says. "Just different ladies who used to come and help her." There's a beat of uncomfortable silence as we all think about Mary Ann. Luis breaks it: "She didn't seem to be a very happy lady. She was lonely most of the years. She had two dogs with her, and that's it."

Moments later, we run into another neighbor, George, who has a different take. "She was a nice person," he says. "All the time she talked to us. She talked with my son. Every day I come to work, sometimes I'd see her on the porch. We'd say, 'Hi, Mary.' 'Hi, George.' That's it."

Talking with George and Luis helps me understand something about what happens when truly isolated people die alone. In most cases, we can't actually know whether their solitude was a source of sadness, or satisfaction. Whether they lived and died without friends or family nearby because they preferred it that way, or because something went wrong once and they couldn't get it right. When we hear about someone like Mary Ann, we can't help but project some of our own feelings into her story. And our reactions say as much about each one of us as they do about the deceased.

THE NEXT MORNING I meet Emily at the public administrator's office, where she's busy making phone calls from her cubicle. She's tracked down the number of Terry, whose name was the one clue she found in Mary Ann's house, on that thirty-year-old Christmas card. But when Emily gets him on the phone, there's a problem: He's got no idea who Mary Ann is. Terry tells Emily to call his ex-wife. She's the one who actually wrote the card.

Moments later, Emily's talking to her.

"Ohhh," Emily remarks. "He's the one who gave me the phone number for you, and he said he'd never heard of her. So you think she was his aunt. I see."

The ex-wife was partly right. Mary Ann was a relative of Terry's, but a distant one. Her mother was Terry's great-aunt. But Terry had never met Mary Ann, never even spoken to her. And he knew virtually nothing about her. "We've been just going back and forth on this trying to find out who she was," Terry explains. He says he felt sad when he heard about Mary Ann's situation, but he admits it is hard to feel emotional about her death. "My only feeling toward this right now is I feel responsibility to try to resolve her situation, to kind of tidy up her life, I guess."

One month after Mary Ann's death, Terry and his cousins were still deciding whether they wanted the county to settle the estate or handle it themselves. Emily tells me that because Mary Ann's assets total more than $6,000, the public administrator could arrange for her to be buried in a local cemetery.

If Mary Ann didn't have $6,000, LA County would still take care of things. When people die alone here without the money for burial, their bodies are cremated and their ashes are stored in individual boxes for four years. After that, if no one claims them, they're buried together in a mass grave. The burial takes place once a year, in the corner of a massive cemetery near the USC medical school in East LA.

The ceremony for all the unclaimed people from 2003 takes place just a couple weeks after Mary Ann's death. A chaplain officiates the service. "Honored guests, on this day, December 6, 2007, we're gathered here . . . One thousand, nine hundred eighteen brothers and sisters of humankind." It's a heartfelt occasion, but it's a little empty, too. Besides the chaplain, only about ten people—all county employees—show up for the mass burial. One of them points out the tiny plaques that mark each year's grave site.

The remains of nearly two thousand people fill a hole that's only ten feet long, eight feet wide, eight feet deep.

And I can't help thinking: Right here, all these thousands of people who lived and died alone, they aren't alone anymore.

5.
TOGETHER ALONE

O N AN UNUSUALLY HOT Monday night in June 2008, a long line of singles—mostly women, many in heels—snaked around the edge of San Francisco's Kabuki Cinema until it reached a long pink carpet in the lobby. Ordinarily, the first night of the workweek is slow at the Kabuki, but this was a special occasion. Five local women, all of whom had written about being single, had organized a special screening of *Sex and the City*, complete with Carrie Cosmos, goody bags (translucent shoe boxes, actually, whose contents included gym passes, a makeup kit, and a prepaid card for thirty minutes of adult videos online), and an after-party in the theater's bar. The women had met two months earlier, when they were copanelists at a sold-out forum called "Single in the City." The event was so successful that they decided to organize a follow-up, and what could be better than gathering to watch the ongoing exploits of that fabulous foursome, Carrie, Samantha, Miranda, and Charlotte? The Kabuki was willing to host, on the condition that the five authors agreed to buy every ticket for the theater in advance and handle the sales. This turned out not to be cause for concern: The gala sold out less than four days after it was announced on the authors' home pages and social network sites, and the crowd was so eager to get there that scores showed up an hour before screen time. The group even included a singular Bay Area celebrity: Craig Newmark, the founder of Craigslist.

The buzz surrounding the party came as no surprise to co-organizer Sasha Cagen, the author of *Quirkyalone: A Manifesto for Uncompromising Romantics* and the leader of an incipient movement that advocates for those who enjoy being single and are not particularly anxious about finding a partner. Cagen, a creative and charismatic Barnard graduate who's now in her mid-thirties, took up the cause ten years ago when she wrote an essay called "People Like Us: The Quirkyalones." "I am," she wrote, "what you might call deeply single. Almost never in a relationship." Cagen had always considered herself an oddball, but then she noticed how many lonely romantics were out there, unaware that, together, they had inadvertently become a social force. "We are the puzzle pieces who seldom fit with other puzzle pieces. Romantics, idealists, eccentrics, we inhabit singledom as our natural resting state. In a world where proms and marriage define the social order, we are, by force of our personalities and inner strength, rebels." Cagen estimated that about 5 percent of the population was Quirkyalone, and she realized that they need not feel lonely or isolated: "A community of like-minded souls is essential . . . When one Quirkyalone finds another, oohh la la. The earth quakes."

The article hit a nerve. The *Utne Reader* requested permission to reprint it, and Cagen says she got "thousands of letters, e-mails, mix tapes, with the chorus 'Thank God, I thought I was the only one on the planet who felt this way.'" She started a Web site, Quirkyalone.net, which includes her own writing, media coverage of the movement, and a number of "Quirky-forums," including discussion threads on friendship, politics, sex, and work. By 2003, Cagen had secured a book contract to write a full-fledged manifesto, and she decided to turn February 14 into a counterholiday, International Quirkyalone Day. Cagen organized events in San Francisco, New York, Providence, and Glasgow that year, and by 2010 the growing ranks of Quirkyalones had planned holiday celebrations in forty cities on four continents. By the end of that year, more than 6,700 people had registered to post items on Quirkyalone forums, and tens of thousands more had visited the Web site. Calls for local events issued from Indianapolis,

Istanbul, and Iceland, as well as all the big cities where singletons come together to be alone.

Cagen is now something of a hero for the growing ranks of singletons who are learning to feel secure with their status, and she is often their public face. She appears frequently on popular national television and radio programs to explain that going solo is a viable, legitimate, and not necessarily lonely way to dwell in a city—a point that is surprisingly controversial given how many people are already living alone. And she seems to be everywhere on February 14, because the media never tires of contrasting the Quirkyalones with couples who are paying dearly for roses and prix fixe meals at romantic restaurants. (The singles don't suffer from the comparison, since they usually celebrate their counterholiday in crowded dance clubs where everyone appears to be having fun.) But recently Cagen has been feeling increasingly uncomfortable with her role in the movement, and her responsibilities to those who see her as a symbol of independent womanhood have become burdensome, even oppressive. I have met with her a few times over the years to discuss her evolving relationship to the Quirkyalone concept and to the community she helped bring into existence, and in every conversation she has dwelled on the fact that her very public liberation has been personally restricting.

Cagen has sustained her passion for promoting the status of singletons, though she sometimes finds it repetitive because, as she puts it, "organizing Quirkyalone Day has become a bit like throwing the same wedding every year." She has grown tired of living alone, and as she approaches her late thirties she finds herself longing for a long-term romantic partner. A husband, even. "I've always been open to the possibility of finding the right guy and getting married," she tells me as we share lunch in San Francisco's Mission District. "And Quirkyalone was never about being *alone*—it was about being connected, to yourself and to other people too. Now I'm ready for a different experience. I've lived alone for a long time, and at this point in my life I'd grow a lot more if I were partnered. To be honest, I worry that if I keep on making this the center of my life I'm going to wind up being single forever."

Her experience helps illuminate a fundamental feature of the singleton society, one that poses problems for those who try to improve the status and well-being of those who live alone: Few people who live alone are inclined to define themselves that way, let alone to organize political campaigns that enlist those who share their fate. Many, including Cagen, of all people, are willing to push back against the cultural pressure to marry and advocate for those who prefer to go solo, but also see living alone as a temporary, if perhaps recurrent, stage in the cycle of life. Others expect to be on their own much longer but simply do not identify as singletons because other categories—man or woman, black or white, rich or poor, young or old, gay or straight—frame their self-perceptions.

In the abstract, at least, there is no reason that domestic status should figure into someone's identity. In practice, however, people who live alone have discovered that others—from friends and family to the growing number of businesses that are beginning to create special products to suit their needs and interests—do define them that way. Many believe that they are treated unfairly in their personal and public lives, and a growing number have decided that they'd be better off coming together as a group. Some, like the Quirkyalones, seek acceptance, legitimacy, and community, but others want more: Better access to health care, housing, and social security. More fairness in the tax code. Less workplace discrimination. Greater representation in politics. A stronger public voice. These things don't come easily for any group of people, and particularly not for one that's as heterogeneous as singles (who, after all, include people from eighteen to one hundred, some of whom live alone and some of whom do not). It's not yet clear whether it's possible to form a collective identity based on being a singleton, or to inspire a movement for social change with the slogan "Solo dwellers of the world, unite!" But there's no shortage of entrepreneurial singletons who see themselves as a vanguard and are committed to trying.

KIM CALVERT IS AN UNLIKELY ACTIVIST, or at least that's my first impression when she and her chatty white cockatoo, Mimi, greet me in her elegant Santa Monica home. Mimi is not her only daytime companion. A few months before my visit, Kim had converted several rooms near the entryway into office space for the small staff she'd recruited to launch Singular Communications, which published *Singular* magazine until 2009 and now produces the Web site and social networking service SingularCity.com, targeting affluent Angelenos who live alone. A journalist and dot-com veteran in her late forties, Kim counts herself among the ranks of people who live alone but are resolutely opposed to identifying themselves as single. "It's a word that just has horrible associations for me," she says as we sit in her verdant court-yard garden. "It makes me think of desperate, unhappy people who can't get a date, and that's never been who I am."[1]

I hardly need convincing. Calvert is a New Yorker's vision of Los Angeles beauty, with long blond hair, a well-toned body, perfect skin, and warm brown eyes. She's dressed fashionably but casually, in jeans, a tie-dyed long-sleeve shirt, a silver necklace, and large brown sunglasses flipped to the top of her head. Her demeanor is professional and serious, but the venture we are there to discuss was inspired by profoundly personal experiences, and her tone lifts noticeably as she explains it. Calvert belongs to a women's group designed for professionals who want help living up to their aspirations. Soon after joining, she noticed that they were spending a lot of their time together discussing relationships, or their lack thereof. "There are about fifteen of us," she explains, "but only three are married. And the rest of us would always use some of our speaking time to justify to everyone what we were doing to find a husband. At some point I was listening to a friend who was clearly happy without being married, and I started to ask, 'What are we doing? Why can't we just accept that this is who we are and get on with our lives?'"

Marriage hadn't done much for Calvert, anyway. She had given it a try fifteen years earlier, despite the fact that she had never pictured herself settling down, and it was an unmitigated disaster. "I'm a free spirit," Calvert tells me. "And when I got married, I suddenly felt like I had to report where I was going, who I was with, what time I was going to be home. It was like being a child again. I'd known this man for years and always loved talking with him. Suddenly, I wanted to push him out of my life."

Calvert believes that there are millions of men and women who are better off going solo, and her Singular enterprise, which she cofounded with the wealthy sixty-five-year-old divorcé and entrepreneur David Wright, could help some of those who live alone appreciate what they already have. "There is a mission to this," she explains. "We want to liberate single people from the bondage of old ideas that are blocking their ability to have a great life today. And that means fighting against the huge industry out there that makes money by making single people feel bad about who they are. Think about those TV shows that do makeovers so people can finally be desirable, finally get married, finally be happy. They program us to think that it's awful to be single and tell us that we need to be fixed. We have to overcome that."

At Singular Communications, the first step involved redefining the experience. "Singular," Calvert says, connotes someone special and distinctive, so on each cover the words "SEXY SAVVY SINGLE" ran above the magazine's name. Then she targeted an audience: people more or less like her. In an editor's letter for the premiere issue, Calvert wrote, "I like being single. I like my life. I have great friends, I'm active, involved in my community and have the career of my dreams. I love my alone time—to read, write, meditate and be me without compromise. I don't need another half to be whole. I am complete. And yes, I love men, I love romance, I love intimacy—but it's so much better now that I've banished the marriage agenda . . . So if you can identify with me, if you're comfortable being single, if you enjoy an active, social lifestyle . . . *Singular* magazine is for you."

Actually, getting a copy of *Singular* involved more than identifying with Calvert's message. The thick, glossy magazine was mailed only to affluent single Los Angeles residents, and was designed for high-end tastes. There were full-page ads from Jaguar, Beverly Hills Porsche, Residences at the Ritz, Bang & Olufsen, Greystone charter jets, and Fiji water. Cover stories profiled glamorous unmarried celebrities such as Leonardo DiCaprio and Serena Williams. Contributors named their favorite self-indulgences in their bios, with responses including massage (one man says he prefers Hawaiian massages with two therapists at once), good red wine, chocolate, and new gadgets from Apple. There were pages of product reviews and endorsements, for everything from personal concierge service to health clubs and new dental technologies. But most of the content was decidedly singular: an article criticizing singles for "sit[ting] back passively" in public affairs rather than organizing as a political bloc; a column on the "Myth of the Perfect Catch," which warns readers about falling in love with their fantasy of who a person is rather than with the real human being; and a story about a psychologist who witnesses so much dishonesty and infidelity in her patients' relationships that she grows skeptical of marriage.

As for SingularCity.com, it includes original content (such as a feature on "The Rules for Staying Single") and a forum where members can meet. Calvert describes it as "an online city with citizen members, a place where you can start old-fashioned relationships in a high-tech environment, which is important in a city that can feel as alienating as LA." SingularCity also sponsors regular get-togethers, from movies to happy hours to more formal parties. While Calvert insists that these are completely different from ordinary singles events "where people who can't get a date go in hope of finding the person they'll marry," she concedes that "people are probably trying to hook up there, just like everywhere else." Her agenda, after all, is to connect people and help them feel comfortable no matter how they choose to live. "We're not opposed to marriage," she tells me. "But people need to realize that singles are the new majority, and our job is helping to establish their voice."

A FEW MONTHS AFTER I record these words in Santa Monica, I hear them repeated, almost verbatim, in a one-room office on a busy commercial street in Brooklyn, from a woman who couldn't possibly look or sound any less like Kim Calvert. Nicky Grist, who until mid-2011 was the executive director of the Alternatives to Marriage Project, or AtMP, has a cool, analytic intelligence, as well as degrees from Yale and Princeton and twenty years of work experience with community organizations and government agencies. She's a light-skinned African American Jew in her early forties, and when we meet the first time she's wearing a stylish blue suit, striped purple socks, and closely cropped black hair with a few specks of gray. Her voice is soft and a bit squeaky, but it gains depth and volume when she speaks out about a charged political subject. This happens often during our interview, because we're discussing the topic that has consumed her for five years now: the fair and equal treatment of the nearly 100 million unmarried adult Americans, nearly a third of whom live alone.

Grist says she discovered AtMP in 2005 the way most people do: searching the Internet to learn the costs and benefits of marriage. It was not an academic investigation. Grist's domestic partner, a New York City fire lieutenant, had proposed to her, partly because getting access to his health insurance would allow her to quit her job and look for something better. Yet Grist had always been opposed to marriage, on the grounds that it was discriminatory against gays and, historically at least, a bad deal for women. "I had billions of reasons for being skeptical about marriage," she tells me. "One of them being that my parents' marriage would have been illegal in sixteen states when they did it, because she was white and Jewish and he was a Caribbean black. But this time there was a good reason to consider it. I needed a way out [of my job]." She started googling the topic, and within a few minutes she found that the AtMP Web site had answers for nearly all of her questions. "I also thought, 'Wow! This is an incredible organization.' It was the only place out there helping single people figure out the consequences of being unmarried. It's not just access to health insurance. There are workplace discrimination issues, housing discrimination issues, estate planning issues, political issues, tax issues. And they had it all laid out for you. It was great."

As she scanned through the Web site, Grist noticed that the Alternatives to Marriage Project was looking for an executive director, and suddenly she started thinking that she might have found yet another excuse to leave her job. Even though the organization was based in Albany, where a young unmarried couple had founded it in 1998, Grist decided to apply anyway. They liked her so much they not only hired her, but also let her move the headquarters to Brooklyn. "I took a 50 percent pay cut," Grist says. "And I went from a good-sized organization to one with an annual budget of about $35,000 per year. But it's worth it because it's such a luxury to work for an organization where none of my values are being compromised." Advocating for alternatives to marriage may sound like a radical occupation, but Grist insists that it's utterly mainstream. "Most Americans aren't married, and most households do not contain a married couple. If you look at it that way, we're promoting the interests of the majority. And it's not like we're making outrageous demands. All we want is a society that recognizes how many of us are living outside of this institution, and has laws that support us."

The Alternatives to Marriage Project works on behalf of unmarried people in all kinds of situations, including gay and straight domestic partnerships and families led by single parents. These constituents usually have a story about why they've opted out of marriage or been denied the option, and they see themselves as part of a group with common interests. People who live alone aren't like that. One reason, Grist explains, is that a lot of them are looking for a partner and can't identify with those who are not. "There are really two potential groups: those who are happy or at least accepting of singlehood, and those who are just saving up for their weddings. The first group, which we call the 'solo singles' or 'unmarried unpartnereds,' cares about marital status discrimination and gets involved in what we do. The second group— much of it anyway—doesn't have a problem with that discrimination. They just want to hop over to the other side of the marital divide so it'll all be fine." This poses serious problems for AtMP's political work. "It's hard to organize any group," Grist says, "and it's especially hard when they don't have a shared identity or interests." In the aggregate, people who live alone endure many of the same problems and penalties. But since they rarely form an aggregate, it's unclear how any organization can help to improve their fate.

Consider one potential bloc of singletons whose status has garnered attention in policy circles during the 2000s: the African American middle class. According to research led by University of Maryland sociologist Kris Marsh, African Americans who have never married and live alone are the fastest-growing segment of the black middle-class population, and women are especially likely to be part of this group. African

Americans who live alone, Marsh argues, are "not just a phenomenon of early adulthood," but are instead "on a trajectory to becoming the most prominent household within the black middle class if not the entire black community."[2]

What's driving this increase? Harvard sociologist William Julius Wilson argues that two major social changes—the dramatic disappearance of industrial jobs once occupied by African American men, and the subsequent mass incarceration of men from these same communities—has generated a rising class of "unmarriageable males" and thereby reduced the intraracial marriage market. But this is not the entire story. For decades, marriages between black men and white women have been more common than marriages between white men and black women, and in the 2000s they were more than twice as common. This is one reason why, as Yale sociologists Natalie Nitsche and Hannah Brückner report, "black women are twice as likely as white women to never have married by age forty-five and twice as likely to be divorced, widowed, or separated." Another is the expanding gap in education. Today black women are far more likely than black men to obtain a college or graduate school degree, and they're also more likely to discover that the price of their success is that it's harder to find a spouse.[3]

Faced with such bleak options, the emerging

generation of African American professionals increasingly shuns marriage as a means of securing middle-class status and, as Marsh argues, "stabilizes its position by not marrying and continuing to live alone."[4] But gaining stability in one dimension of their lives can bring suffering in another. In her study "The Sexless Lives of College-Educated Black Women: When Education Means No Man, Marriage, or Baby," Yale sociologist Averil Clarke claims that conventional measures of inequality fail to register the personal costs of educational attainment and economic achievement among black professionals. The stigma of being single and childless can be especially severe for black women, she shows, because of the expectations of their families and communities. But so is the stigma of being a single mother, which means unmarried black professionals lose, whatever they do.

The plight of single black professionals, whether male or female, means they have a lot to gain by participating in groups like the Alternatives to Marriage Project. Yet, to Nicky Grist's consternation, recruiting them into the organization's campaigns against marital status discrimination has been difficult; they have other political priorities and personal aspirations to pursue. Moreover, groups like AtMP have to compete with far wealthier organizations—

including religious institutions and the federal government—whose marriage promotion campaigns only further marginalize people who live alone. "It drives me crazy to see things like Black Marriage Day," Grist says. "Or, to name my real pet peeve, the use of public antipoverty funds to pay for billboards saying marriage is good for you. What kind of message does this send to people who might want the privileges and benefits that come with marriage but can't get them? It denies and stigmatizes the real-life experiences of most taxpayers. It's completely unfair."

Though the challenges are daunting, more and more political organizations are attempting to build bases of constituents who identify with the real-life experiences of going solo. The sheer numbers of unmarried people make them too tempting a target: *If only they could be mobilized . . . imagine the power they could exert!* This logic drove Page Gardner to found Women's Voices, Women Vote (WVWV), the first organization dedicated to increasing civic participation among unmarried women across the United States. Gardner, a Democratic political strategist and married mother of two in Northern Virginia, started WVWV in 2003 after learning that 20 million single women did not go to the polls in the historically close 2000 election, making them—by some estimates—the nation's largest group of nonvoters. "In their day-to-day lives, surely these women knew of their individual power," Gardner wrote. "With WVWV, I wanted to convince them of their individual and collective power."[5]

When the 2008 presidential campaign started, Gardner did everything in her power to turn single women into the new soccer moms or NASCAR dads. Yet single women are not typical swing voters. On the contrary, Democratic pollster Stanley Greenberg's firm calls them "the largest progressive voting bloc in the country," and they have a long record of supporting liberal candidates who favor causes such as gun control, public education, expanded access to health care, and prochoice policies. In 2008, Gardner's main challenge was persuading single women to register and turn out on election day, and she knew this wouldn't be easy. Compared with married women, single women were about 9 percent less likely to register and 13 percent less likely to vote in 2004. They were also far more likely than married women to vote for John Kerry than for George W. Bush, and Gardner believes that getting even a slightly higher fraction of unmarried women to the polls could have changed the outcome of that election.

During the 2008 primaries, the prospect that Hillary Clinton would top the Democratic ticket boosted WVWV's initiatives. Clinton may not be single, but she was hugely popular among unmarried women and her candidacy inspired a burst of engagement. But when Barack Obama won the nomination and pundits began arguing that sexism had played a role in her loss, the organization had to keep its constituents from losing faith. Women's Voices, Women Vote stepped up its voter registration campaign, which included a "20 million reasons" public service announcement recorded by celebrities, single mothers, and widows, as well as more than a million direct mailings and countless media appearances in which Gardner urged candidates to help rally single voters. By election week, the organization had generated more than 900,000 registration applications and sent about a million vote-by-mail forms to single women in the swing states of Ohio, Colorado, Iowa, Nevada, and Montana. Gardner predicted that a record number of unmarried women would make it to the voting booth, and that thereafter political officials would recognize them as a powerful interest group.

Did the campaign make a difference? According to WVWV's numbers, in 2008 single women were just 2 percent more likely to register and 1 percent more likely to vote than they were four years earlier. But in absolute numbers the increase looks more substantial, from 27.9 million single female voters in 2004 to

30.5 million in 2008, and their margin of support for the Democratic candidate rose from 62 percent (for Kerry) to 70 percent (for Obama). (Married women, by contrast, voted 50 percent for John McCain to 47 percent for Obama.)[6] Soon after the election, Women's Voices, Women Vote issued a report whose title, "Unmarried Women Change America," conveys Gardner's view of their impact. "Unmarried women played a pivotal role in making this history and changing this nation," it stated. "Barack Obama would have lost the women's vote and the 2008 election if it were not for the contribution of the unmarried woman."[7]

Not everyone shares this interpretation. Nicky Grist, for instance, says that Alternatives to Marriage actually dropped its voting project after the election because the organization had invested so much energy in it but was disappointed by the modest increase in turnout. Moreover, the political issues that matter to her constituents, such as decoupling health insurance from marital status (so you don't lose your coverage if you divorce or become widowed from a partner whose employer provides it) and getting marital status discrimination included in the Fair Housing Act, got little traction in the early years of the Obama administration. In the media, not many analysts credited unmarried women with helping provide Democrats their margin of victory, and, with the exception of WVWV, not many organizations claimed it. As they prepared for the 2010 midterm elections, Gardner and her colleagues worried that the single women's voting bloc had still not solidified. "Based on our nationwide projections, there are likely to be 35.3 percent fewer unmarried women voting in 2010 than in 2008," warned one of their reports. "That's 10.8 million voters."[8] But since unmarried women remain the nation's fastest-growing demographic group, there's good reason to believe that others, including Republicans and conservative get-out-the-vote groups, will soon begin competing for their allegiance. The incentives for engaging unmarried Americans are too great to ignore.

WHILE GROUPS LIKE ALTERNATIVES to Marriage Project have struggled to organize singletons as a political bloc, producers of consumer goods and services are finding that they can effectively organize those who shop solo into an emerging market segment. They also have real incentive to do this, since singles (not all of whom live alone) account for more than 35 percent of total consumer spending, or about $1.6 trillion annually.

The Packaged Facts market study "Singles in the U.S.: The New Nuclear Family" compares the lifestyle and consumption patterns of all variety of unmarried adults, including those in Gen X and Gen Y, seniors, childless singles, blacks, Hispanics, Asians, and those who live alone. The report notes that while singles are hardly absent in the media and in advertising, they are generally depicted as stereotypes: glamorous young professionals who spend their evenings in clubs and fancy restaurants or, conversely, lonely old people who suffer home alone. These images, Packaged Facts warns, turn off the very consumers that advertisers are trying to attract. "It's important for marketers to realize that singles are increasingly viewing their unmarried state as a choice, rather than a temporary and undesirable situation," the study explains.[9] The solution? Packaged Facts offers plenty of strategic advice on how to target-market each of the singles market segments, and the $3,500 price tag on its report suggests the value of this information.

A similar study, published in 2008 by Euromonitor International, offers a global guide to the emerging market of singles and singletons, identifying not only their generic tastes and habits but also specific products that appeal to their demographic in different settings. "Single Living: How Atomisation—The Rise of Singles and One-Person Households—Is Affecting Consumer Purchasing Habits" reports that the rise of living alone has generated unprecedented demand for apartments (not houses), compact furniture and appliances (no need for an oversize refrigerator, dishwasher, or coffee machine when you cook alone), one-seat automobiles and motorbikes, and all kinds of personal services. The global "ready meal" market, for instance, does more than $73 billion in business, up nearly 40 percent since 2002. In Sweden, the nation with the greatest proportion of people who live alone, a company called GOOH! has developed a "home meal replacement concept," offering "fresh, restaurant-quality dishes with the pricing and convenience of fast food . . . which can be reheated on-site or taken home." In Japan, the market for dried ready meals has expanded rapidly, driven by single women's demand for simple, healthy nourishment such as dehydrated savory porridge. Throughout the developed world, singletons are proving to be heavy users of mobile media, as well as of cafés, bars, and restaurants. They may not show the signs of their indulgences, however, since they are also more likely to exercise at the gym.[10]

With marketing analysts tracking their behavior so closely, it's no surprise that entrepreneurs are developing new businesses that cater to the needs of people who live alone. One of these is Singelringen, which is Swedish for "single ring." Designed in 2005 by Johan Wahlbäck, who was born in Stockholm and spent much of his youth in New York and Texas, the turquoise and sterling silver ring allows singles to publicly signal their status. According to the company's Web site, "By wearing your Singelringen, you declare that it is OK to be single. You may wish to find the one, or you are quite satisfied with life as it is. Regardless, you will show to everyone that you accept and stand for what you are." Not many rings get feature coverage on national television, but in 2006 the *Today* show reported that the Singelringen "comes without commitment" and had become "a pretty hot item." It has been mentioned in *People*, *OK!*, and *In Touch* magazines and was promoted at that San Francisco *Sex and the City* event. Like Sasha Cagen, who wore a Singelringen that night, Wahlbäck says he's hoping to help build solidarity.

But selling to a community is hardly the same as organizing it, and not many entrepreneurs have the interest and will to do both. One exception is Sherri Langburt, who we met in chapter two when she faced discrimination in her office and her housing search. Langburt launched Single Edition in late 2007 after spending most of her twenties and thirties on her own. "I started the company because everything online for singles was about dating," Langburt tells me as we sit in her "second office," a café near her apartment on Manhattan's Upper West

Side. "But when I lived alone, my life wasn't all about dating. I had a lot of other concerns, things I wanted to learn about or try, and there were no resources to support my lifestyle. No good information about things like traveling alone or cooking for one. Obviously I wasn't the only person interested in content like that. Every day I hear more stories of people who are living alone and figuring out how to enjoy themselves. People who were married and then divorced and now say, 'I do *not* want to do that again.' Single Edition is for them."

Langburt had spent years as an executive at Weight Watchers, a for-profit corporation that prides itself on building communities and improving people's lives. Single Edition is based on a similar model. When Langburt started the company, she had produced a lot of editorial content, including advice on everyday challenges, such as controlling your portion size when eating alone or finding the right products for a one-person home, as well as on more momentous issues, from career management to financial planning and dealing with parents who pester you about not being married. She had also lined up a network of experts who were willing to contribute in exchange for the recognition, since they too ran businesses—in fitness, law, fashion, nutrition, and, yes, dating—that catered to single clients. And she found a Web designer who was willing to build the site on the barter system. After the launch, Langburt dedicated herself to finding companies interested in marketing to singles. "I was calling ad agencies and saying, 'We need a sponsor. How about Kraft Singles? They'd be perfect. Or Häagen-Dazs, which has those single-serving cups?' I called everyone, met with everyone. And there were days when no one would even talk to me. I could hardly sleep."

The problem, Langburt discovered, was that advertisers insisted that singles didn't identify primarily as singles and couldn't be targeted that way—except by dating services. They market to boomers or to thirtysomethings or to affluent city dwellers, any of whom may happen to be single, but they always aim to convey an aspirational message, and they don't think anyone aspires to be on their own. "I just disagree with this strategy," Langburt tells me. "And my whole business is based on a bet that I'm right. Singles do identify as singles—it's often the first thing they say about themselves. There's no reason to be ashamed of it anymore, especially if they're in a big city. No one cares. You can be anything. You can eat alone. Go out alone. It doesn't matter. You just have to be okay with it." Her theory is that once advertisers recognize this, they'll immediately have access to a rapidly growing market of singletons who are likely to stay that way long enough to make some major purchases. Clothing. Vacations. Cars. A home.

By 2010 Langburt was making progress. She had organized three sold-out events in which hundreds of singles gathered to hear speakers discuss issues such as health, security, and adventure when you're on your own. Fox was interested in developing videos for the singles marketplace. Spark Networks, which runs specialized dating services such as JDate, made her a columnist. Norwegian Cruise Line, which had just announced plans to offer special rooms for solo travelers, was considering a deal with her company, and marketing executives who'd refused her phone calls two years earlier were now taking her concepts to their clients and partners. "My fantasy is that once a few big advertisers get it, then everyone will follow and the business will just take off. Someday, I'd like Single Edition to be for singles what the AARP is for seniors. I'm sure that when they started people said that no one wants to identify as a senior, too. That was fifty years ago. Think about how much has changed."

CHANGING THE WAY we think about singles is the life's work of Bella DePaulo, who coined the term "singlism" to raise consciousness about prejudices toward the unmarried majority. DePaulo has helped Langburt and Kim Calvert develop their businesses, but she is clearly motivated by cultural rather than commercial concerns. "Crusading against singlism is not a great way to get wealthy," she tells me. "I wish it were! The organizations that invite me to speak have no money whatsoever. Last week I visited a community college that asked me to take the train rather than fly and then could only put me up for one night. And for my blog, which takes a huge amount of work, I probably get less than a penny a click. Sometimes I laugh about it. I've got a PhD from Harvard, after all! But I love doing this. It feels completely necessary, because there's so much misinformation out there, so little awareness. I do this because it matters."

Since 2006, when her book *Singled Out: How Singles Are Stereotyped, Stigmatized, and Ignored, and Still Live Happily Ever After* was published, DePaulo has become something like the minister of truth for the solo nation. When a politician makes a baseless claim about the hazards of living alone or the benefits of marriage, it's only a matter of hours before she's posted a refutation on her blog for *Psychology Today*. When a scholar or serious journalist does it, she sharpens her razors and attacks. A few days before our conversation, DePaulo took umbrage with a *New York Times* op-ed about Sandra Bullock's post-Oscar marital humiliation in which David Brooks mentions a study that claims (in his words) that "being married produces a psychic gain equivalent to more than $100,000 a year." This infuriated DePaulo, and she immediately fired off a response: "Studies that compare the currently married to everyone else (which is the vast majority of marital status studies) can tell us nothing about the implications of getting married for happiness, health, or anything else. That's because the currently married are the people who are left after setting aside the 40-some percent of people who got married, hated it, and got divorced. It is like saying that the new drug Shamster is very effective, based on a study in which the experiences of nearly half the people who took the drug were discounted, because it most certainly did not work for them."[11]

At the outset of her career, DePaulo had never imagined getting involved in the public debate about married and unmarried America. She was a scholar of deception, and didn't get interested in the marriage literature until she noticed that colleagues, with whom she enjoyed lunches and formal interactions on workdays, never included her in their more casual weekend and evening plans. "I didn't know if it was personal or because I was single," she recounts. "I started talking with my single friends and they'd say, 'Yes! The same thing happens to me.' Then they would add other stories about the ways they were treated. And all of us felt that we were being excluded—not just from social events, but from networks that shaped our professional lives. Clearly I had hit a nerve."

At the time, DePaulo's only knowledge of the marriage literature was what she saw in the media. "The headlines always said that being married was the best thing for you. I had no reason to doubt it. I just thought I'd hunt for the weak spots, the cases when it wasn't true." But when she scrutinized the literature, she found more than just a few unfounded arguments—it seemed to her that nearly all the claims about the benefits of marriage could be easily refuted by anyone with advanced knowledge of statistics. The comparisons were misleading because they failed to account for the fate of people whose marriages ended in divorces. And even the more careful studies didn't definitively establish whether being financially, physically, and emotionally healthy was the cause or the consequence of marital longevity. DePaulo says she remembers thinking to herself, "Journalists aren't the only ones being sloppy. Almost everything in the so-called science on marriage is bunk!"

Before long, DePaulo found herself thinking less about deception in the abstract and more about the ways that the public, and singles in particular, had been deceived by claims about

223

the benefits of being married. The issues weren't merely academic, after all. The federal government and religious organizations were investing millions of dollars in marriage promotion campaigns, and their messages, she believed, did more to marginalize the unmarried majority than to lead them to the altar. These campaigns aren't merely wasteful, DePaulo argues. They do damage. Not only do they make people feel bad about themselves, they also give the false impression that there's no way to be a good or happy or worthy person when you're single and living alone, and that shapes the way everyone perceives people who are on their own. "The truth," she tells me, "is that today a lot more people than we realize are not looking to become unsingle. They date. They have close friendships. They have successful careers. They've just chosen not to be married, and we shouldn't be trying to change them."

DePaulo is impassioned and persuasive, but when we talk I cannot help asking her about the wrinkles in her own argument. It's one thing to live alone when you're healthy and successful, I offer. But what happens to people living alone when they get sick or lose their jobs and need someone to support them? Do their friends come through as if they were family? If you're in that situation, are you better off with a spouse?

"I wish we had more systematic research on

that," DePaulo answers, before explaining that this is a policy issue as well as a personal one. "Under the Family and Medical Leave Act, you can't take time off work to care for a loved one if they aren't related, and obviously that makes it harder for singles to get assistance. That's something that needs to change." In her research she has collected anecdotal accounts of singles whose networks deliver. She refers me to an essay in *Health Affairs* by the sociologist Margaret K. Nelson, who chronicles her experiences helping to care for a fifty-seven-year-old friend who was single and living alone when she was diagnosed with terminal cancer,[12] as well as to time use surveys showing that Americans spend considerable time assisting friends in need. "None of this is definitive," she concedes. "But what I've learned so far makes me believe that this is not a clear-cut issue. And it's not as if getting married guarantees that you'll have someone there when you really need them, is it?"

SASHA CAGEN, still ambivalently Quirky-alone, has been struggling with this question. At our lunch in San Francisco, she explains that she's always believed that having security while living alone requires building "families of friends" who will support each other during times of need. And although today her

225

relationships feel stable, a recent experience has made her question whether her community is as durable as she'd like to imagine it. "My favorite aunt lives in Los Angeles," Cagen tells me. "She's a casting agent, and she's been incredibly successful. She had a partner for about twenty-five years, and they separated about a decade ago. But she's been single, and living alone, ever since then, and she's always been totally connected—to friends, to colleagues, to her community. She has had this incredibly rich life." The aunt, who was then in her sixties, was a role model for the Quirkyalone concept. She showed that it was possible to be alone but not lonesome, independent while immersed in collective life. "But the last few months have been a disaster," Cagen says. "She got diagnosed with brain cancer, and before we knew it she had gone from being on top of everything to being pretty much incapable of taking care of herself. She needs someone there with her, taking her for treatment and making sure she's okay. All these things that we normally take for granted, she can't do them on her own anymore."

A debilitating terminal disease is the ultimate test of a support network. In the United States, where women are integrated into the labor force and relatives are often separated by thousands of miles, not many families are equipped to handle the challenge. In theory, Cagen had always thought, locally based "urban tribes" could be well suited for intensive caretaking. (Gay men in San Francisco during the AIDS crisis were her model.) In her aunt's case, however, the family of friends proved unable to meet her growing list of needs. "Her friends were amazing," Cagen explains. "There were all these people there to support her when she got her diagnosis, and they took turns taking her to the doctor or bringing her meals." But fighting terminal cancer can be overwhelming for everyone, whether they live alone or are married, and when there are extensive treatments to undergo those who are most involved have no choice but to restructure their lives. The process can take months, even years, and in her aunt's case the prospects were bleak. Her friends had been so generous and attentive that Cagen's aunt felt revitalized, and she said she'd never experienced so much love. But her friends had full-time jobs and problems of their own to manage. Someone had to take charge of the situation, and when it became clear that none of her friends could do it, Cagen and her sister did.

Cagen left her job in San Francisco and began commuting to Los Angeles, where she planned to stay for a few months. She had been eager for a change—for a "life churn," as she calls it—and for a time she considered settling down there so she could continue attending to her aunt. But, like the others in her aunt's network, Cagen ultimately realized that she couldn't handle the responsibility. Los Angeles wasn't her city, and she didn't want to rebuild her life there. She had also been saving up to travel in South America for a year or so, and she worried that if she didn't do it then, she never would. Cagen's family in Rhode Island gathered to devise a new arrangement, concluding that the only way they could be there for her aunt was if she moved back to the East Coast to be there with them. Her aunt agreed, even though it meant leaving her doctors, her friends, her home—her life, really—behind. She wanted to be taken care of by her family, and it was a relief for her to know that, in addition to her friends in Los Angeles, she had her family's love and support.

For Cagen, her aunt's situation has raised difficult questions. Her aunt had led an exemplary Quirkyalone lifestyle—indeed she was its inspiration—but it was hard not to see a cautionary tale in her fate. "I just didn't know what the tale was," Cagen tells me. "Was it that she lived alone? That she lived far from her family? That she was single and childless? I still don't really know." To be sure, it was an improbable situation. Her aunt, who ultimately died in Rhode Island, got sick at a young age, when her friends were still working, and her illness, which ravaged the brain, quickly undermined her capacity to care for herself. Cagen knew that most people who live alone are unlikely to wind up this way, and she didn't want to interpret her aunt's tragedy as a consequence of going solo any more than of bad luck. But the entire situation added new urgency to her attempt to make a life churn, part of which involved publicly redefining Quirkyalone in a blog post so that it emphasized the possibilities for being in relationships.

Cagen decided to leave the country, bought a ticket for Brazil, put her things into storage, and set out to live a more anonymous, adventurous life. Before leaving, she posted a message on the Quirkyalone Web site: "More and more quirkyalone is about connection for me, the idea that it's impossible to be connected to others without being comfortable alone . . . For many of us, I think being quirkyalone is a prerequisite to being in a healthy relationship. It's about confidence and presence, so you can be fully present for someone else and appreciate them for who they are without judgment or squeezing them into a predefined box or list. Solitude can be experienced alone or with others. With others: it's just about focusing on the world which you inhabit together."

The post generated a minor controversy among Quirkyalone's followers, with some voicing their support for Cagen's honesty and others condemning her for abandoning the cause. "I was really worried about what would happen when I posted it," she tells me. "But it turned out to be a great experience—it brought back a lot of the feelings I had when I published the original Quirkyalone article ten years ago. I've been dealing with these issues for so long that it was liberating to share what I was thinking. I know that a few people out there are upset with me. But I'm human, and this is my life. I need to do what's best for me."

6.
AGING ALONE

I F SASHA CAGEN'S ACCOUNT of how her family scrambled to support her chronically ill aunt sounds familiar, it's because situations like this have become increasingly common throughout the developed world. In recent decades, both the number and proportion of people aging alone has skyrocketed, and yet the challenges stemming from this extraordinary transformation fall squarely on the shoulders of individual families like the Cagens, and are rarely discussed in public or political debates. Consider that, in 1950, only one in ten Americans over sixty-five lived alone, whereas today about one in three do, and the prevalence is far higher among the older elderly, those seventy-five and above. The situation is similar in Europe. Despite some national variation, the European Commission estimates that one in three elderly people on the continent lived alone in 2010. In Japan, only one in ten men and one in five women over sixty-five lived alone in 2010, but even this represents a dramatic increase from 1950, and the national government is expecting a "surge" in the next two decades. The same is true in India, China, and South Korea, where demographers are already worrying about the rise of aging alone.[1]

Worrying is not the only appropriate response to this emerging phenomenon. After all, the longevity revolution, which is the driving force behind the rise of seniors living alone, ranks among the greatest achievements in human history. In fact, until 1930, there was not a single European nation in which 10 percent of the population reached the age of sixty-five. As the Nobel Prize–winning economist Robert William Fogel writes, during the past century "nothing has been more remarkable . . . than the extension of life expectancy, which has increased by about thirty years since 1900 in England, France, and the United States and in equal or larger amounts in such countries as India, China, and Japan."[2] Longevity is just one measure of this achievement. The majority of us don't merely survive far longer than our predecessors, we also maintain our physical health and capacity for independence for a span of years that would have been unimaginable a century ago.

But alas, our most astounding accomplishments are all too often the sources of our most difficult challenges—think of industrialism, nuclear energy, or the automobile—and longevity is by no means an unqualified good. One problem, for instance, is that at an individual level our lifetimes have expanded unevenly, which means that today it is not uncommon for one spouse or domestic partner to outlive the other by years or even decades, leaving her—and it's usually her—without a partner when she is most in need of com-panionship and support. Another problem is that aging alone requires learning to live differently, since challenges that might be simple and mundane during other stages of life—getting to the doctor, filling up free time, maintaining one's strength—can become unmanageable as our capacities diminish.

This is why being old, alone, and isolated does not merely render us vulnerable when we're sick or during a crisis, it can also dramatically diminish the quality of life every day. Consider the findings from a study conducted by Australian researchers who distributed diaries to a large sample of people in different age groups and asked them to record how they spent each part of the day. The average adult is alone for about three hours a day. But the story is different for a typical older person who lives alone. Elderly Australians who live on their own spend 12.5 hours a day alone, roughly 80 percent of their waking time. In 2001, Japanese researchers conducted a similar study. It's not uncommon to hear Americans praise the Japanese for the respect they pay to the elderly. This praise may be deserved, but not because the Japanese do an unusually good job of attending to seniors who live alone. The study found that Japanese people who live alone after age sixty-five spend about twelve of their waking hours by themselves daily; when sleep is included, the number of hours they spend alone rises above twenty.

American senior citizens who live alone have more social contact—but not much more. According to the American Time Use Survey, between 2003 and 2006 the typical elderly singleton spent an average of 10 hours a day alone, 2 hours with family, 2 hours with friends or acquaintances, and 1 hour in some other activity, while the typical married senior spent an average of 5 hours alone, 7.3 hours with a spouse, 1.3 hours with other family, 1 hour with friends or acquaintances, and 1 hour in another activity. The word "average" is important here, because the fact is that older Americans who live alone do not spend two hours every day with family and two hours every day with friends and acquaintances. On many days they see no family and no friends. On some days they have no social contact. They are isolated, not merely alone.

Not many people want to end up this way. Most of us hope to spend our golden years living actively, with loved ones—a spouse, family, good friends—nearby. But we all know that life is unpredictable, particularly once you hit sixty-five or seventy. No one, rich or poor, can fully control their social fate. Marriage is a strong buffer against the threat of isolation. Yet most aging couples are well aware of the unwelcome fact that they are just a heartbeat away from terminal separation. And no one struggles more with solitary living than the recently widowed elderly, whose own risk of sickness, death, and institutionalization increases significantly immediately after a spouse dies.[3]

What's puzzling, in light of all this, is that the majority of the single elderly believe that living alone beats any other available option, such as moving in with children or, far worse, a nursing home.[4] Most Americans and Europeans (and a rising number of people in other parts of the world, too) place great value on independence, so much so that their sense of integrity and self-respect depends on how autonomous they feel. Giving up their own place to move in with family or professional caretakers decreases the risk of loneliness, isolation, and the related health hazards, but if it comes at the expense of dignity it may not be worth the price. Our cultural preference for living autonomously is a key reason why today more than 11 million elderly Americans and 72 million elderly Europeans live alone, and why in the coming decades many millions more will do so.

The time use studies of older Americans

235

suggest a bleak outlook for those who age alone, with endless hours of solitude broken only by rare and brief visits from friends or family. If these diaries were our only source of information, it would be hard to avoid the conclusion that most older people who live alone would benefit from more social contact, and that if we don't find ways to provide it, our rapidly aging nation faces severe and widespread troubles. Indeed, during my research I've observed so many cases of severe isolation and vulnerability among the solo-dwelling elderly like Mary Ann that it's hard to see it as anything other than a haunting social problem, one that deserves far more attention than we give it today.

But I've also come to appreciate that aging alone is not always a social problem. A number of recent studies report that while living alone is now rampant among the elderly, social isolation may be less pervasive than we think. Drawing on a survey of more than 3,000 older Americans between ages fifty-seven and eighty-five, Cornell University sociologist Benjamin Cornwell confirmed that those who live alone have less overall social contact and weaker relationships than those who are married. Surprisingly, however, he also discovered that single seniors have the same number of friends and core discussion partners as their married peers, and that they are actually more likely to socialize with friends and neighbors. In England, one team of medical researchers reported that the overall level of loneliness "has shown little change in the past fifty years" despite the incredible rise of aging alone; another group found that elderly people living alone don't suffer more mental or physical illness than those living with others and, even more surprisingly, that "stated satisfaction with life was somewhat higher in those living alone."[5]

None of this should imply that, in the abstract, most single elderly people would rather go solo. On the contrary, those who have lost a spouse or domestic partner with whom they've grown old wish things had turned out differently and that their companion was still beside them. But they are also realistic about the options they face after a loss, and they understand that getting their partner back isn't one of them. What's new and intriguing is that in recent decades the great majority of older widows, widowers, and divorcees have found ways to remake their lives as singletons and to stay that way as long as they can.

ONE CRUCIAL REASON that so many elderly singles are going solo is that the experience need not be either miserable or isolating. In the United States, where remarriage is far more common than it is in comparable nations, a startlingly low

2 percent of elderly widows and 20 percent of elderly widowers ever remarry. (The gender disparity is largely attributable to the fact that at ages sixty-five and above there are about three women for every two men, and three women for every one man at ages eighty-five and above.) Studies show that these low rates of remarriage are due not only to a shortage of available partners, but also to a lack of interest in coupling up again. According to the sociologist Deborah Carr, at eighteen months after the death of a spouse, a mere one in four elderly men and one in six elderly women say they are interested in remarrying, one in three men and one in seven women are interested in dating someday, while one in four men and only one in eleven women are interested in dating now.[6]

Single senior citizens are also uninterested in moving in with family. Although a century ago nearly 70 percent of elderly American widows lived with a child, today—thanks to social security, private pensions, and more widespread prosperity—only 20 percent do. As Kathleen McGarry, a UCLA economist quoted in the *New York Times* story "They Don't Want to Live with You, Either," put it, "When they have more income and they have a choice of how to live, they choose to live alone. They buy their independence."[7] Older singles still value their relationships with their children; indeed these relationships are often the most important parts of their lives. But they would rather have what gerontologists call "intimacy at a distance" than a bedroom beneath their grandchildren. They want to live close to their family, but not too close; to see them often, just not all the time.

Nor do elderly singletons show much interest in living with close friends. *Golden Girls* may well have been entertaining, but by no means did it inspire the widows of the world to share homes. Increasingly, even those single seniors who get involved in romantic relationships prefer "living apart, together"—keeping places of their own so they can avoid the kinds of emotional, financial, and physical entanglements that proved to be so difficult when they lost their last partner.

This is not to say that close friendships are unimportant for the widowed elderly. On the contrary, being connected to a supportive social network is precisely what most seniors who live alone need to make peace with their condition, or even to enjoy it. And this is where men's and women's experiences of aging alone differ most sharply, especially after the loss of a spouse. On average, women are considerably more skilled at building and sustaining relationships. Women are far more likely than men to age alone, mostly because they usually outlive their spouses. But older women are also far less likely to grow estranged from their friends, family, and neighbors and to become socially isolated. Carr, the sociologist, was surprised to discover that although (as we have seen) in general men are more interested in dating and remarrying than women, those who have high levels of friendship support express the same relatively low desire to remarry as their female peers. "Friendships," she concludes, "may provide at least some of the same rewards as marriage for older adults."[8] The Harvard epidemiologist Lisa Berkman has confirmed this through studies showing that, for example, singletons who have strong social ties outside the family have fewer health risks than those who are married but otherwise disconnected, and that women who live alone are actually less likely to experience mental health problems and diminished vitality than their married peers.[9] This is precisely what we learned from seniors in my interviews, too.

Ava, a retired bookkeeper, lives by herself in a one-bedroom apartment where the walls and tabletops are adorned with photographs of her five grandchildren, but she does everything possible to spend time away from home. She's in her late seventies, and remarkably fit and energetic. Ava is the remaining survivor of five siblings, most of whom died young, including a twin brother. "God has kept me around for a reason," she says. But she also attributes her vitality to her naturally occurring retirement community, which developed as she and her neighbors aged in place while living in their sprawling publicly subsidized housing co-operative near Coney Island. Ava moved into one of the complex's 2,585 units more than a quarter century ago, after her fifty-two-year-old husband died of a heart attack and her two children had settled into places of their own. She was living on Long Island at the time, and suddenly she no longer needed the space she had there. When her sister-in-law told her she could get a subsidized rental unit, she decided to make a change. "I had to watch my money," she recalls. "I really didn't know many people here. Just one woman through someone I knew from the Rockaways, and when she found out I played mahjongg, she came and rang my bell. We're still friends today."

Ava kept her job with a construction company on Long Island when she first moved to the complex. She recognized that her neighbors, along with the building's staff, were organizing more and more social activities as they aged, but she was too busy to participate and, as a self-identified working woman, not all that interested, either. When she retired, though, her friends from mahjongg persuaded her to come to their senior group, and it quickly became a gateway for other activities: walking the boardwalk and the neighborhood; taking exercise and yoga classes; attending meetings of Hadassah, the women's Zionist organization; and volunteering through a program that helps frail and isolated old people nearby. "You have to be involved," she explains. "Otherwise, what do you do with yourself? You need something to look forward to when you get up in the morning. It keeps you going."

Spending time with her girlfriends has always been an important part of Ava's life, and after a decade in her senior groups she has "at least five really close friends I can confide in" at the complex, plus many casual acquaintances from her classes and activities. In recent years, though, her most absorbing relationship has been her romance with Victor, a widower of twenty-five years who has lived in the housing complex since it opened in 1964. The two had been acquaintances before they started dating, when neither was available. For years, Ava had been in a relationship with Jason, who had been trying to persuade her to marry him, yet she broke things off when his health began to fail—not to be heartless, but because she didn't want to become his caretaker as things spiraled downward.

For many of us, this decision may seem surprising, since there's a myth that older women who live alone are constantly searching for a new husband. But in fact Ava's choice not to marry

Jason is quite typical, because women in her situation know how quickly their lives can come apart once a husband gets seriously ill. Victor, who's in his early eighties, had a similar experience with his ex-girlfriend, Susan. "I used to kid her about getting married and she said she wouldn't do it," he says. "Her husband had had Alzheimer's, and she'd had enough trouble taking care of him for ten years. 'I'm not looking after anyone anymore,' she'd tell me. And I said, 'No problem.' We lived two blocks away, so we didn't need it."

The winter after Susan died, Ava saw Victor at a local restaurant and asked him if he was seeing the same woman. "He said, 'No, she passed away in July,' and I told him that I was available," she recalls. "Lo and behold, two days later we saw each other at a Jewish group meeting and he says, 'What did you mean, you're available?' So I'm thinking maybe he took it the wrong way, and I said, 'Not what you think!' I said I was just available for dating, and he said, 'Oh, that's good.' That was it. That night he called me again and we started going out."

The couple wasted little time with courtship. They quickly started spending their weekends together, taking the subway into Manhattan to see plays and movies. By summer, Victor was bringing Ava to Lincoln Center for outdoor concerts and dancing. "We went this past

Saturday in horrible one-hundred-degree weather," she reports. "I just sat under a tree while Victor danced. I have asthma, so I'm not taking any chances." They helped to organize a talent show at the local senior center, and their joint performance of "Yankee Doodle Dandy" earned an award. Recently they've started cooking for each other, once a week at her place, once a week at his.

But Victor and Ava keep strict limits on their relationship. "I see her Friday night, Saturday, and Sunday," Victor explains. "The rest is my time." Ava is similarly protective. On an average day she goes to two morning classes with other women in the complex, then goes home for lunch—"I can't eat out like some of the women here. I don't have a pension," she says. She spends the afternoon walking, volunteering, shopping, or going to the doctor, and in the evening plays mahjongg, talks on the telephone, reads, or watches TV. Occasionally, Ava thinks about what it would be like to live with Victor. She gets lonely some evenings and regrets that she lacks the intimate companionship of a husband. But then she remembers what happened with Jason and thinks about the odds that she'd wind up the full-time caretaker of any man who'd be interested in moving in with her. She considers how busy she is already and recognizes that, like so many of her female contemporaries, she's more interested in having someone to go out with than in having someone to come home to.[10] Inevitably, she concludes she's better off going solo. "Also," Ava jokes, scanning her tidy apartment, "I really don't have much room here for a man. I mean, I have no closet space! Where am I going to put him?"

BOTH AVA AND VICTOR ARE HEALTHY and financially secure, having so much success aging on their own that they've never had to contemplate moving in with, or even closer to, their children. In fact, recently Ava has cut down on her visits to her children: a daughter on Long Island with three teenagers, and a son with two young children who took a job with the Defense Department and moved to Virginia. Spending time with them is just not as rewarding as it used to be. "My son is very busy," Ava explains. "And I try to see my daughter, but her three boys are all big now. Also, she gives me a lot of aggravation. She's unhappy with her marriage—I think she's going to leave him. That's all she talks about."

Ava's not lost any love for her daughter, but these days being with her can be a hardship, and at this point in her life she has little energy to attend to her family's needs. This is quite common. Elderly singletons often report that one reason they prefer living alone to living with family is that their children do not merely host them, they put them to work—with child care, help with the cooking, even cleaning. Some of these activities are pleasurable for seniors, of course, but most prefer to do them on their own terms, not to meet their children's demands or expectations. There is also the problem of getting caught up in family dramas, which, again, can make an older person feel integrated or alienated, depending on the situation. For her part, Ava says she's thankful she doesn't have to deal with any of this on a daily basis. She believes things will eventually get better for her daughter's family, but Ava is not embarrassed to say that, at this point, having her own friends, her own home, and her own life is exactly what she wants.

Other seniors we interviewed harbor more negative feelings about the prospect of living with or moving closer to their children. Joan, an eighty-year-old retired psychologist, divorced her husband decades ago and has been on her own for four years now, ever since her boyfriend died. She enjoys being in the city, likes walking around her neighborhood with a shopping cart, traveling to the bank or the doctor on foot. But recently she needed help when the elevators in her apartment building broke and she couldn't get up and down the stairs. She was also grateful when her family brought her down south for a six-week visit; she got angry, however, when her daughter and son-in-law insisted that she look for an apartment in the area. "I don't want to live with them," she declares. "I love my daughter. I know she loves me. But I don't wanna be that close to the kids. I don't trust 'em." Joan has similar feelings about her son's family. "For the first time, we are not connected in any way, shape, or form. My son's very depressed. He plays video poker all the time, talks to nobody. He and his wife have two girls, eleven and seventeen years old. And their eleven-year-old is cute, sweet—but manipulative, incredibly manipulative. Not to be trusted an inch. I stay out of their way for the most part."

As Joan sees it, her daughter's attempts to move her from New York City to the South are motivated by her needs, not Joan's. "She'll go, 'If you were down here, I'd feel so much better about you. You could come over to the house a couple times a week for dinner. Ralph [her son-in-law] could do your shopping for you, and we could take you out once a week.' But I don't get along with either of them that well. They both drive me kinda crazy." Like many other old people, as she's aged Joan has become less concerned about what other people think she should do and more interested in doing what she wants, even if that means paring down the time she spends with certain friends and relatives, the ones whose companionship she never really enjoyed.[11]

Joan believes the real issue facing her children is control. Will her daughter have to live with the anxiety of knowing that her elderly parent lives alone with no family nearby? Or will Joan have to surrender her autonomy, leave her home and her city, to strengthen family ties that she'd rather keep loose? In the end there's no contest. "I love it here," Joan exclaims. "I can do what I want, when I went, and how I want. I'm responsible for myself. I've made all my arrangements. I've made my will, even picked where to be cremated. I suppose as I get weaker I'll have to be moved somewhere. But I hope I die in New York. I really do."

Dee, a petite, light-skinned ninety-year-old African American who has lived alone in a well-maintained one-bedroom apartment in Harlem since her husband died in 1983, also prizes her domestic autonomy and worries about the other options. "This is my house," she explains. "I'm in charge. I can do whatever I want to do. The idea of a nursing home and—what is that other thing?—assisted living. I dread the thought of it. I want to stay on my own at home."

Dee acknowledges that some of her peers would get lonely and isolated if they were in her situation, but she also thinks that many people—social workers, relatives, friends—overestimate her needs for companionship at this stage in life. "People think you should have company all of the time," she complains. "I don't mind my own company. I do things when I'm ready to do them." Decades ago, Dee was a community activist, on the board of her housing association, involved in fights over integration, engaged in organizations like the NAACP. Now most of her friends have died or moved to warmer climates, and she has discovered that she's content if she sees those who remain in New York City every few weeks or so, for lunch dates or trips to a museum. Most days, Dee spends her time reading—biographies, novels, and magazines, mostly. (She says she stopped reading the newspaper regularly because she realized that, at ninety, she has only so much time left for learning and she wants to focus on "serious things" with enduring value, not on the random events of the moment.) She talks on the phone regularly, watches a little television in the evenings, and goes out into the city as much as her body allows her, about three or four times a week. "I try to live with my limitations," Dee tells me. "I'm just happy doing what I do."

Not everyone has the emotional capacity to be alone in this manner. But Dee has been on her own for nearly three decades, and she's fortunate enough to have the skills and disposition that help singletons flourish. Her only child, a daughter who lives alone in Massachusetts, respects her commitment to solitude. Dee says the two are "extremely close," and yet the idea of moving closer is unappealing. "I don't want to live with my daughter," she explains. "We have different approaches to things. When I visit her, of course I'm congenial. I do things the way she wants them done, and she tries when she's here. But she's beginning to supervise me." Like Joan, Dee gets upset when her daughter tries to mother her. It's demeaning, she says, but also threatening. Dee prides herself on being independent, and when someone suggests that she needs special assistance, it makes her feel she's losing control.

FEAR OF LOSING one's independence haunts most of those who grow old in contemporary societies, as does anxiety about becoming dependent on other people or institutions. These are among the deepest insecurities generated by the cult of the individual. For when our dignity and integrity require the self-perception of personal autonomy, we experience profound humiliation—a loss of face—if we are forced to acknowledge that we can no longer make it on our own.

At some level, of course, none of us is truly independent. Collective belief in the myth of autonomy obscures the fact that our prized individualism is directly underwritten by social institutions: the family, the market, the state.[12]

Related fantasies—of self-reliance, or the self-made man, for instance—lead us to ignore the webs of interdependency that give even the most antisocial among us the strength to go it alone. Yet there is a clear distinction between people like Dee, Victor, and Ava, who can care for themselves and maintain a high quality of life while in their own apartments, and their many less fortunate contemporaries, who suffer immensely from living alone but do not have any relatives who could help them or who fear that moving in with others—and thereby admitting their need for special assistance—would be even worse. Elena Portacolone, a young medical sociologist who assisted me on this research, calls this predicament the "tyranny of independence." And the stories of less healthy elderly singletons illustrate why.

Take Edith, a self-defined "shut-in" in her late seventies, who has spent thirty years dealing with the physical repercussions of strong radiation treatments that her doctors used to combat her aggressive ovarian cancer. She was a teacher specializing in the education of deaf children when she was diagnosed and first treated, and she says that no one understood the consequences of heavy radiation exposure until years after her treatment ended. "They got the cancer," Edith explains. "But it was a mixed blessing. They burned me until most of my insides were gone. I had to retire at fifty-two, and I've been disabled ever since."

Edith complains about the poor quality of her life now. She lives off disability insurance and she's constantly stressed about her finances. She endures nearly constant physical pain, struggles with depression, and is losing her teeth from malnutrition. She has trouble moving and rarely leaves her home. She is lonely, and yet reluctant to acknowledge her emotional hardships to her few remaining friends, lest they abandon her. And on the one recent occasion when she agreed to have a volunteer from an outreach program visit her home and take her outdoors in her wheelchair, she wound up tripping over him and getting hospitalized with a compound fracture in her arm. Now she has nurses and social workers coming to assist her, and they're urging her to move into an institutional facility. "I'm angry at everybody at this point," Edith confesses. "I'm just stuck."

She's also scared, because, in a life that often feels empty and cruel, Edith has always taken pleasure in her capacity to live independently—or at least on her own. "I was always so blessedly independent," she says. "Now I'm saying, 'How am I gonna take care of myself?'"

From an outsider's perspective, it appears that she cannot. Edith's weight has dropped to around 80 pounds since the accident, down from 132.

With her teeth falling out and no dentures in place, she has been relegated to a liquid diet—"like a baby," she says. A nutritionist advised her to grind foods in a blender, but her arm injury makes it hard to use her hand, and the help she's gotten hasn't been sufficient. Part of the problem is that Edith distrusts the Medicaid system, because she fears that a government agency will refer her case to the human services divisions, which will force her out of her home. Her fierce will to remain independent has led her to refuse much of the public assistance that is available to her. "I want to keep my apartment," Edith insists. "And I'm just in a panic that they want to shove me into a nursing home. I don't think it would work."

Edith, who's done her share of time in medical institutions, has legitimate concerns about what her life might be like in a nursing home: Poor care from indifferent staff members. Physical confinement in a drab setting. The sheer boredom of living in a place where nothing happens except death. "Mentally, I'm still very alert," she argues. "I'm afraid I'd be miserable there." And who can deny this risk?

Certainly not John, who's homebound, in his eighties, and doing everything he can to stay in his apartment. He's a retired social worker who'd spent part of his career caring for residents in a nursing home, as well as a tough part of his life taking care of his mother when she was in one, too. John is adamant: "Anyone who has any idea of what a nursing home is will try and make every effort to stay in their home and their community. I *really* know that, from firsthand experience." The problem, John says, is not only that nursing homes rarely have sufficient staff to address their residents' many needs. It's also that the social environments they produce are consistently boring, dreary, alienating, and, above all, depressing. As a social worker, John recalls observing that old people who moved into nursing homes had virtually no chance of getting better or becoming more independent. "It's the last stop," he says. "That's it."

John regrets that he and his sister had to move their mother into a nursing home, but after she fell and broke her hip at home they had no other option. "I got one of the best," he reports, "but after three years it started to sink. The food, the menus—they were always the same and the people there used to complain. I came once on a holiday—there was one nurse or one attendant for twenty patients, and when she had to go to the bathroom it was terrible. That's not fair, you know? They cut their staff to save expenses, and then it stank." After that visit, John and his sister were so upset that they decided to move their mother to another home, but the change proved traumatic. "She only lasted a week," he says, his voice betraying self-doubt and perhaps some shame about what happened. "She couldn't take the change."

For Edith, the scariest thing about nursing homes is not the quality of care they offer, but the fact that moving into one would cut her off from her family and friends. "I have friends coming once or twice a week now," she tells me. "And I have two cousins who are close to me. They call a lot." She still gets lonely quite often, and she wishes she had more companions, people who could be her sounding board, who would understand her need to complain and vent. But she also knows she has more friends and family than other people in her situation. "Some older people don't have anyone coming to visit," Edith remarks. "Nobody to check in on them. I'm lucky there."

It's strange to hear this from an elderly shut-in who's struggling with loneliness and depression. But it's true. Some seniors do become deeply isolated after outliving their family and friends, and typically the most isolated seniors are men. The gendered nature of social isolation is, by now, a well-documented social pattern.[13] We know, for instance, that at all stages of adulthood men are less adept than women at making and maintaining friendships, and they are similarly less able to sustain ties with family members, including children. These abstract social facts became more tangible during my study of the great Chicago heat wave, in which one of the most surprising findings was that elderly men, who were far less likely to live alone in the city (mostly because their spouses tended to outlast them), were far more likely to die alone in the disaster. Moreover, by at least one intriguing measure, they were much more likely to be thoroughly cut off from family as well: Of the fifty-six victims whose cases were handed over to the Cook County Office of the Public Administrator because no one came to claim the body or the estate, forty-four of them—roughly 80 percent—were men.

WHETHER MALE OR FEMALE, it's never easy to identify the most isolated elderly. During the heat wave, the most vulnerable among them became visible only after they perished in their sweltering homes, sometimes several days after their final breath. By definition, the truly isolated do not participate in the senior centers, religious organizations, and volunteer networks where scholars and journalists who investigate the older population usually recruit their subjects. We spent years combing New York City in search of shut-ins and socially withdrawn seniors who would speak openly about their situation, and although each of the men we found had his own individual story, together they had much in common: a spouse lost to death or divorce; weak ties to children and other family, or no children at all; a small or nonexistent friendship network; physical or mental illness; a repellant personality. And although many longed for more companionship, they, too, preferred living alone.

"I lead a dull life," Guy says, just a few minutes after agreeing to be interviewed in his drab Chinatown apartment, a place he's struggled to maintain since his second wife left him five years ago. "I don't talk to nobody. I don't contribute to any causes. I like to sit in the courtyard, walk the streets at night. I recite poetry. And I drink—the best thing is Canadian vodka." He conveys a deep sense of anger about the world and the way his life has turned out: "Miserable—I told you that fifty times!" During the conversation he rails against President George W. Bush and Mayor Michael Bloomberg, says the Russians have no good poets ("they're all rhymers"), claims blacks are "too stupid" for higher education (and then says he's joking), and declares that "any hospital with a cross or a Star of David is bad." At times he's playful, but in a cruel, disdainful way. Although he says he enjoys having company, he cannot help but drive you away.

Guy is childless, but he's not entirely friendless or isolated. His sister lives in his building, albeit on a different floor, and when his wife left him she moved into his sister's apartment, so they are separated yet tantalizingly close. They don't spend any time together, but now that Guy, who struggles with arthritis, has trouble walking without his cane, his ex-wife will occasionally come by to drop off food or bottles of water. It's an odd arrangement, but Guy says he's happier with it than he was with their marriage. "Things are much better now," he insists. And of all the people he complains about, his ex-wife is not among them, nor is the one who'd left him before she did.

His closest friends are from his student days, about sixty years ago, and his service in the navy. It's a psychological closeness, not a physical one, though. One of the men he speaks of, a high school classmate who lives in California, rarely visits. The other, a cartoonist who lives in Connecticut, used to join him for lunch in Manhattan every once in a while. "But now he's busy trying to bring over a Russian wife," Guy says. "He's not in the neighborhood much, and I've never visited him."

Long ago, when the Lower East Side was more Italian and Jewish, Guy knew more people in the neighborhood. In recent decades, the area has become more heavily Chinese and far more gentrified. He's aged in place, but the place has changed with age, too. If, on the one hand, the change makes him feel culturally estranged from the community, it also makes him feel more comfortable on the streets. "It used to be vicious here," Guy says. "The Italians terrorized the place. The Chinese keep it safe." These days, his most regular companions are the people from Meals on Wheels, who come by every weekday, with a double meal on Friday to help him through the two days on his own.

As the interview winds down, Guy apologizes for not having a more compelling life story. "I'm sorry to bore you so much," he says, and then he offers to share his "secret of life": "If you are miserable, imagine a good life and imagine that you are having that life. I didn't know that before. Now I do, and I'm not afraid."

Guy's secret wouldn't do much to help Paul, a widower of four years in his eighties who also lives alone in Chinatown, in the same large apartment where he raised his son and cared for his wife as she succumbed to metastatic cancer. Once, the living room was clean and neatly decorated. It's still spartan, but now the table is piled with old photographs, pens, and notebooks. And the floor is lined with tubing from the machine that Paul, who's losing his battle with chronic obstructive pulmonary disease, needs to get oxygen at all hours of the day. Before his wife died, Paul enjoyed walking through the neighborhood, shopping, and socializing with the other old-timers who'd aged in place as the Chinese and then the young hipsters moved in.

Now he says, "I spend my days on this couch, watching television. I can't read because of the medications I'm taking. My eyes are blurred. My breathing is better when I'm not doing anything. If it's not too hot, I'll look out the window. If it's too hot, I'll just sit here or lie down on the bed."

Unlike Guy, Paul admits that he's suffered from his neighborhood's ethnic turnover and from what feels like the steady disappearance of his longtime friends. He has lived in the area for more than fifty years now, and he fondly recalls the days when he and his neighbors would drop in to each other's apartments to socialize, when he was surrounded by good friends and infused with the sense that he belonged. "It used to be Italian, Irish, Spanish, Jewish. Then they tore down tenements and put up the housing projects," Paul remembers. "The Irish people and Spanish people who lived there before never came back, and the kids we raised grew up, bought houses, and left the neighborhood too. It's just Chinatown now. I like it here, but the neighbors don't have anything to do with each other. It's not like it used to be."

The social distance from his neighbors is difficult, Paul says, because being homebound is isolating, and he wishes more people would stop by to visit or at least see if he has any needs. He has one old friend who has stayed in the neighborhood, who, fortunately, has volunteered to take Paul to the doctor and come by regularly with coffee or a meal, or to help pass the time. Paul's son, who lives in Staten Island and has two children, divorced recently and is so wrapped up with his own issues that he comes by only every two weeks or so. (When it comes to visits from children, at least, Paul might have been better off if he'd had a daughter, since in the typical division of domestic labor women tend to be more active caretakers of their parents than men.) "My wife and I used to go to their house and spend the day with the grandchildren," he recalls. "Now they come here for a few hours a couple times a month."

The absence of friends and family from his daily life has made Paul dependent on professional service workers. He gets two meals delivered each weekday because his social worker noticed that he'd become frail and emaciated and made special arrangements to supplement his diet. A home aide comes every week to clean. Paul is eligible for a home health attendant from Medicare, and he can get additional care when he returns from a stay in the hospital. Most of the elderly people we interviewed expressed great interest in this kind of service, because visits from home care workers offer personalized attention and face-to-face interaction—sometimes the only one they get in a day. Paul, however, complains that the people they send him can't speak English. Their company makes him feel alienated, so he usually sends them out to get him fresh fruit, which has become a real luxury, thereby leaving him even more time to be alone.

Paul says that trying to fill the endless cycle of open, unscheduled hours is one of the great challenges of living this way. His mind wanders everywhere, and while sometimes it takes him back to better times and warmer feelings, at others it lands on the rough spots: his wife's illness, his spells in the hospital, the time the power went out in his building and six paramedics had to carry him down before bringing him to the emergency room. He also gets anxious: What will happen if his friend gets sick and can't help him any longer? What if there's an emergency? What if the electricity goes out again and the paramedics can't fix his respirator in time?

Paul tries not to fixate on these questions. At some level, he says, we all have to make our peace with worries like these. "I mean, I can't sit here with a sad face all the time. That's not gonna help me at all. This is it, and I've got to look at the brighter side, to make the best of it. That's what I try and do."

STORIES LIKE PAUL'S AND GUY'S make it clear that being male is not the only risk factor for social isolation. Others include being childless, or living far from your children; being sick, particularly if the illness leaves you homebound; being depressed, or struggling with another mental illness; and being poor, which increases the odds of facing nearly all the risks of winding up old and alone. According to an influential report from the Commonwealth Fund's Commission on Elderly People Living Alone, of all seniors living alone and below the poverty line, one out of three sees neither friends nor neighbors for as much as two weeks at a time, and one out of five has no phone conservations with friends.[14] None of these qualities are distributed equally, of course. Elderly Latinos and African Americans who live alone are much more likely to be poor than their white or Asian counterparts, for example.[15] They're also less likely to get appropriate medical care and treatment for mental illness, and more likely to feel that the place they live is unsafe.

This feeling matters, because, as scholars, policy makers, and advocates for the elderly have begun to recognize, certain neighborhoods can be inhospitable for older singletons. Neighborhoods that are far from family and friends aren't the only places where older residents face heightened risks of isolation. So, too, are those that have become abandoned, impoverished, or violent, such that street-level conditions—a lack of grocery stores, well-maintained sidewalks, or safe public spaces, for instance—give elderly singletons little incentive to escape from their private burrows and participate in local life.[16]

Unfortunately, poor and depleted urban neighborhoods are now quite common in American cities, particularly in the regions that suffered most from deindustrialization: the Rust Belt and the Northeast. The old residents of such places are twice removed from public attention: first because of their age, and second because of their location. And while this is true in cities across the United States, it seems especially cruel in New York City, where the most dangerous and isolating neighborhoods lie in the shadows of the most safe and prosperous communities on earth.

In the mid-2000s, United Neighborhood Houses (UNH), which provides funding, policy research, and program support for more than three hundred New York City settlement houses and community centers, took up the challenge of determining precisely which parts of the city were especially likely to isolate older singletons. The organization had been serving New York's seniors for more than eighty-five years at the time, but never before had it made a special point of assisting those who lacked companionship and social support. As Jessica Walker, the program officer who led the project, recounts: "The agencies and social workers in our network kept telling us how many isolated people they were seeing, and we knew there were even more isolates out there who were essentially out of sight. This used to be something that everyone took for granted. We started to see it as an emergency in slow motion, and we needed to understand just how bad it was."

The UNH research staff reached out to leaders in the government agencies that were also spending more of their time and resources responding to the needs of seniors who live alone, including the city's Department for the Aging. "You have to understand that this issue affects almost everything that we do now," the department's former commissioner Edwin Méndez-Santiago tells me. "It's not just doing outreach during blackouts or heat waves. It's the senior centers, housing, Meals on Wheels, home care. The older population that lives alone drives a lot of this, and when they're isolated, that's the hardest thing of all." Needless to say, he was eager to have his agency cooperate when UNH called.

Drawing on the city's best available data (but not, alas, any measures of neighborhood-level residential or commercial density, nor of crime), UNH determined which parts of the city contained high proportions of both old people living alone and old people with special needs living in poverty. "You can't do a survey of isolation," Walker explains, "because you'll probably miss the most isolated people. So we tried to find out which neighborhoods had the biggest risks of isolation. And what we found was not a complete surprise."

"Aging in the Shadows," a UNH report published in 2005, revealed that residents of Central Harlem, where 50 percent of all elderly people live alone, and East Harlem, where 40 percent do, face the greatest threat of isolation. If you factor in the prevalence of psychological distress, as Lloyd Sederer, New York City's deputy commissioner for mental hygiene at the time of the study, did, a few more risky neighborhoods pop out. "The most vulnerable was the South Bronx, where we actually began a special outreach program to screen for depression," Sederer tells me. "But the Lower East Side of Manhattan, Bedford-Stuyvesant in Brooklyn, and Coney Island have problems as well. We would love to do more in those areas, and in many others, too. Right now it's a question of resources, and when money is tight, finding money for this kind of problem is not easy to do."

COMPARED WITH OTHER CITIES, New York City offers unusually generous public assistance for the elderly and the isolated. Practically every neighborhood has a senior center that serves lunches, organizes social events, and helps senior citizens enroll in public programs. Community groups and neighborhood organizations encourage people to age in naturally occurring retirement communities, which keep them from losing touch with friends, family, and local institutions; rent control policies, while weaker than they once were, allow retired people on fixed incomes to stay in their homes. Volunteer programs connect the retired healthy elderly with their less mobile counterparts, so that the visitors maintain a sense of purpose while the visited get a break from the monotony of long, solitary days. The Office of Emergency Management does special outreach for the elderly when the weather is dangerously hot or cold, and local postal workers check in with residents when mail accumulates in the box of an older person.

But New York City has nearly a million senior citizens—its elderly population alone outnumbers the total population of all but the nine largest U.S. municipalities—along with hundreds of thousands of others who live alone. It is, no doubt, a wealthy place, yet when the economy is sluggish the city government struggles to fund its public programs, and the cutbacks can be painful.

Meals on Wheels is one of the nation's most popular public service programs. Who, after all, could oppose a policy that delivers hot food to sick or homebound residents? No one ever demanded that New York abandon its commitment to feed the hungry, but in 2004 the city announced that, to save money, it would terminate the contracts of sixteen nonprofit senior centers that handled the delivery program in the Bronx and turn them over to three large contractors who could do it more efficiently. Gaining efficiency required one simple change: Rather than delivering hot meals on a daily basis, the contractors would deliver frozen meals once or twice a week.

News of the plan incensed the city's old people and their political advocates. Mayor Michael Bloomberg had anticipated that they would be upset about the loss of hot meals. But he failed to recognize that the program delivered human companionship and well-being checks as well as food, and that the coldest consequence of the change would be depriving New York's most vulnerable residents of the rare occasions when they could see and be seen by another person. The controversy made it into local papers and TV news shows, and it didn't look good for the Bloomberg administration. Soon the two sides reached a compromise: Residents of the Bronx would be enrolled in a pilot program called

Senior Options, which would offer those capable of heating frozen food with a choice to get daily delivery of a hot meal or frozen meals delivered once or twice a week.

Community organizations in the Bronx criticized the program for deepening the isolation of local seniors, but in spring 2008 Mayor Bloomberg's office declared that the pilot program had been a success—so much so that it would soon end daily delivery of hot meals to most residents and instead offer frozen meals in all five boroughs. Bloomberg insisted that his motivation was not the overall cost savings. The budget would remain fairly constant, keeping in mind that the city needs to provide far more meal delivery service to meet growing demand. Regardless, another political fight began, only this time the governor's office got involved, demanding that the city answer a number of questions: How will the city address the problem of social isolation? How will it ensure that seniors are able to manage frozen meals? (Some elderly people should not be encouraged to use their ovens regularly, for fire safety reasons.) Will the city guarantee that seniors will still receive quality meals? And what will the city do when there is inflation in the prices of food and gas?

The New York City Council organized a hearing on the proposed change, and in early

June the New York State Assembly threatened to pass special legislation to block Bloomberg's plan. Bobbie Sackman, policy director for the Council of Senior Centers and Services of New York City, encouraged the state to do "the right thing to protect and defend the long tradition of neighborhood-based senior services that have made New York City a model for the nation." Home meals are especially important for the frail and the very old, Sackman noted, because they have trouble getting out to the local senior centers that broker programs. "For an eighty- or ninety-year-old person, a daily knock on the door is important."

In fact she was understating the issue. Isolates like Guy and Paul are not the only ones who need attention. These days most of us know someone—a parent, grandparent, neighbor, or friend—who's on their own and could use some extra care or another daily visit. And none of us—no matter who we are, how much money we have, where or how we live—can escape the possibility that someday the person waiting for that knock on the door will be someone we love—perhaps even us.

7.
REDESIGNING SOLO LIFE

THE EXTRAORDINARY RISE of living alone is not in itself a social problem. But it is a dramatic social change that's already exacerbating serious problems for which there are no easy solutions: Social isolation for the elderly and frail. Reclusiveness for the poor and vulnerable. Self-doubt for those who worry that going solo will leave them childless, or unhappy, or alone.

Today our species has about 200,000 years of experience with collective living, and only about fifty or sixty years with our experiment in going solo on a massive scale. In this brief time, we've yet to develop any serious public responses to the challenges related to living alone. Occasionally, a political official, religious group, or cultural critic tries to reverse the tide of history by persuading us that we are, in fact, better off together: The marriage promotion campaigns sponsored by President George W. Bush's administration. The divorce prevention programs run by churches. The popular books like *Marry Him*, *The Case for Marriage*, and *The Lonely American*. Or the calls for adult children to take in their elderly parents, lest they be left to spend their golden years alone. But these attempts at moral suasion are destined for failure—and not only because their strongest proponents tend not to practice what they preach when their own happiness is on the line. The case against living alone simply runs counter to our modern sensibilities. And when millions of people from all parts of the globe believe they're better off solo, it's hard to convince them they're wrong.

What would happen if we spent less energy on these futile campaigns to promote domestic unity and focused instead on helping people live better—healthier, happier, and more socially connected—if they wind up in places of their own?

We could, for instance, begin thinking about how to redesign our metropolitan areas so they better meet the needs of the people who live and work in them. As the Yale historian Dolores Hayden has shown, most modern cities and, especially, suburbs were designed for nuclear families in which the mother stayed at home to do domestic work while the father labored elsewhere; so, too, were most residential units, both apartments and stand-alone houses.[1] These old forms don't suit today's world, where women work outside the home and millions of people live alone. And from an environmental perspective, they may even be dangerous, because sprawling, sparsely populated, car-dependent metropolitan areas dominated by large private houses require greater energy consumption than densely populated urban centers. How might the physical places that we call home be redesigned to suit the new metropolitan population, in which most adults are workers and singletons are ubiquitous?

Answering this question is especially urgent for the most vulnerable of those who live alone, the frail elderly and the poor. Today the two most common forms of specialized housing for these groups are the nursing home and the single-room occupancy dwelling, or SRO. But both of these housing options scare off more prospective residents than they attract—and for good reasons.

Nursing homes, the places of last resort for old people who require assistance with basic activities (such as bathing and getting out of bed) and can no longer live by themselves, need not relegate their residents to a sentence of living death. Although most of the 3 million or so Americans who move into one each year are likely to get good care, far too many of them will not.

Most old people who live alone have a catalog of nursing home horror stories at their disposal, which they'll share in interviews after just the smallest provocation. "One woman I know very well had to go to a nursing home," says Edna, who's in her eighties and clings to her independence as if her life depends on it. "She wanted to see me, so I went up there. Ugh! It was horrible! She sat there in this room. And there was one woman screaming her head off. Right over here—" She points to a spot nearby. "I don't know what was with her. Somebody else was howling over here—" She points to a spot in the other direction. "There were noises all around us. Oh God! So she said to me, 'I know it may not be easy, but will you *please* see if you can get me out of here?'" Edna promised to do her best, but she lacked the clout or the resources to do much about the situation. Before long, she got news that her friend had died. "All I could say was 'Thank God!'" Edna remembers. "Oh, it was terrible!"

A neighbor of Edna's had a similar experience. She lived alone, had retired early, and then got sick before she had a chance to enjoy it. "They sent her to that terrible place, and she was there a long time. Anyone who went up there came back and said, 'My God, how does she stand it?!' *Finally* she died. *Finally*. I don't know how she stood it there. So you live alone. And like it. Get along as best you can." Do anything, Edna says, to avoid a nursing home, because in her view it's tantamount to being buried alive.

I've seen nursing homes of all kinds and levels, from well-maintained (though still quite lifeless) places where residents get private rooms and attentive care to those that I'd turn down if my only other option was a grave. The Amsterdam Nursing Home, a handsome brick high-rise that abuts the Columbia University campus on Manhattan's Upper West Side, could easily be mistaken for an expensive co-op apartment building. Not only does it have good doctors, nurses, and social workers, it also offers the kinds of programs and facilities found in a high-end assisted living facility: wireless Internet access, live concerts twice a week, a library cart, an arts and crafts group, day trips of all kinds. This is unusual. Harlem is just a few blocks away from the Amsterdam; the South Bronx is just a few miles farther. Although there are some well-managed nursing homes in these neighborhoods, there are more that get disturbingly low ratings for nurse staffing, health inspections, and overall quality.[2] This may not be surprising, but it certainly isn't acceptable—particularly not for the people who live in them.

Unfortunately, most older people who need a nursing home have trouble avoiding low-quality facilities. According to a 2006 *Consumer Reports* analysis of 16,000 nursing homes across the United States, some two decades after the federal government passed historic legislation to improve conditions for nursing home residents— the 1987 Nursing Home Reform Act—"bad care persists and good homes are still hard to find." The study's key findings confirm the horrific stereotypes that strike fear in everyone searching for a facility where they, or their parents or grandparents, can get good care and assistance. On their site visits investigators found scores of abuses: Unattended residents getting bedsores, even when they have no risk factors. Workers ignoring doctors' orders. Medication errors. Unsanitized dishes and utensils. Widespread failure to comply with laws that require homes to make inspection records available to anyone who requests them, including prospective residents and their families. The problems are worse in certain states, including Illinois, where the government allows nursing home operators to admit young people with severe mental illnesses, including those with criminal records. The result, as the *Chicago Tribune* reported, is not just "compromised care," but a spike in crimes against elderly residents, from robbery to rape and homicide.[3]

Bad social policies and weak regulatory oversight aren't the only sources of trouble for nursing homes—so too are some of the companies that have acquired them. The *Consumer Reports* study is but one of many to report that the lowest-quality facilities tend to be managed by for-profit corporations, and that independently run, nonprofit nursing homes are more likely to provide good care. A *New York Times* investigation of private equity firms that recently acquired nursing homes reports that "at 60 percent of homes bought by large private equity groups from 2000 to 2006, managers have cut the number of clinical registered nurses, sometimes far below levels required by law." And that "during that period, staffing at many of the nation's other homes has fallen much less or grown."[4] Is it a coincidence that, compared with the national average, the investor-owned homes also have more serious health deficiencies cited by regulators, a higher percentage of long-term residents whose need for help with daily activities has increased, and a higher proportion of long-term residents suffering from depression or anxiety? These outcomes have been facilitated, if not promoted, by federal officials whose weak penalties for offending companies send a laissez-faire message to everyone in the industry. And although meaningful reforms are clearly in the public interest, they are difficult to enact now that the nursing home industry has established an influential lobbying presence in the key sites of government power, from state capitals to Washington, D.C.

But reforms are necessary. After all, if nothing changes, what will happen when you, your partner, or your parents find yourselves searching for a nursing home, with no place else to go?

Recent changes in the nation's stock of single-room occupancy buildings have made many of them similarly inhospitable, to the extent that they are even available. The supply of SROs has been dwindling for decades, largely because they've tended to be located near downtown areas that have been revitalized and owners across the country have sold their buildings to developers or converted them into luxury properties on their own. The remaining buildings have transformed from their historic role of sheltering mainly migrant workingmen. The massive deinstitutionalization of the mentally ill, along with the growing number of people who cycle in and out of the criminal justice system, has produced a new population of marginal men in need of SRO-style accommodations. Today, most SROs contain an unstable mix of the poor, the old, the mentally ill, substance abusers, and ex-convicts. SROs may work for some, but for others they are impossible communities, and in all but the best-managed facilities both residents and staff struggle to maintain decent conditions. Like nursing homes, SROs are in desperate need of redesign.

Redesigning the places where people live alone is only one way to address the challenges of a singleton society. Another is to improve the material objects we keep around us, and to design new ones to help those most at risk of isolation become better connected to networks of social support. This, of course, is something we are already doing quite effectively. Massive investments in communications technologies have helped usher in what we alternately call the Network Society and the Digital Age. These technological innovations haven't merely benefited people who live alone; they've also produced the conditions that make solo living attractive, because cheap, accessible communications systems, from the telephone to the Internet, allow us to remain connected while living alone. The next frontier of this ongoing technological transformation is home-based robotics, from "smart home" devices that assist with everyday tasks such as cleaning and getting entertainment to even smarter machine companions that could be particularly helpful for the homebound. These technologies aren't cure-alls. They'll be expensive, and the prospect that they could be used to substitute for human contact raises serious ethical questions. But this hasn't kept engineers and computer scientists from developing new machines that might someday help compensate for our social failures. We need to understand what they are making, and to get people with different backgrounds and experiences to help them, since we all may be touched by the outcome of their work.

PEARL IS JUST A FEW INCHES over four feet, and her hearing, speech, vision, and memory are far from perfect. She moves slowly and has trouble with stairs. She loses energy quickly, and occasionally she crashes from overexertion. Still, Pearl can be tremendously helpful to people who want to live on their own but need special assistance. She is steady, so they can use her to stay balanced when walking. She knows when they should take medications, and provides reliable reminders if they forget. She can help them get connected to the Internet, or to contact family, friends, and health care providers. She monitors their activities and recognizes unusual behavior, such as failing to get out of a chair or neglecting to go to the bathroom. If they don't respond to her prodding, she'll ask for an explanation. If she doesn't get one, she'll call for help.

Pearl is still developing. She may get taller, but even if she doesn't, her arms will soon grow long enough to reach items stored on top shelves or pick up things from the ground. She'll be able to do a few onerous household chores by herself, and to help with others. Her speech will improve, as will her ability to understand language. She'll play interactive games, and music and TV programs. She'll be able to warn about threatening weather, answer the phone, program the DVR, and control the lights. When she has access to high-speed wireless service, she'll transmit remote video and audio signals, mediating virtual meetings in real time. She'll become a better companion and caretaker—still a robot, but one with a more human touch than her peers today.

Pearl is a prototype for a robotic personal assistant, with origins in a collaborative research and design experiment conducted by computer scientists, nurses, gerontologists, and psychologists at Carnegie Mellon and Stanford universities. Sebastian Thrun, who organized the project in Pittsburgh and now directs the artificial intelligence laboratory at Stanford, says that building machines that can live with and adapt to human beings is now "the cutting edge in robotics." In a research paper, he and his colleagues, who have also engineered a robotic nurse prototype called Flo (in honor of Florence Nightingale), offer a simple explanation for why they focus on developing machines for the elderly and the isolated: The population of old and very old people (age eighty-five and above) is soaring, the costs of home care and health care are skyrocketing, and there is little political will to provide more help. "Thus," they explain, "we need to find alternative ways of providing care . . . The vast majority of independently living elderly people is forced to live alone, and is deprived of social interaction. Social engagement can significantly delay the deterioration and health-related problems. While robots cannot replace humans, we seek to understand the degree at which robots can augment humans, either by directly interacting with the person, or by providing a communication interface between different people that is more usable than current alternatives."[5]

According to new research led by the gerontologist William Banks and his wife, Marian, a nurse at the Veterans Affairs Medical Center in St. Louis, robotic pets can be just as effective as living ones—at least when it comes to reducing loneliness and establishing feelings of attachment. The Bankses arranged for one group of residents in a long-term nursing home facility to have weekly thirty-minute one-on-one visits with a floppy-eared, trained therapy dog named Sparky, while another had the same number of visits with AIBO, a robotic dog (made by Sony) that wags its tail, vocalizes, and blinks lights when spoken to or touched. A control group had no exposure to either Sparky or AIBO. Marian, who delivered the dogs to the nursing home, did not make personal contact with the residents, but she observed that those who visited with Sparky were quick to build rapport with the canine, whereas those who were placed with AIBO took a week to pet him and talk with him as they would a living dog. Surprisingly, at the end of the eight-week study, the groups who visited with Sparky and AIBO reported similar levels of relief from loneliness and attachment to the dogs, while those who didn't visit with a dog reported that they were just as lonely as they had been when the experiment began.

When I visit the Stanford University artificial intelligence laboratory, a team of young researchers led by Thrun and Andrew Ng convey great interest in the Sparky experiment. They're even more excited about their own machines, whose components are scattered around the lab like auto parts in a repair shop, with a few more polished projects on display in a large central room. "We've lived with robots for a long time," Ng tells me. "We call them things like dishwasher, dryer, and microwave. Now we have machines that are mechanically capable of doing household chores and even providing some interaction. But they can't be all that helpful until we develop software that makes them smarter. We need them to hear and understand, to find the bathroom or know what to pick up. When they can do that, it's going to be a very exciting change."

Not everyone shares this enthusiasm for robotic companionship. "The prospects for the ethical use of robots in the aged-care sector are far fewer than first appears," write the ethicists Robert and Linda Sparrow. They perceive "a profound disrespect for older persons" in even the most well-meaning artificial intelligence research, because it ignores old people's strong preference for human caretakers and advances projects that will substitute machine companions for human ones. The Sparrows acknowledge that social robotics is a flourishing field, and they recognize that machines could be helpful for certain routine tasks, such as using appliances, opening doors, and fetching food. But they warn that robot designers have a long history of setting unrealistic expectations, and they doubt that there is a technological solution to the problem of caring for the isolated.[6]

The questions raised by critics like the Sparrows should be directed at all of us, not merely at artificial intelligence researchers: Is there really a shortage of living pets to accompany people? Will robots ever be able to meet the complex needs of people, particularly those who suffer from a lack of social interaction and long for emotional connection? Will machines be able to navigate through the often cluttered rooms of homebound people, let alone clean the floors? Will robotic pets provide enough stimulation and affection to sustain their owners' interest when the novelty wears off? (The nursing home residents in the robotic dog study had access to AIBO for only eight thirty-minute sessions.) If the robots can be turned on and off, won't that make it impossible for them to establish what the Sparrows call "the inde-pendent presence that is a necessary condition of meaningful relationships"? If the robots can't be turned on and off, will that make them threateningly invasive, and unappealing?

Skeptics of robot care for the elderly and frail also argue that machines capable of interacting with singletons will be prohibitively expensive —unless, as they predict, the robots ultimately displace human caretakers, deepening the isolation of those they serve. After all, many of the most vulnerable older people we inter-viewed report that paid caretakers, from cleaners to meal delivery workers and home health attendants, are their most regular sources of social contact. They value the presence of another human being just as much as the labor that the person provides, and they long for more company, not less. Substituting a machine for these already rare visitors would be devastating. Hence the Sparrows' emphatic conclusion: "We believe that it is not only misguided, but actually unethical, to attempt to substitute robot simulacra for genuine social interaction."[7]

But machines need not substitute for social interaction, and with the right design they can even promote it. Consider Kompaï, a robotic companion being developed by the French company Robosoft. Although the machine is still a work in progress, its 2010 incarnation featured a short, sleek human form with a head, a cartoon face, and a video camera on top; a box with two large wheels at its base; and a large touch-screen monitor at its midsection, which its human companions could use for a wide range of Internet-mediated communications. The designers of Kompaï envision the family, friends, and health providers of the machine's user contacting them through an Internet-based program such as Skype or Facebook or an instant messaging service. When completed, Kompaï will be able to locate and move to its owner, and its speech recognition software will allow physically impaired people to communicate by voice.[8]

Machines like Kompaï may appeal to homebound and elderly singletons because they provide greater access to a kind of communication that people who live alone are already enjoying. (And by the time the current generation of young adults reaches old age, their comfort with machines will make robotic companions even more attractive.) Senior citizens are not only the fastest-growing segment of Internet users, they are also heavy users of its interactive features, from e-mail to dating and social networking sites to video calling programs, which they now use to enrich their communications with family and friends. There's not much good research on the effects of this activity. But one report, by economists at the Phoenix Center for Advanced Legal and Economic Public Policy Studies, finds that older people who used the Internet experienced a 20 percent reduction in depression and that the change was actually caused by their online activity.[9] Not all old people have good access to the Internet, and many who do lack the training they need to master its most important social features. But there are clear payoffs to helping them get online, and projects designed to do this—from the British old-age advocate Valerie Singleton's six-button touch-screen desktop computer, the SimplicITy, to state-subsidized programs that bring Internet access to public housing for seniors—will deliver immediate rewards.

There's also no questioning the value of using machines to link isolated or homebound seniors with health care providers and social workers. Videoconferencing with doctors and nurses is never as good as a face-to-face consultation, but it can be helpful, if only as a way to maintain better contact between visits or to evaluate whether patients are following medical advice at home. New technologies are already enhancing these interactions. Increasingly, health care providers are giving their more frail and isolated patients wireless monitors that convey vital physiological information—pulse, temperature, and breathing levels—to a remote office, where medical technicians can detect potentially serious conditions before they become emergencies. Elderly singletons who are in good health but still worry about a sudden fall (approximately 13 million older Americans fall each year) or some other crisis can benefit from more mundane technologies, like the medical alert systems activated by the touch of an alarm that fits into a pocket or around the neck. And since devices like these bring some peace of mind to those who love or care for seniors who live alone, the rest of us benefit from them, too.

NO MACHINE, be it a compact alert bracelet or a human-size robot, can provide what so many old people and their families need most these days: a home that allows them to maintain the feeling of autonomy while also offering genuine sources of social connection and access to services and amenities. Places like these do exist, and they're not nursing homes. They're called assisted living facilities—or, alternatively, independent living facilities, a telling conceptual distinction for a place without a difference—and roughly one million elderly Americans live in them today.

Typically, assisted living facilities are located in large apartment buildings that carve out spaces for communal activities: a dining room for shared meals, a gymnasium, classrooms, or a garden. They also tend to have large support staffs, from cooks to cleaners, security guards to home care assistants. About one-third of assisted living residents occupy smaller places, including houses, that have fewer than sixteen tenants. They may not offer all the amenities of larger facilities, but these homes can offer more personal services, and they lack the institutional feel that can be off-putting to people who are fighting to retain their dignity as they age.

Whether large or small, high-quality assisted living facilities share at least one characteristic: They are prohibitively expensive for all but the most affluent individuals and families. A report published by the trade publication *Assisted Living Executive* estimates the monthly rent for a typical room at about $3,500, or $42,600 per year. In one recent post on the *New York Times* blog The New Old Age, Paula Span explains that, at $4,000 a month, a small residential home in New Jersey is a bargain compared to a neighboring facility with ninety-eight beds and fees starting at about $65,000 per year. (Residents pay more for services like home care or medication reminders.)[10] In another post, the reporter Jane Gross recounts her own family's expenses for the nine years that her mother (who, it should be noted, held an expensive long-term insurance policy) spent in two assisted living facilities and one nursing home: "All in all, I figure the years from 1994 to 2003, when my mother died, cost our family $500,000, easy, even without accounting for her lesser expenses or, more important, the emotional and physical wear and tear of so many moves on an old lady."[11]

The wear and tear related to moving could be avoided, Gross writes, if families encouraged their elderly relatives to move into a special kind of assisted living facility: a continuing care retirement community, which can accommodate residents no matter how much special care they need when they lose the capacity for domestic independence or approach the end of life. The catch, however, is that these facilities demand a large up-front payment; the one Gross visited, in Tarrytown, New York, asked for about a $200,000 payment against which future costs would be deducted, just to get in the door. Those rich enough to afford this may well benefit in the long run. Then again, they may not, since there's no refund if the resident dies soon after moving in, as many inevitably do. It's "a dilemma many can only wish for," Gross acknowledges. But that doesn't make it any less difficult for the families that are affluent enough to consider a continuing care facility.[12]

For the past dozen years my own family has experienced the stress of this fortune. Until her death in 2011, my grandmother Esther had always been humorous, mischievous, and full of life. As a child during prohibition, she learned to make bathtub gin; as a young mother, she was the president of the local school parents' association and the synagogue women's auxiliary, and she also threw enormous, occasionally raucous parties where she taught her friends to dance; as a grandmother, she taught me how to hit a baseball and drive with my left hand so I could put my right arm around a date. But for the last twenty-five years of her life, she spent much of her energy in a daily battle with Parkinson's disease, and the fight became more difficult after her second husband, Irv, died in 1997.

For most of their marriage, Esther and Irv lived in small rental apartments in Los Angeles; among the countless ways that Irv helped her, driving her around town was particularly important, because their city, like so many others, demands mobility, and she could no longer drive. When he died, quite unexpectedly, the quality of Esther's life in Southern California diminished immediately. She had a few friends in the area, but they too were beginning to suffer from various illnesses and the deaths of their husbands, and it was hard for them to visit. Her three children lived elsewhere: my mother in Chicago, my aunt in Milwaukee, and my uncle in Silicon Valley. After a few scary mishaps, including one where she tried driving a golf cart and accidentally crashed it into the local senior center, we decided she would be better off coming back to Chicago, where she had been born nearly eighty years before.

My grandmother didn't own a home and had little savings, but her children had been successful and they agreed to share the costs of a luxury assisted living facility on the lakefront. It's a gorgeous high-rise building, with a sweeping, glass-enclosed atrium on the ground floor; an open, sun-drenched dining room; generously sized apartments, many with water views; and a kind, attentive staff. It's expensive: about $50,000 per year for a one-bedroom apartment with two meals a day and access to the building's services and amenities, and more for those, like my grandmother, who need additional care. But when it's your own parent, who has given so much of her life to you and the family, it's hard, if not inconceivable, to give back anything but the best.

Esther's first years in the Breakers went smoothly. Of course, she missed her deceased husband and her life in California. But as a spritely newcomer, she had little trouble making friends and joining in various activities at the complex. She was witty and engaging, and within days she was getting invitations to dine with her new neighbors. She had always been a good bridge player, and once she made that known a small group of women let her into their game. The facility, which is located on the far north side of Chicago, offered shuttle service to the downtown shopping district, and although she didn't have much to spend, she'd often go just to be social. Moreover, she was close to family—daughters, grandchildren, cousins—as well as old friends, and visits with them made her feel like she was back home.

Things got complicated as her disease progressed, however. Although Esther retained her mental acuity, her Parkinson's made it difficult for her to walk, speak clearly, and control her hands. Most of her neighbors were sympathetic, and helpful. But as her body failed, she was forced to acknowledge a brutality in the culture of assisted living complexes that she hadn't previously registered: They are organized around a social hierarchy, with the healthiest and most independent at the top and the sick and frail at the bottom, stigmatized and marginalized, lest their company remind others how vulnerable they really are.[13]

In her telling, my grandmother's stories

sounded like dispatches from the front lines of junior high school, not a retirement community. Women who had always included her in their social outings began planning them without her. When she confronted them, they'd usually be evasive, but sometimes they could be nasty, too. Friends who once held a place for her at the dining table allowed others to fill her seat. The greatest insult came from her bridge group, whose members decided that her problems communicating made her an impossible partner and barred her from their game. Suddenly she was an outcast, forced to find a new set of friends.

There was no shortage of possibilities, since assisted living facilities are full of people who, like Esther, are physically compromised but intent on preserving their dignity and maintaining their social lives. Remarkably, she quickly found her way into another small community, and repaired a few of her older friendships, too. Yet her enthusiasm for the assisted living facility diminished. She complained more: about the food, the staff, and other residents. She began reporting the times when paramedics would arrive to assist a neighbor, and told us about all the friends who would fail to show up for breakfast one day and turn out to be dead.

By the time she reached her late eighties, my

grandmother's disease had rendered her incapable of living independently, even with the extraordinary support that her building offered, so her children hired someone to move into her apartment. Five years later, Esther was turning ninety-two, and on her birthday, July 4, my mother hired a small bus to bring about fifteen of her neighboring friends to her home for a party. Nothing was easy for my grandmother in those days. She was weak, occasionally depressed, and sometimes disoriented. She was spending ever more time in her apartment, and she said that on some days the effort to go downstairs for dinner demanded more than she could give. Her children faced a different kind of struggle. Her care costs reached more than $80,000 per year by the end of her life, and they'd spent a fortune to help her get through the last decade—a fact that made her feel embarrassed, and perhaps a little proud as well. But that day there was still a lot to celebrate. After all, there she was, still spirited in her nineties, surrounded by family and embraced by friends who lived only steps away. Sitting beside her at our Independence Day ritual, I found myself asking how more of us could wind up this way.

In recent years a number of groups have tried answering this question with projects designed to democratize the experience of "independent living" beyond the most affluent communities.

No one believes that affordable independent living is going to come from the private sector. But in 1992, two nonprofit organizations, NCB Capital Impact and the Robert Wood Johnson Foundation (which funded the research for this book), launched Coming Home, a $13 million initiative to develop new models for assisted living that middle-class and even low-income seniors could afford.

The challenges were formidable, because developing, let alone managing, these facilities requires different kinds of economic and political expertise. In most cases, dealing with complicated bureaucratic matters—securing subsidies and low-cost credit from government agencies, or integrating services with Medicaid—proves difficult enough to discourage all but the most motivated parties. And in their final report, the program reviewers noted that the local groups who remained committed to the project were rewarded with an endless series of punishments from the very public agencies that were supposed to help: "slow Medicaid eligibility determinations, slow payments, insufficient payments, delayed licensing processes, adversarial survey agencies and disinterested or unapproachable finance agencies."[14]

Ultimately the Coming Home project resulted in fifty completed assisted living complexes in thirteen states. Although most are in rural and suburban areas where development costs are low, a few are in cities—including San Francisco, Milwaukee, Tampa, and Burlington—where local agencies offered land or special loans and showed a genuine interest in solving the housing problems of their solo-dwelling senior citizens. The facilities are typically mixed-income communities, with some residents paying market rate and others no more than their social security insurance affords. And although some of the projects struggled in the late 2000s when the Great Recession arrived and states slashed funding for the elderly, while other projects that had been planned were deemed "infeasible" and never broke ground, the Coming Home staff says they found eager local partners in all parts of the country, and the number of residences they built actually exceeded their expectations.

THERE ARE FEW GOOD MODELS of affordable housing for younger and middle-age singletons, and as a consequence the most marginal of them often live on the edge of homelessness, where a single misstep can result in disaster. Rosanne Haggerty first noticed this problem in 1982, when she graduated from Amherst College, moved to New York City, and began working with Covenant House, a Catholic charity that served the poor. The job came naturally to her. Haggerty had grown up outside of Hartford, Connecticut, in a large religious family that attended church in a congregation made up largely of poor old-timers, many of whom lived in cheap apartments and SROs. "I spent a lot of time in their apartments helping out or just visiting," she tells me. "They weren't especially nice places. But they were modest and dignified. Respectable. I came to appreciate that places like that could be decent homes."

In New York City, Haggerty encountered a very different kind of housing stock. Homeless shelters were makeshift places where nonprofits had squeezed in as many beds as they could fit. The SROs were dilapidated and dangerous. Though she was only in her early twenties and a relative newcomer to the city, Haggerty sensed that the housing problems in New York had become urgent. "It was the moment when our understanding of homelessness was starting to change," she tells me. "It had always been a Bowery bum issue, confined to a small group of men and just a few places. We treated it like we treat hurricanes: Get them through the crisis and they'll be fine. But it was getting bigger, and that didn't work anymore. There were homeless people all over the city, and we'd see young adults come back to our clinic again and again because they didn't have a place to go. That's when I realized that no one had an exit strategy.

Neither the city nor the charities knew what to do."

Haggerty left Covenant House for a full-time job at Catholic Charities in Brooklyn, and her first major task was helping to convert three church buildings into housing for the homeless and poor. During the planning process, she visited various shelters and SROs around the city, and she always came away disturbed by how they looked and felt inside. The SROs were particularly upsetting, because many were in beautiful old buildings with terrific bones. They had been neglected, even abused. Public areas had been divided and darkened so that no one would feel comfortable in them. The original molding and fixtures had been replaced with the cheapest materials available. "The problem wasn't the buildings," Haggerty explains. "It was the management and the design. I knew we could do it better. We could restore and maintain these places so that they'd look as good as everything else in the neighborhood, maybe better. We could renovate the public spaces inside so that the residents would want to use them. We could create housing that didn't feel stigmatizing, places that people wouldn't be ashamed to call home."

In the late 1980s, Haggerty got her first opportunity to try this experiment on a large scale. A few years earlier, Covenant House had purchased the neighboring Times Square Hotel as a real estate investment, but the project collapsed because the organization, beset by internal conflicts and a pedophilia scandal involving Father Bruce Ritter, failed to maintain the property and its 652 units. "It had once been a gorgeous residential hotel," she recalls. "But it was in shambles, on the cusp of bankruptcy. I'd spent some time there when I volunteered next door, and I knew it had possibilities. I started a campaign to save it and convert it into low-income housing for people who lived alone, and a lot of people signed on. The problem was I couldn't find an organization that would do it. That's when I decided to start my own."

Haggerty launched Common Ground in 1990, with help from a board made up of other homeless advocates and an attorney whose firm did pro bono work to establish its charter. Although she was not yet thirty, Haggerty had seven years of experience renovating buildings for the homeless, and she knew exactly how to get city funding for the Times Square project. After three years of renovations, Common Ground reopened the hotel in 1994 as an entirely new kind of SRO. About half the residents are formerly homeless, and they struggle with everything from substance abuse to mental illness and HIV. But the other half is made up of the working poor, including aspiring actors and artists and a variety of blue-collar laborers who have a hard time finding a place for themselves in the local rental market. Haggerty hoped that those who were used to working every day would mix with those who weren't. The groups can help each other, whether it's dog walking or helping find a job. "The hotel is designed to be a vertical village," she explains. "The rooms are small, but everything else is as grand as we could make it. There's a garden roof deck and a large community room on the top floor with amazing views of the city. We built a library, a computer room, an art studio, a medical clinic, and a gym. We restored the lobby so that residents would feel proud when they came home or met visitors."

In addition to these architectural renovations, Common Ground remade the SRO's service delivery system, offering everything from health care to counseling to job placement, so that residents wouldn't have to rebuild their lives on their own. Haggerty says that most low-cost housing for poor singles may rescue people from homelessness, but they also remove tenants from their network of family, friends, and neighbors. "In those places residents often wind up feeling even more alone than they did on the streets," she explains. "So we needed to strengthen their support systems—to create a substitute for the aggressive daughters—to help them navigate the system and get back on their feet."

The redesigned SRO proved to be more

effective than anyone at Common Ground had imagined. As word of its success spread through news stories and glowing policy reports, foundation officers and local officials throughout the United States came to visit The Times Square, and the organization won funding to expand its model on a larger scale. By 2011, Common Ground had renovated twelve SROs and nearly three thousand individual units in the New York metropolitan area, and six other buildings were under construction. It had established partnerships with organizations in Los Angeles, New Orleans, and Washington, D.C., and branched out into larger projects, including a neighborhood-level initiative to prevent homelessness in Bedford-Stuyvesant. "It's been totally consuming," says Haggerty, who's now working on a doctorate in sociology at NYU (where I teach) in whatever spare time she can find. "But obviously we haven't even scratched the surface of this problem, because there are just so many people on their own who can't afford to live in our cities. The housing option we're trying to create is going to become more and more necessary. Our biggest challenge isn't keeping up with the demand, it's catching up. And right now we're not even close."

THE MAIN REASON that there's not enough affordable housing for people who live alone is that our metropolitan areas weren't built for them, and we've failed to redesign cities and suburbs to meet the needs of a singleton society. Compact residential units in apartment buildings, not single-family homes. Walkable and densely populated neighborhoods. Proximity to a range of commercial goods and services, attractive public spaces, and restaurants, bars, and cafés where residents can meet. Good public transit. These are important for people who live in all kinds of domestic arrangements, but they are especially important for those who live alone, because they are such heavy users of the places that support local social life.

As it happens, these metropolitan amenities are also the key elements of more environmentally sustainable cities. For although, as one British study recently reported, singletons tend to consume more land, energy, and household goods than those who live with others, these statistics are misleading.[15] After all, a family of four with two cars, long commutes, and a 2,500-square-foot house in the suburbs will leave a greater carbon footprint than four individual city dwellers who live in compact apartments and use public transportation (or, better, walk) to reach work. That's why Manhattan, the capital of America's singleton society, is also the nation's greenest city.[16]

Manhattan is not the only urban center that's

begun adapting to the new social environment. Planners and developers in cities across the United States are starting to build better accommodations and amenities for the unprecedented number of singletons who live in them. Some urban officials have made special efforts to attract the coveted demographic of professional singles that Richard Florida calls "the creative class," in hope that they will stimulate the local culture and economy. Cities in Europe, Japan, and Australia have made even more progress. In Stockholm, where 60 percent of all households have just one occupant, a generous supply of publicly subsidized housing in urban centers and a rich, locally based neighborhood life make living alone an affordable and often quite social experience. Tokyo, Paris, Sydney, and London offer not only robust public transit systems, but also an increasing number of small residential apartments, many of them rental units and condominiums designed for young professionals, the fastest-growing segment of the singleton society.

Unfortunately, the fastest-growing part of the American metropolis is the suburb, and that's also the place that's proved most inhospitable to people who live alone. While many singletons prefer cities, others share the cultural preference for suburbia that's so common in the United

States and are frustrated by the paltry housing options now available. Rollin Stanley is the director of planning for Montgomery County, Maryland, an affluent area just north of Washington, D.C., and southwest of Baltimore and home to popular commuter havens such as Silver Spring, Germantown, and Rockville. Stanley, who's in his early fifties and lets the bangs of his wavy brown hair fall across his brow, spent his early career in Toronto, where he got support for promoting more walkable, ecologically sound neighborhoods, places where residents could live, shop, and socialize without traveling far to work. "Coming to an American suburban area has been an entirely different experience," he tells me. "And this is the fundamental problem: People here are scared to death of traffic. They don't want to build apartment buildings or expand the commercial districts because they think it will bring congestion. They honestly believe it's a threat to their way of life."

But the current arrangement, a sprawling landscape of large single-family homes accessible only by automobile, is unsustainable—and not just for environmental reasons. "Washington, D.C., has more people living alone than almost any other city," Stanley explains. "And the parts of Montgomery County that have refused to make a place for them are already suffering.

Housing prices are down. Tax revenues are way down. The municipalities here need revenue and it's not clear how they'll get it." The places that have best weathered the downturn are what he calls "urban lite" communities, such as Silver Spring and Bethesda. In Montgomery County, the average home is a single-family house that sells for around $500,000. But these places have a range of housing options, at different sizes and prices, and their mix of amenities entice the people who are still hunting for housing: young singles, senior citizens trying to downsize their domestic arrangements, and immigrant workers.

"This isn't a fleeting issue, and it's not just about the recession," Stanley adds. "We're dealing with a major demographic change. Montgomery County has enough single-family housing to last forever. Today only about a quarter of our households have married couples with children. And almost two-thirds of our seniors live in private houses. When they die, or decide to move into something smaller, we'll have more single-family houses than we know what to do with."

As he sees it, what Montgomery County and others like it clearly do need is more diverse and affordable housing choices, as well as more small-scale commercial development—not big-box stores or strip malls, which require automobiles and do clog up local roadways, but stores and restaurants that residents near modest downtown suburban areas could reach on foot. "We're starting to see some development for the DINKS—dual income, no kids—families. Now I want to get some projects for SINKS [single income, no kids] to break ground, and I've told everyone that Generation Y wants to move here. They grew up in suburbs, and they'll stay here for a long time if we can give them the taste of the city that they need."

This vision for the future of the suburbs outside the nation's capital is not widely shared by the people who've lived there longest, however, and they tend to be the ones who are most invested in civic affairs. When Stanley rolled out his master plans for Montgomery County, he got fierce resistance from home owners, particularly those near the areas where he wants to promote urban lite developments. Each project generates a mini controversy, he says, so the pace of change is painfully slow. Now, after a few years in the region, Stanley says he's developed a new strategy for debating the issue. He's started warning those who refuse to make room for singletons that their resistance is bad for everyone, including, perhaps especially, themselves. "There's a real risk that we'll miss the chance to adapt suburbia for the way we're currently living," Stanley insists. "And we're all going to suffer, because as we get older we'll find that it doesn't work for us anymore. We'll want less space and better proximity to amenities when we can no longer drive. And you know what will happen? We'll wind up having to move to Florida or California. We literally will no longer fit in our hometowns."

CONCLUSION

ANXIETY ABOUT BEING DISCON-nected is an age-old condition. It's in Genesis, when God, concerned about the potential power of a unified human community, "confounds" the language shared among residents in the Tower of Babel, leaving them unable to communicate or understand each other. It's in Plato's *Symposium*, when Aristophanes explains that Zeus, who also feared the power of a united human species, split us in half. Before then, the story goes, every person had four arms, four legs, and a two-sided face, with integrated male and female qualities. Now each of us is an incomplete individual, condemned to feel alone unless we find the companion who makes us whole.

Concerns about various forms of alienation and social fragmentation are also hallmarks of modern culture, as are debates on why we wound up this way and how we might come together again. In fact, inquiries into these very issues helped inspire the first major works of social science, including canonical works in economics, psychology, political science, and sociology, by big thinkers as diverse as Adam Smith, Karl

Marx, Max Weber, and Sigmund Freud.

Contemporary social scientists have taken the study of human disconnection in new directions. Instead of grand philosophical theories, today's number-crunching academics traffic in surveys, using powerful statistics to convey who we are and what troubles us now. In recent years, blockbuster findings about our purportedly heightened social isolation have sent commentators into a new cycle of anxiety-laden debates about the reasons we've become so atomized. Some, such as the startling discovery that one in four Americans has no one with whom they can discuss important matters, turn out to be unfounded. Others, like those documenting the number of hours we spend in front of screens rather than in face-to-face interaction, seem to discount the social nature of what we do online. But if we often exaggerate the extent of our disconnection, there is no mistaking the fact that today more people throughout the world live alone than ever before, and that even more will likely join them when they are affluent and secure enough to pull it off.

The meaning of these facts can be debated, however, and making sense of them requires looking beyond the numbers. The cultural critics and political officials who worry about the rise of living alone don't acknowledge that living alone is an individual choice that's as valid as the choice to get married or live with a domestic partner. Nor do they recognize that it's a collective achievement—which is why it's common in developed nations but not in poor ones. They tend to overlook the fact that neither individuals nor societies see living alone as a goal or an end point—which is why social movements to promote the interests of singletons are so difficult to organize. And they don't admit that living alone has *not* led to the "decomposition" of collective life and the end of meaningful social commitments, as the economist Joseph Schumpeter and many others feared.

More pragmatically, those who caution against the shift toward living alone need to grapple with the fact that the social changes driving it—the emergence of the individual, the rising status of women, the growth of cities, the development of communications technologies, and the expansion of the life course—are unlikely to be reversed. At this point in history it's clear that living alone will be an enduring feature of the contemporary developed world. States and societies that recognize this, and particularly those that give singletons the kinds of support that they now offer to those who are married, will be better able to meet their citizens' needs.

CONSIDER SWEDEN, where about 47 percent of all households have just one resident (compared to about 28 percent in the United States), or more specifically Stockholm, where a staggering 60 percent of all dwellings are occupied by someone who lives alone. Like the United States, Sweden has a deep-seated cultural legacy of individualism and self-reliance. But it's the nation's ongoing commitment to collectivism, not its problems with atomization or social isolation, that most impressed me when I traveled there to learn about how and why so many Swedes live alone today.[1]

For decades, scholars of the modern world—and of the family in particular—have turned to Sweden for a preview of trends (the bad as well as the good) that may emerge in their own societies. In the 1980s, the American sociologist and marriage proponent David Popenoe noted that Sweden had made a "world-leading move away from the nuclear family." Popenoe highlighted the fact that Swedish marriage rates were down and nonmarital cohabitation was up, as well as the fact that family dissolution, whether from divorce or nonmarital separation, happened more frequently than before. But he also called attention to another surprising social change: that the number of one-person households had more than doubled between 1960 and 1980, with young adults leading the way. Popenoe questioned what would happen when the once universal human experience of living in groups was no longer assured. He worried about whether the rise of living alone would change the quality and character of social relationships, resulting in more loneliness or anomie. But he also acknowledged that this seemed unlikely: "It is not that Swedes are misanthropes, living their adult lives with no intimates. The evidence suggests that the propensity of adult Swedes to form a dyad with another person, at least for part of their lives, is as strong if not stronger than elsewhere . . . Nor is it that Swedes necessarily lack intimate social contacts, even if many of these contacts are outside of their immediate household."[2]

The intensity of Swedish social life is most evident in Stockholm, a prosperous city that is also the global capital of living alone. I arrived there during a damp and cloudy week in the fall of 2010, but the weather did nothing to diminish the vitality of the city's sidewalks, waterways, parks, restaurants, and cafés. More remarkable than the crowds of people, though, was the density of the city's handsome, functional residential buildings, including prewar complexes designed specifically to promote communal living among singletons and postwar high-rises that, if not especially attractive, created an abundant supply of decent places to live.

These buildings were not developed by

commercial realty companies for which success is measured solely by revenues. They were designed to meet the needs of quite specific populations, including the ranks of those who live alone. In the 1930s, for instance, a group of modern architects, social planners, and feminists conceived a new style of collective housing, one that offered single women (young and old) a private residence within a building that also supplied services such as cooking, cleaning, and child care. The "collective house," designed by architect Sven Markelius and social welfare champion Alva Myrdal (who won the 1982 Nobel Peace Prize), opened its doors to single women and single mothers in 1935. Located in central Stockholm's Kungsholmen district, the building contained a restaurant (with a small elevator system that could deliver meals into every unit), a communal kitchen, a laundry (with chutes for sending down dirty clothing and a paid staff of launderers), and a nursery. It was a resounding success, perhaps too much so, because demand for a place there has always exceeded the modest supply of fifty-seven units (eighteen with one room, thirty-five with two rooms, and four four-room "mansionettes"). Fortunately, there are several similar buildings in the same neighborhood, some catering to single mothers, others to all singletons regardless of sex or age. And while in some the services are no longer available, the restaurant and pastry shop in the Markelius and Myrdal collective house remain extremely popular. After I sampled the fare there, the outgoing staff delighted in showing me that the meal delivery elevator still works.

Between 1965 and 1974, Sweden embarked on a far more ambitious housing project: the Miljon-programmet, or Million Program. At the direction of the Social Democratic Party, the government invested in the construction of roughly one million new residential units (and the demolition of about 350,000 others), including high-rise apartment complexes, many of which were packed together in inner suburbs, as well as less conspicuous, small-scale developments scattered throughout the city. The Social Democrats initiated the program because Swedish cities lacked sufficient housing for the continuous stream of migrants who had abandoned their rural and small-town communities in the previous two decades. Social planners believed that the massive construction project would assure Sweden its role as an ultramodern nation, a place where citizens would benefit from their nation's collective prosperity and the privileges it afforded.[3] Thereafter, one of those privileges would be the chance to live alone.

The abundance of small apartments available in cities like Stockholm is just one reason that going solo is so pervasive. Like the other

Scandinavian nations, all of which have unusually high rates of people who live alone, Sweden has both a dynamic market economy and a strong welfare state, and citizens can pursue their autonomy with confidence that the safety net will catch them if they fall. "Do you know why so many of us live alone?" a Swedish statistician I interview in the charming Old Town district asks me. He quickly answers his own question: "Because we can."

For middle-class Swedes who came of age after the Million Program, moving into a place of their own after leaving their childhood home has become a rite of passage into adulthood, a luxury that sometimes feels like a social right. Until recently, when the government changed the system for allocating apartments, parents would register their newborn children on the waiting list for a small apartment (in the same way that Manhattan parents sign up their infants for nursery schools), to assure that there would be one available when they graduated from gymnasium (high school). What's more, Swedish parents will often exchange their own family-size apartments for a smaller, "empty-nest" unit so that they can help pay for their child's first go at domestic autonomy. "It's our responsibility," the father of a teenager who's approaching graduation tells me. "And we're trying to figure out how to make it work."

During my visit to Stockholm I interviewed a dozen middle-class men and women between the ages of twenty-nine and forty-seven. It was by no means a large or random or remotely scientific sample, but I was still impressed and surprised by what I learned from them. Not only had every single one of them begun living alone in their late teens or early twenties, but nearly all of their friends and family members had, too. Under these conditions, going solo is a tremendously social experience. "I got my first apartment when I turned twenty," a forty-three-year-old man in Stockholm recounts, "and so did just about all of my friends. That was one of the best times of my life. Most nights we'd meet up at someone's apartment and drink for a while, because we didn't have enough money for more than one drink in a bar, then go out somewhere to meet women and other friends." A thirty-year-old woman who's studying anthropology reports a similar experience. "We all kept our own places, even when we were dating someone seriously and spending a lot of nights together. It's only recently, now that we're all turning thirty and moving in with partners, that my friends are starting to sell or give up their apartments. But even that's hard, because so many of the people who are just a little older than us have already divorced or separated. And we all want a place that's ours."

Just as Swedish social planners like Alva Myrdal built special housing complexes for female singletons in the 1930s, contemporary planners are designing new collective dwellings for the growing ranks of young people, divorcés and divorcées, and seniors who live alone. In Stockholm, I spent one afternoon with Ingela Lindh, the CEO of Stockholmshem, which manages more than 25,000 residential units from the city's public housing stock, and her colleague Björn Ljung, who is also a liberal (of the free-market variety) representative in the municipal government. (He is a distinctively Swedish free-market liberal, though, which means he says things such as "We pay a lot of taxes and we think that's a good thing, because it allows us to take care of each other.")[4] Lindh is petite but has a commanding presence, which she honed during her ten years' tenure as Stockholm's chief urban planner. Since taking over Stockholmshem, she has pledged to develop more housing for young adults and students, as well as for the growing number of elderly Swedes who have aged in place but now seek a more communal way to live alone. "Housing has gotten too expensive here in the past decade," Lindh tells me. "Stockholm residents used to spend a quarter or a third of their income on their apartment. Now people who are getting into the market are paying 40 or 45 percent, and a lot of young and old people won't be able to afford it unless we do something."

As we sit around her conference table, Lindh and Ljung show off the architectural plans for a number of projects, including an office tower they've converted into an apartment building full of "starter" units for young singles. "We want to make sure that young people have the chance to get their own apartment," Lindh says. "Because if they have that experience, they'll have a fuller life, a more social life, and they'll develop closer connections to friends." Sweden's Social Democrats, who until recently controlled the national government as well as many municipal ones, took the same position in a report issued before the 2010 elections. The party called for the immediate construction of 50,000 units of housing, including 3,000 apartments for students and 11,000 one- and two-room apartments for young adults. The housing shortage, it claimed, is "a serious problem for young people who are prevented from moving away from home, and for students who are not infrequently forced to abstain from studying in the Stockholm region."[5]

Stockholm's municipal government has also acknowledged that it lacks enough housing for the poor and the sick, as well as for the rising population of immigrants and refugees. Stockholmshem is trying to build some. Lindh and Ljung pull out the design for the Swedish equivalent of an SRO, as well as a complex designed and located to allow the children of Somali refugees to move into their own places without leaving their family's neighborhood. "It's not a very Swedish idea, because it treats the Somalis as if they are different from all others. And at first we didn't like it," Lindh acknowledges. "But when they explained how important it was for the families to be connected, I understood that it was the right thing to do."

Lindh seems most excited about a building that she doesn't manage: Färdknäppen, a community-owned facility for Stockholm residents who are above age forty, with no children living at home, and an interest in being alone together during the second half of their lives. "You can move into Färdknäppen when your needs are no longer dictated by family and children," the building's Web site explains. "How much social contact and 'togetherness' one desires varies, from person to person and from one period to another."[6] "It's important that someone can move in at forty, not sixty-five," Lindh adds, "because that means there's real age diversity, with middle-age adults who work full-time as well as retired people. You can see how different it is from a retirement home the moment you walk in." I tell her I'd like to see it sometime, perhaps on another visit. "How about now?" she asks me. "We can visit my mother, who's lived there for fifteen years."

A few minutes later we're in a taxi heading to Stockholm's Södermalm district, a leafy, densely populated area where Färdknäppen, with seven floors and forty-three residential units, blends in neatly. The building, which was designed in 1989, is clean and modern, with large windows, a brick exterior at street level, and white walls with red trim above. The ground floor is spacious and inviting. Lindh's mother, Siv, who's lively at eighty-five, greets us at the front door and offers me a tour. We begin in the bright dining room, with seating for sixty people, where on most nights the majority of the residents eat together (for about four dollars), next to the large, open kitchen where four people are busily preparing dinner. There's also a library and television room, a computer room, a laundry room, a weaving area, a carpentry and hobby room, and an entry to the communal garden and outdoor seating area. We take the elevator to the top floor, where there's a roof deck and a party room; then we descend to the basement, which features an exercise room large enough for group classes as well as a sauna, before we head up to a residential floor, where a group photograph of the floor's residents hangs prominently in the hall. Siv lives in an airy corner unit, with a bedroom, a living room, and a compact kitchen. "I have enough space to cook for myself," she tells me. "But usually I eat downstairs in the dining room and spend an hour or so after dinner talking with friends. Of course I don't have to, which is what makes being here so nice."

Residents of Färdknäppen are obligated to participate in some activities, however. Every six weeks each resident must help with the cooking and cleaning. "This doesn't mean, though, that everyone must be a good cook or that everyone must do exactly as much as everyone else," the building's Web site explains. "'From each according to their ability' as it's stated in the rules of the association." Occasionally, residents may experience these tasks as onerous, but there's little question about whether they detract from or enhance the appeal of the place. Today there is a long waiting list of Stockholm singles who are eager for a spot in the building. "We obviously need a lot more places like this," Lindh tells me. "It's a great model for bringing people who live alone into a real community. Now the question is whether it can be replicated on a bigger scale, because more and more of us are going to want what it offers."

Lindh, who's divorced, has two children, and as they reach the age where they expect to move into their own apartments, she is thinking more about what kind of arrangement will suit her best. "They will both be out of my apartment soon," she explains. "But I've realized that the way we live is never permanent. Sometimes we're with a partner, sometimes with children, sometimes alone. In Sweden we know that the family is always changing, and so are our own lives. We're not especially lonely—not at all. We're actually quite social, and we've learned how to be okay when we're on our own."

IN SWEDEN, as in many other nations where singletons are now ubiquitous, living alone is not merely a condition to be okay with. It's an arrangement that people have come to appreciate, value, and even pursue. Young people believe that moving into a home of their own is essential for becoming an adult, because the experience will help them grow more mature and self-reliant. Middle-age adults believe that living alone is important after a divorce or separation, because it helps them regain their autonomy and self-control. The elderly believe that living alone allows them to maintain their dignity, integrity, and autonomy, and to determine how they will live.

One reason that so many find living alone appealing is that the choice is hardly binding. Most people could find roommates, from strangers on Craigslist to friends, family, prospective romantic partners, or coresidents in a group-living facility. But the fact is, most of us prefer living alone to these other options, and—since we've all been shaped by the cult of the individual—we're unlikely to change our minds.

What if, instead of indulging the social reformer's fantasy that we would all just be better off together, we accepted the fact that living alone is a fundamental feature of modern societies and we simply did more to shield those who go solo from the main hazards of the condition? Isolation and insufficient care for frail, old, or impoverished singletons. Disconnection for those who want to participate in social activities but have lost their companions and don't know how or where to find others. Stress and anxiety for single women who want a child but are nearing the limits of their reproductive years. Economic insecurity for those who lose a job and have no partner to support them. These are practical problems for which there are good solutions, not causes for vague and fuzzy proclamations—the death of community! the collapse of civil society!—which are notoriously difficult to assess.

One reason that singletons are so prevalent in the Scandinavian countries is that their welfare states protect most citizens from the most difficult aspects of living alone. Consider one of the issues that makes going solo so much more stressful for young women than it is for young men: planning one's life around the biological clock. In my interviews, American women in their late thirties and early forties consistently reported that their anxieties around reproduction led them to wonder whether they had made good decisions about their personal and professional lives. They tear themselves up asking questions that few young American men who live alone ponder: Should they have settled, or settled down, earlier? Would they have been happier if they had lowered their professional ambitions and invested more time in their personal lives? Young Swedish women who live alone share some of these anxieties, but for them finding the right partner feels less urgent or consequential, because they know that if they have a child on their own they are entitled to meaningful support: sixteen months of paid parental leave, with costs shared by employers and the state; heavily subsidized child care, for which no family can pay more than 1 to 3 percent of their income; and public health care that ranks among the finest in the world.

It is, of course, unlikely that the United States would adopt such generous social policies in the foreseeable future, and perhaps it is folly to suggest that we emulate them now that nations throughout the developed world are trimming down their welfare programs. But it's important to note that the social rights of citizenship in places like Sweden dramatically improve life for all young women and provide even more benefits for those who live alone. It's also important to identify the costs of relying on the market to satisfy the needs of individuals and societies in which so many people live alone. One of these costs is the problem of overwork among aspiring young professionals whose security hinges on their professional achievements and who often end up "married" to their job. Another, as we have seen, is that the private sector, whose innovations enhance and even enable the lives of successful singletons—consider smart phones, solo vacation packages, prepackaged meals, and luxury condominium complexes, among others—has done far less to help the sick, the poor, and the elderly, all of whom need the kinds of support that even "socially responsible" corporations are unlikely to provide.

What should societies adapting to the emergence of singletons ask of the private and public sectors? To what extent could our policies promote or demand genuine social responsibility for those who live alone? Citizens and political leaders in the United States have asked these kinds of questions during previous historical moments when they faced up to the challenges posed by major demographic changes. Think of the post–World War II baby boom, when public support for suburban home development and highway construction to accommodate the growing population of middle-class families reshaped the urban landscape. Or the late nineteenth and early twentieth centuries, when progressive reformers invested in municipal services and public health agencies in response to the wave of immigrants who had settled in centralized cities. The extraordinary rise of living alone is a less publicly visible but equally dramatic transformation, and it will be impossible to manage it well without bold policy initiatives. In the United States, we've discussed "settling" as if it is exclusively a personal matter concerning our choice of a partner. In fact it is also a political issue, concerning what we expect from our public and private institutions, today and in the future.

The question of what we expect from the state and society extends to the domain of housing, and our answer will affect the future of all of us who might live alone someday. There's little question that residential environments that are better designed for singleton societies could greatly reduce the most serious risks related to going solo. People who live alone do not need as much interior space as nuclear families. As Alva Myrdal recognized in the 1930s, young adults as well as the elderly are often willing to live in relatively small but functional apartments if they are located in buildings with well-designed public spaces and common facilities for eating, socializing, exercising, and the like. And when people choose to live in these places, they increase the available supply of family-size housing, bringing down the price for those who could use some extra room.

There are some buildings that are laid out this way in contemporary America, particularly high-end condominium developments for urban professionals and assisted living facilities for retirees. But these tend to be exclusive enclaves for the nation's most affluent people, inaccessible to those who would benefit most from the social integration and high-quality services they offer. These places so thoroughly segregate—especially by age and by class—that they impoverish the experience of those fortunate enough to inhabit them. Better architectural designs for today's singleton societies are therefore necessary but not sufficient. We also need new models for integrating people of different life stages and social positions. And of course we need more buildings, too.

This is the insight that helped Rosanne Haggerty and Common Ground develop SROs that are more successful than any others in New York City. Their best projects are not merely well crafted, with the kinds of handsome public spaces we associate with opulent hotels and prewar apartment buildings, they are also centrally located, professionally managed, and exceptionally diverse. The Times Square, for instance, houses struggling young actors and professionals as well as the retired elderly, the unemployed, and those who are coping with illness and substance abuse. It offers high-quality services for those who need them, and encourages those who don't to lend a hand when they can. It's not for everyone. But it's far more attractive than the other alternatives for people who live alone and need low-cost housing in New York City.

Supportive housing facilities like those built by Common Ground are cost-effective and, as a number of scientific studies have shown, cost-saving ways to help people who are on their own and in trouble; they can even produce benefits for the communities in which they are located. Consider findings published in two top medical journals, *Psychiatric Services* and *JAMA: The Journal of the American Medical Association*. One article, an analysis of homeless single adults with psychiatric and substance abuse disorders in San Francisco, reports, "Providing permanent supportive housing . . . reduced their use of costly hospital emergency department and inpatient services, which are publicly provided." A second, which tracks chronically homeless singles with severe alcohol problems in Seattle, reports that those who were placed in a supportive housing complex—one that allows residents to drink in their rooms and offers a range of voluntary services—cut their consumption of alcohol, their encounters with the criminal justice system, and their use of expensive health services. The authors, researchers at the University of Washington, conclude that the savings from these changes—specifically, the reduction in overnight visits to hospitals, mental health and substance abuse clinics, jails, and shelters— more than offset the costs of the housing program: "At twelve months, the ninety-five housed individuals had reduced their total medical costs by more than $4 million, compared with the year prior to enrollment, or $42,964 per person per year, as compared with a cost of $13,440 per person per year to administer the housing program."[7]

Surprisingly, these facilities can also contribute to local economic development. A study of supportive housing in New York City by NYU's Furman Center for the Study of Real Estate and Urban Policy reports that properties within five hundred feet of a facility "show steady growth relative to other properties in the neighborhood in the years after supportive housing opens," while those between five hundred and a thousand feet away decline initially "but then increase steadily, perhaps as the market realizes that fears about the supportive housing turned out to be wrong."[8]

Supportive housing for solidly middle-class

people produces a different set of benefits. Recall Stockholm's Färdknäppen, which integrates people of different ages and life stages, and the city's historic collective houses made for singletons living en masse. Alas, these kinds of facilities are even more uncommon than supportive housing programs for the formerly homeless. Even in Sweden, the supply of cooperative housing like Färdknäppen is not nearly large enough to meet the demand, and today the state housing agency lacks the budget it needs to replicate the model on a large scale. But the current economic crisis will not last forever, and when government agencies around the world regain their fiscal health they should be encouraged to develop housing that's appropriate for the way we live now. These need not be exclusively public endeavors. After the housing bubble burst, real estate developers regained some incentive to collaborate on projects for which there is both market demand and a clear social need. And all of us have an interest in increasing the supply of housing that works for people who live alone, because whether or not we need it for ourselves, the odds are that someone we love—a parent, a spouse, a sibling, a child—will.

Of all the people who live alone, those who are old and infirm face the most difficult challenges, and finding affordable housing that connects them with sources of social support is one of them. Most elderly singletons haven't been fortunate enough to live in a naturally occurring retirement community or to have aged in a place that continues to suit their needs. Those who could use more help usually find that high-quality assisted living facilities—those providing extensive personal and social services, a communal environment, and private apartments—are prohibitively expensive. (In some states, those who are eligible for Medicare and Medicaid are guaranteed funding for a spot in an assisted living facility. Yet they are typically given a bed in a shared room of a lower-quality institution, and they are not assured readmission if they are hospitalized or otherwise forced to leave.)[9] It's unlikely that many viable alternatives, let alone attractive ones, will come from for-profit corporations competing in the free market. In fact, what's happened when for-profit corporations enter the nursing home business suggests that, left to their own devices, they might only make things worse.

The market's failure to provide decent care or attractive housing options for older people who live alone has generated a serious social problem. Today we live longer than any generation before us, yet none of us can be certain of whether we will age on our own or with a companion, and few of us know whether we will be financially stable or insecure (as millions of retirees who planned on living off their investments before 2008 can attest). Wouldn't everyone feel less anxious if they knew that their loved ones would have a place where they'd be comfortable and well cared for if they wound up old and alone someday? Wouldn't we all feel more secure if we knew there were residential options for elderly seniors beyond the solitary private apartment or the lifeless nursing home?

One relatively simple way to begin addressing this problem involves increasing the public support for caregivers, including some of the 38 million Americans who provide uncompensated care to aging family members. I say simple because the U.S. Congress has already passed a bill that authorizes this very thing. The Lifespan Respite Care Act, which Congress passed in late 2006, created a modest pool of funds—about $290 million over five years—for states that were interested in building coordinated systems of community-based services for those who take care of people with special needs. (Although the term "respite" suggests otherwise, care for old adults who live alone but are not near death is covered by the legislation.) President George W. Bush signed the bill into law in December 2006, but neither he nor Congress funded it beyond a onetime $2.5 million appropriation. The Obama administration and the Democratic Congress reversed this decision, opting to fund it "on level" for 2010 and 2011, at $70 million and $95 million, respectively. The Obama administration also introduced a new, $102 million caregiver initiative designed to "ease the burden on families with elder care responsibilities and allow seniors to live in the community for as long as possible."[10]

There's no doubt that these programs will help generate better care and support for the millions of Americans who are aging alone. But there's also no doubt that they will do little or nothing for the majority of people in this situation. The problem is not only that this level of funding is woefully inadequate for addressing the American care crisis, it's also that these programs fail to address the more difficult (and expensive) problem: the shortage of housing where older people who live alone can come together and get support. Building the kinds of assisted living facilities that are now available only to the affluent elderly would require an enormous investment, and in some respects this is a terrible time to advocate for it. The economy is sluggish. The federal government faces record deficits. The cost of other benefits, for things like health and prescription drugs, is already high. But there are other reasons to believe that the timing isn't too bad. After all, building new housing is a useful way to improve our physical infra-structure and create jobs, and managing an assisted living facility will also entail putting more social service providers to work. Moreover, today the baby boomers are beginning to experience the challenges of growing old, and millions of them are learning firsthand that aging alone is much easier when they have good support. If, as it's often alleged, the baby boomers are a distinctively self-interested generation, they may well use their political clout to promote housing programs that benefit them first.[11] But in this case they could be forgiven, maybe even appreciated, because by building better places for themselves today they'll give younger Americans better choices tomorrow. We'll need them, too, since so many of us will be living alone.

ULTIMATELY, the question is not how many of us live alone but how we live with the fact that so many people in so many societies do. It's too early to say how any particular society will respond to either the problems or the opportunities generated by this extraordinary social transformation. After all, our experiment with going solo is still in its earliest stages, and we are just beginning to understand how it affects our own lives, as well as our families, communities, cities, and states.

In theory, the rise of living alone could lead to any number of outcomes, from the decline of community to a more socially active citizenry, from rampant isolation to a more robust public life. I began my exploration of the world's first singleton societies with an eye for their most dangerous and disturbing features, including selfishness, loneliness, reclusiveness, and the horrors of getting sick or dying alone. I found some measure of all of these things in the cities where living alone has become common, and in the pages above I've suggested several ways that we could address them more effectively than we do today. On balance, however, I came away from my fieldwork convinced that the problems related to living alone do not and should not define the condition, because the great majority of those who go solo have a more rich and varied experience. Sometimes, indeed, they feel lonely, anxious, and uncertain about whether they would be happier in another arrangement. But so, too, do those who are married or live with others, and the widespread, often firsthand knowledge of this fact is just one of the reasons that, in my interviews, nearly everyone who lives alone said that they prefer it to their other available options.

Today there is an abundance of pop sociology that associates living alone with the rise of loneliness, the collapse of civil society, and the demise of the common good. I find this line of argument to be worse than misleading. It's damaging, because its vague generalities distract us from the urgent challenge of calling attention to truly isolated people and to the places that most need help.

Moreover, when we treat living alone exclusively as a social problem, we cannot help but overlook the fact that its rapid emergence has also created new possibilities for our personal, romantic, and social lives. The rise of living alone has produced some significant social benefits, too. We have seen, for instance, that young and middle-age singletons have helped to revitalize the public life of cities, because they are more likely than those who live with others to spend time with friends and neighbors, to frequent bars, cafés, and restaurants, and to participate in informal social activities as well as in civic groups.[12] We have seen that cultural acceptance of living alone has helped to liberate women from bad marriages and oppressive families, allowing them not only to reassert control of their personal lives but also to make a spirited return to civic life, where a world of other singletons will welcome them. We have seen that, despite fears that living alone may be environmentally unsustainable, solos tend to live in apartments rather than in big houses, and in relatively green cities rather than in auto-dependent suburbs. So there's good reason to believe that people who live alone in cities actually consume less energy than they would if they coupled up and decamped to pursue a single-family home. And we have seen that living alone has given people a way to achieve restorative solitude as well as the freedom to engage in intensely social experiences. Surprisingly, it has given people the personal time and space that we sometimes need to make deep and meaningful connections—whether with another person, a community, a cause, or ourselves.

COUNTLESS CULTURAL TRADITIONS, from the Stoics to the monastics to the transcendentalists, have emphasized the value of spending time in a place of one's own. So, too, have modern social scientists, from Émile Durkheim, the French sociologist who coined the expression "cult of the individual," to John Cacioppo, the University of Chicago psychologist who, in his innovative studies of loneliness, has noted that the lack of time for oneself "is one of the great complaints of men and women in today's harried marriages" and that "those who feel lonely actually spend no more time alone than do those who feel more connected."[13]

Durkheim argued that the private time that individuals spend on their own allows them to preserve energy and build an appetite for social participation. He recognized the allure of autonomy and independence, but he had a deep and abiding faith in the fundamental human need to come together, and he insisted that individuals, once liberated, would begin searching for something that transcended themselves. The Americans Emerson and Thoreau shared a similar vision. They argued that being alone, and sometimes living alone, was necessary not because solitude grants us freedom from the burden of intimate social ties, which are, in the end, a source of deep meaning and security, but because it allows us the freedom to cultivate our selves, develop original ideas, and make a productive return to the world.

People who live in the world's busiest and most modern societies can easily forget that it's vital to learn how to be alone. But finding solitude is particularly important for those of us who spend ever more of our time online and in social media. Today "friends" are everywhere, distractions are ubiquitous, and all too often our minds are exactly where we are not. Whether online or offline, we are so immersed in social networks that, as *Connected* authors Nicholas Christakis and James Fowler put it, we have begun "to form a human superorganism." In this state, they claim, "we necessarily lose some of our individuality."[14] This is precisely the kind of loss that would have worried the philosophers

Emerson and Thoreau, the sociologists Durkheim and Simmel, or the psychologist Anthony Storr, each of whom, in his own distinctive way, viewed individuality as sacred because it enhances collective life.

Living alone is by no means the only way to reassert our individuality or to discover how and where and on what terms we want to engage the world. But an unprecedented number of people in our hypernetworked, ultra-active, 24/7 culture have discovered that, instead of leading to loneliness or isolation, having a place of one's own gives us time and space for a productive retreat. Solitude, once we learn how to use it, does more than restore our personal energy; it also sparks new ideas about how we might better live together. No matter who we are or how we live at the moment, isn't this our most pressing need?

APPENDIX
METHODS OF RESEARCH AND ANALYSIS

THE PRIMARY SOURCES of original research that I use in this book are ethnographic observations and long-form, semistructured interviews with more than three hundred people who live alone. In addition, I draw on interviews with people who assist, interact with, or design for those who live alone, including social workers, family caregivers, community organizers, political officials, urban planners, architects, and scientists working on artificial intelligence.

All of the ethnographic observations and interviews took place in major metropolitan areas, and it should be clear that this book is primarily about living alone in cities. Those who are interested in learning more about the experience of living alone in rural areas or small towns will need to look elsewhere, for although I too am curious about these issues my work does not allow me to contribute much to our knowledge about them. The majority of the research presented here took place in four boroughs of New York City (Brooklyn, the

Bronx, Manhattan, and Queens), whose diversity allowed for a heterogeneous sample within the parameters of a great city. The fieldwork also extended to other metropolitan regions, including the San Francisco Bay Area, Los Angeles, Austin, Chicago, and Stockholm. And the research included extensive reviews of the secondary literature on living alone in many other parts of the world, such as England, France, Australia, China, Japan, South Korea, India, and Brazil.

I used different methods to recruit subjects from each of the following four groups of people who live alone: young adult professionals (between the ages of twenty-eight and forty); middle-age middle-class adults (ages forty to sixty-five); poor men in SROs (ages thirty to sixty-five); and the old (age sixty-five and above). For the young adults we used a targeted snowball sample, seeking out people from a broad range of backgrounds, neighborhoods, and professional fields (i.e., not simply interviewing a convenience sample of any singletons willing to speak with us, but rather asking subjects to identify other people who lived alone and were different from themselves). We also made special efforts to recruit African American women because of their relatively high rates of living alone. For the middle-age, middle-class adults we used three techniques: poster advertisements, snowballing, and Web-based solicitations. Again, for this group we made special efforts to recruit a diverse sample, by occupation, ethnicity, sex, and location. For the poor men in SROs we worked through referrals from social workers at a supportive housing organization in New York City. For the older subjects, we used referrals from the staff at senior centers and from social workers, as well as direct invitations at senior centers that allowed us to visit and explain our project. None of the subjects were paid to participate. And all but those who are already public figures were guaranteed anonymity, which is a common way to protect human subjects in social science research.

I designed the interview questionnaires for each group of subjects and conducted many of the interviews personally. I also hired and trained a team of graduate students to help with the interviews and the recruitment of subjects. We consulted regularly, especially at the early stages of the project, as we fine-tuned the interview questions to address unexpected topics. The graduate student researchers wrote extensive field notes on their observations and identified their most common observations as well as their most surprising discoveries. These notes, and those that I recorded personally, were crucial to the analytic and interpretive process.

As a sociologist, my aim is not to report the

most sensational stories that I learned from studying the world of singletons, but to uncover the shared experiences and orientations that tell us something about the fundamental features of solo life. To distinguish between common and uncommon experiences, idiosyncratic and widely held views, I entered transcripts for 273 of my interviews into ATLAS.ti, a computer program that facilitates the coding and analysis of large qualitative data sets. I selected the individuals and the stories that appear in this book based on how well they expressed the most interesting and important findings from this analysis. The cost of this approach is that some intriguing personalities, extreme perspectives, and entertaining anecdotes are excluded from your consideration. The benefit is that the themes highlighted herein are general social phenomena, ones we need to understand as we come to grips with a world in which so many of us live alone.

NOTES

INTRODUCTION:
THE SINGLETON SOCIETY

1. Genesis 2:18.
2. Aristotle, *Politics*, Trevor J. Saunders, trans. (New York: Oxford University Press, 1995), p. 11.
3. Carel van Schaik, *Among Orangutans: Red Apes and the Rise of Human Culture* (Cambridge: Harvard University Press, 2004).
4. This quote is in Craig Haney and Mona Lynch, "Regulating Prisons of the Future: The Psychological Consequences of Solitary and Supermax Confinement." *New York University Review of Law and Social Change* 23 (1997): 477–570.
5. Craig Haney, "Mental Health Issues in Long-Term Solitary and 'Supermax' Confinement." *Crime & Delinquency* 49, 1 (2003): 124–56.
6. See Nicholas Christakis and James Fowler, *Connected: The Surprising Power of Our Social Networks and How They Shape Our Lives* (New York: Little, Brown, 2009).
7. George Peter Murdock, *Social Structure* (Oxford: Macmillan, 1949), pp. 2–3.

8. See Pew Social Trends, "The Decline of Marriage and the Rise of New Families," Washington, D.C., November 18, 2010.

9. The data on group quarters are from Robert Ellickson, *The Household: Informal Order Around the Hearth* (Princeton: Princeton University Press, 2008), p. 40.

10. On the durability of one-person households, see Toni Richards, Michael White, and Amy Ong Tsui, "Changing Living Arrangements: A Hazard Model of Transitions Among Household Types," *Demography* 24, no. 1 (1987): 77–97. On their prevalence, see Euromonitor International, "Single Living: How Atomisation—The Rise of Singles and One-Person Households—Is Affecting Consumer Purchasing Habits," 2008.

11. The statistics on living alone are from the 2006–2008 American Community Survey Three-Year Estimates, published by the U.S. Census Bureau.

12. See Harold Bloom, *Ralph Waldo Emerson* (New York: Chelsea House, 1985); David Potter, "American Individualism in the Twentieth Century," in Ronald Gross and Paul Osterman (eds.), *Individualism: Man in Modern Society* (New York: Dell, 1971). On Franklin as the "quintessential American," see Robert Bellah, Richard Madsen, William Sullivan, Ann Swidler, and Steven Tipton,

Habits of the Heart: Individualism and Commitment in American Life (Berkeley: University of California Press, 2007 [1981]).

13. See Barry Alan Shain, *The Myth of American Individualism: The Protestant Origins of American Political Thought* (Princeton: Princeton University Press, 1994).

14. See Philip Gura, *American Transcendentalism: A History* (New York: Hill and Wang, 2008).

15. Potter, "American Individualism in the Twentieth Century."

16. Robert Putnam, *Bowling Alone: The Collapse and Revival of American Community* (New York: Simon & Schuster, 2000), p. 367.

17. The international statistics on living alone come from varied sources and are produced with different methods, and I treat them as good estimates rather than as absolute facts. Here I draw primarily on two sources: Euromonitor International, "Single Living"; and Maria Iacovou and Alexandra Skew, "Household Structure in the EU," in Anthony B. Atkinson and Eric Marlier, *Income and Living Conditions in Europe* (Luxembourg: Eurostat Statistical Books, 2010), p. 84. I use different sources for a few additional cities and nations. For Paris, see Philip Ogden and François Schnoebelen, "The Rise of the Small Household: Demographic Change and

Household Structure in Paris," *Population, Space, and Place* 11 (2005): 251–68. For Japan, see Richard Ronald and Yosuke Hirayama, "Home Alone: The Individualization of Young, Urban Japanese Singles," *Environment and Planning A* 41, no. 12 (2009): 2836–54. The European nations with the lowest rates of living alone are war-torn Kosovo, where in 2003 just 2 percent of all households had one resident, and impoverished Albania, where in 2001 only 5 percent of all households had a single dweller. This is consistent with the observations of Yale law professor Robert Ellickson, who writes, "As a nation becomes more prosperous, its households generally shrink in size." See Ellickson, *The Household*, p. 35. For Kosovo and Albania, see Sasha Tsenkova, *Housing Policy Reforms in Post-Socialist Europe: Lost in Transition* (Heidelberg: Physica-Verlag, 2009), p. 115.

18. See Euromonitor International, "Single Living."
19. See Joseph Schumpeter, *Capitalism, Socialism, and Democracy* (New York: Harper Perennial, 1962 [1942]), p. 157.
20. The survey figures are reported in Frank Furstenberg Jr., Sheela Kennedy, Vonnie McLoyd, Rubén Rumbaut, and Richard

Settersten Jr., "Growing Up Is Harder to Do," *Contexts* 3, no. 3 (2004): 36.

21. Andrew Cherlin. *The Marriage-Go-Round: The State of Marriage and the Family in America Today* (New York: Knopf, 2009), p. 31.

22. The "community of limited liability" concept comes from Morris Janowitz, *The Community Press in an Urban Setting* (Chicago: University of Chicago Press, 1967). I should note that in the 2000s Americans were moving less often than they had in previous decades. See Claude Fischer, *Made in America: A Social History of American Culture and Character* (Chicago: University of Chicago Press, 2010).

23. Ulrich Beck and Elisabeth Beck-Gernsheim, *Individualization: Institutionalized Individualism and Its Social and Political Consequences* (London: Sage, 2002), p. xxii.

24. See Claudia Goldin, Lawrence F. Katz, and Ilyana Kuziemko, "The Homecoming of American College Women: The Reversal of the College Gender Gap," National Bureau of Economic Research, Working Paper 12139, 2006.

25. See Mitra Toossi, "A Century of Change: The U.S. Labor Force, 1950–2000," *Monthly Labor Review* (May 2002): 15–28. Although women's compensation continues to lag

behind men's, a growing number of women do well enough to become financially independent and, in turn, domestically independent, too. As the international trends suggest, when women can live alone without enduring poverty, a great many of them will.

26. Women's economic independence is not the only reason for the increase in divorce. Legal reforms, most notably the no-fault divorce laws that became common during the 1970s, have allowed a dissatisfied spouse to terminate a marriage without accusing the partner of any wrongdoings and likely have given divorce rates a gentle nudge upward. See Andrew Cherlin, *Marriage, Divorce, Remarriage*, third edition (Cambridge: Harvard University Press, 1992).

27. See Michael Rosenfeld, *The Age of Independence: Interracial Unions, Same-Sex Unions, and the Changing American Family* (Cambridge: Harvard University Press, 2007).

28. Telephone use rates are from the U.S. Census and reported in *Inventors and Inventions* (Tarrytown, NY: Marshall Cavendish, 2008).

29. Ethan Watters, *Urban Tribes: A Generation Redefines Friendship, Family, and Commitment* (New York: Bloomsbury, 2003).

30. See Claude Fischer and Michael Hout, *Century of Difference: How America*

Changed in the Last One Hundred Years
(New York: Russell Sage Foundation, 2006).

31. On England, see Steven Iliffe et al., "Are Elderly People Living Alone an At-Risk Group?" *British Medical Journal* 305 (1992): 1001–4. On mental health in the United States, see Robert Michael, Victor Fuchs, and Sharon Scott, "Changes in the Propensity to Live Alone: 1950–1976," *Demography* 17, 1 (1980): 39–56. For the survey, see Emily Grundy and Michael Murphy, "Marital Status and Family Support for the Oldest-Old in Great Britain," in Jean-Marie Robin et al. (eds.), *Human Longevity, Individual Life Duration, and the Growth of the Oldest-Old Population*, Volume 4 (New York: Springer, 2006), pp. 415–36.

32. See Dora Costa, *The Evolution of Retirement: An American Economic History, 1880–1990* (Chicago: University of Chicago Press, 1998).

33. See Ellickson, *The Household*, p. 39.

34. According to one rigorous sociological study: "In general, persons living alone are not fundamentally more socially isolated than others in comparable marital situations, and they are generally more likely to be socially integrated outside the household." See Duane Alwin, Philip Converse, and Steven Martin, "Living Arrangements and Social Integration."

35. See Jacqueline Olds and Richard Schwartz, *The Lonely American: Drifting Apart in the Twenty-first Century* (Boston: Beacon Press, 2008), pp. 2, 135. The article on social isolation is Michael McPherson, Lynn Smith-Lovin, and Matthew Brashears, "Social Isolation in America: Changes in Core Discussion Networks over Two Decades," *American Sociological Review* 71 (2006): 353–75. The response is Claude Fischer, "The 2004 Finding of Shrunken Social Networks: An Artifact?" *American Sociological Review* 74 (2009): 657–69.

36. John Cacioppo has done the most cutting-edge research on loneliness. For a synthesis, see John Cacioppo and William Patrick, *Loneliness: Human Nature and the Need for Social Connection* (New York: Norton, 2008).

37. Linda Waite and Maggie Gallagher. *The Case for Marriage: Why Married People Are Happier, Healthier, and Better Off Financially* (New York: Doubleday, 2000).

38. See Debra Umberson, Kristi Williams, Daniel Powers, Hui Liu, and Belinda Needham, "You Make Me Sick: Marital Quality and Health over the Life Course," *Journal of Health and Social Behavior* 47 (March 2006): 1–16.

39. One great exception is the writing of Vivian Gornick, and in particular her arresting book

Approaching Eye Level (Boston: Beacon Press, 1996).

40. Jenna Appelbaum, Jill Conte, Jane Jones, Sarah Kaufman, Isadora Levy, Allison McKim, Elena Portacolone, Nerea Puzole, Jason Stanley, and I conducted interviews with people who live alone, as well as with service providers and family members who care for them. Throughout this book, I use phrases such as "my interviews" and "tells me" rather than "our interviews" or "tells us." The reason is primarily stylistic, but in the social sciences it is not unusual for the principal investigator of a large-scale interview project to use this language.

CHAPTER 1: GOING SOLO

1. See Jemele Hill, "Kickball Carnival in Las Vegas," ESPN.com. October 16, 2009; and "Nobody Lost Their Virginity at Hipster Kickball Prom," Gawker, September 22, 2008.

2. Rosenfeld, *The Age of Independence*, p. 6.

3. Younger adults, between the ages of eighteen and twenty-four, are also not much more likely to live with their parents than they were several decades ago. In 1960, for instance, 52 percent of young men and 35 percent of young women lived at home, compared with 53 percent of men and 46 percent of women

in 2005. The data on young adults living with parents are from the U.S. Census Bureau and are publicly available at www.infoplease.com/ipa/A0193723.html.

See Rosenfeld, *The Age of Independence*; and Sharon Jayson, " 'Boomerang' Generation Mostly Hype," *USA Today*, March 14, 2007.

The historic data on living alone come from Wendy Wang and Rich Morin, "Home for the Holidays . . . And Every Other Day," Washington, D.C., Pew Research Center, November 24, 2009. See also Elizabeth Fussell and Frank Furstenberg Jr., "The Transition to Adulthood During the Twentieth Century," in Richard Settersten Jr. et al. (eds.). *On the Frontier of Adulthood: Theory, Research, and Public Policy* (Chicago: University of Chicago Press, 2005), pp. 29–75.

Peter Brown, 1971. "The Rise and Function of the Holy Man in Late Antiquity," *Journal of Roman Studies* 61 (1971): 82–83. On China, see Aat Vervoorn, *Men of the Cliffs and Caves: The Development of the Chinese Eremitic Tradition to the End of the Han Dynasty* (Hong Kong: Chinese University Press, 1990), p. 3.

For a rich account of the monastic tradition in several world cultures, see Isabel

Colegate, *A Pelican in the Wilderness: Hermits, Solitaries, and Recluses* (Washington, D.C.: Counterpoint, 2002). And see Anthony Storr, *Solitude: A Return to the Self* (New York: Free Press, 1988).

8. Georg Simmel, "The Metropolis and Mental Life," in Donald Levine (ed.), *On Individuality and Social Forms* (Chicago: University of Chicago Press, 1971 [1903]).

9. Ibid.

10. See Howard Chudacoff, *The Age of the Bachelor: Creating an American Subculture* (Princeton: Princeton University Press, 1999). The data on single men between ages twenty-five and thirty-four are from George Chauncey, *Gay New York: Gender, Urban Culture, and the Making of the Gay Male World, 1890–1940* (New York: Basic Books, 1991), p. 136.

11. Quoted in Paul Groth, *Living Downtown: The History of Residential Hotels* (Berkeley: University of California Press, 1994), p. 7.

12. Quotes are from Groth, *Living Downtown*, p. 23. Walt Whitman, in Emory Holloway and Ralph Adimari, eds., *New York Dissected* (New York: Rufus Rockwell Wilson, 1936 [1856]), pp. 96–97. Harvey Zorbaugh, *The Gold Coast and the Slum: A Sociological Study of Chicago's Near North Side*

(Chicago: University of Chicago Press, 1983 [1929]), pp. 73–80.

13. Zorbaugh, *The Gold Coast and the Slum*, pp. 73–80.

14. Christine Stansell, *American Moderns: Bohemian New York and the Creation of a New Century* (New York: Metropolitan, 2000), pp. 6–7. Ross Wetzsteon, *Republic of Dreams: Greenwich Village: The American Bohemia, 1910–1960* (New York: Simon & Schuster, 1998).

15. Stansell, *American Moderns*, pp. 14, 27–28, 33. Judith Walkowitz, *City of Dreadful Delight: Narratives of Sexual Danger in Late-Victorian London* (Chicago: University of Chicago Press, 1992).

16. "The place where everything happens first" is from Wetzsteon, *Republic of Dreams*. See Anna Alice Chapin, *Greenwich Village* (New York: Dodd, Mead, 1917); and Luther Harris, *Around Washington Square: An Illustrated History of Greenwich Village* (Baltimore: Johns Hopkins University Press, 2003). On converting tenements and houses into small apartments, see Caroline Ware, *Greenwich Village, 1920–1930* (New York: Octagon, 1935), p. 19. Groth (*Living Downtown*, p. 63) writes that by the 1920s women were the majority residents of many hotel residences, from New York City to Seattle. It's worth

noting that Shakespeare's Benedick ultimately reverses his position on matrimony. By the end of *Much Ado About Nothing*, he is ready to commit to Beatrice.

17. See Ware, *Greenwich Village*, pp. 38–43.
18. Chauncey, *Gay New York*, chapter six.
19. Richard Sennett, *The Fall of Public Man* (New York: Norton, 1974), pp. 40–41.
20. Helen Gurley Brown, *Sex and the Single Girl* (New York: Bernard Geis, 1962), p. 13.
21. On Brown, see Jennifer Scanlon, *Bad Girls Go Everywhere: The Life of Helen Gurley Brown* (New York: Oxford University Press, 2009); Betty Friedan, *The Feminine Mystique* (New York: Norton, 1963); and Brown, *Sex and the Single Girl*, pp. 12, 18.
22. Brown, *Sex and the Single Girl*, pp. 12, 16.
23. Sharon Marcus, "Placing Rosemary's Baby," *Differences: A Journal of Feminist Cultural Studies* 5 (1993), no. 3: 121–40.
24. Brown, *Sex and the Single Girl*, p. 16.
25. Bill Osgerby, "The Bachelor Pad as Cultural Icon," *Journal of Design History* 18 (2005), no. 1: 99–114; Barbara Ehrenreich, *The Hearts of Men* (New York: Vintage, 2005), p. 42.
26. See Susan Thistle, *From Marriage to Market: The Transformation of Women's Lives at Work* (Berkeley: University of California Press, 2006), p. 102. Mitra Toossi, "A Century of Change."

27. The divorce statistics are published by the National Center for Health Statistics, "Advance Report of Final Divorce Statistics, 1981," *Monthly Vital Statistics Report* 32 (1984), no. 9: 5. The statistic on divorces from 1970 to 1977 is from Chudacoff, *The Age of the Bachelor*, p. 271.
28. Barbara Dafoe Whitehead, *The Divorce Culture: Rethinking Our Commitments to Marriage and Family* (New York: Knopf, 1996), pp. 4–5.
29. Nikolas Rose, *Powers of Freedom* (Cambridge, UK: Cambridge University Press, 1999), p. 84; Anthony Giddens, *Modernity and Self-Identity: Self and Society* (Stanford: Stanford University Press, 1991), p. 89; Elisabeth Beck-Gernsheim, *Reinventing the Family: In Search of New Lifestyles* (Oxford: Polity, 2002).
30. David Sarasohn, "Modern Love: A Joint Account That Underwrites Our Marriage," *New York Times,* December 11, 2009.
31. John Adams, *Housing America in the 1980s* (New York: Russell Sage Foundation, 1988), p. 48.
32. The data are from the U.S. Census, and are available at www.census.gov/hhes/www/housing/census/historic/livalone.html.
33. The data on rooms per child are from Rosenfeld, *The Age of Independence*, p. 135;

the data on square feet in the typical home are from the National Association of Home Builders.

34. Waln Brown and Thomas Newman, "Latch-key Kids," Tallahassee, FL: William Gladden Foundation, 2005.

35. European Commission, "Demography Report: Meeting Social Needs in an Ageing Society," chapter two. Data for Canada come from Statistics Canada; for Japan, see the Statistics Bureau and the Director-General for Policy Planning of Japan; for the increase in floor space within homes, see Ann Waswo, *Housing in Postwar Japan: A Social History* (London: Routledge Curzon, 2002), p. 110; and for the U.S. see the Bureau of Labor Statistics (www.bls.gov/opub/uscs/1950.pdf).

36. Annette Lareau, *Unequal Childhoods: Class, Race, and Family Life* (Berkeley: University of California Press, 2003), p. 39.

37. Benjamin Spock's book is now in its eighth edition, and is currently called *Dr. Spock's Baby and Child Care*. See the discussion of this in Rosenfeld, *The Age of Independence*, p. 133.

38. Richard Ferber, *Solve Your Child's Sleep Problems* (New York: Simon & Schuster, 1986), pp. 38–40.

39. See Lisa Chapman, "MU Housing Creates

Dorm Singles to Meet Students' Privacy Demands," *The Miami Student*, February 17, 2006; Shimmy Edwards, "Single Dorms Are in High Demand," *The GW Hatchet*, March 3, 2008; Tracy Jan, "BU Dorm Offers a Study in Luxury," *Boston Globe*, September 2, 2009.

40. Quoted in Tracy Jan, "BU Dorm Offers a Study in Luxury."

CHAPTER 2:
THE CAPACITY TO LIVE ALONE

1. Bella DePaulo, "How I Discovered That Living Single Was My True Happily Ever After," Onely blog, September 26, 2009.
2. Ethan Watters, *Urban Tribes*.
3. See Lori Gottlieb, "Marry Him! The Case for Settling for Mr. Good Enough," *Atlantic Monthly,* March 2008; and the book by the same name (New York: Dutton, 2010).
4. In fact, as DePaulo reports, those who stay single and live alone over time are relatively successful at managing the challenges that stem from their lifestyle. Consider a long-running (more than twenty years) German survey that asks more than 30,000 participants to rate their happiness annually. On average, those who remain single throughout the study self-report slightly lower happiness than those who get and remain married, but they also

report higher happiness than those who marry and then divorce or become widowed. A similar study, conducted by Dutch demographers over eighteen years, got similar results. Respondents who had remained married or remained single reported relatively high happiness, whereas those who had coupled up and then separated experienced a sharp drop in life satisfaction, followed by a gradual increase over time. DePaulo discusses the German study in *Singled Out: How Singles Are Stereotyped, Stigmatized, and Ignored, and Still Live Happily Ever After* (New York: St. Martin's, 2006), pp. 35–40; she also compares the two studies in her *Psychology Today* blog at www.psychology today.com/blog/living-single/200912/another-longitudinal-study-satisfaction. The Dutch study is Judith Soons, Aart Liefbroer, and Matthijs Kalmijn, "The Long-Term Consequences of Relationship Formation for Subjective Well-Being," *Journal of Marriage and the Family* 71 (2009), no. 5: 1254–70.

5. Rose M. Kreider and Jason M. Fields, "Number, Timing, and Duration of Marriages and Divorces: 1996," U.S. Census Reports, 2002.

6. See Matthew Bramlett and William Mosher, "First Marriage Dissolution, Divorce, and Remarriage: United States," U.S. Centers for

Disease Control and Prevention, 2001. The statistics on never-married Americans are reported in Eduardo Porter and Michelle O'Donnell, "Facing Middle Age with No Degree, and No Wife," *New York Times*, August 6, 2006.

7. See Laura Kipnis, *Against Love: A Polemic* (New York: Pantheon, 2003), p. 23.

8. See Matthew Crawford, *Shop Class as Soulcraft: An Inquiry into the Value of Work* (New York: Penguin Press, 2009); Daniel Pink, *Free Agent Nation: How America's New Independent Workers Are Transforming the Way We Live* (New York: Warner, 2001), pp. 10–11, 103.

9. For an extensive report on the appeal of social life in professional office spaces, see Arlie Hochschild, *The Time Bind: When Home Becomes Work and Work Becomes Home* (New York: Metropolitan, 1997).

10. One important study of social networks and time use found that "persons living alone appear to be no less attached outside the household, and in some instances have higher levels of such contact." Duane Alwin, Philip Converse, and Steven Martin, "Living Arrangements and Social Integration," *Journal of Marriage and the Family* 47 (1985): 319–33.

11. See the Pew Internet & American Life Project

report "Social Isolation and New Technology: How the Internet and Mobile Phones Impact Americans' Social Networks," Washington, D.C., November 2009, pp. 3–4.

12. See "Singles in the U.S.: The New Nuclear Family," Rockville, Md.: Packaged Facts, 2007.

13. The concept that loneliness is a social pain comes from the psychologist John Cacioppo, who has also argued that those who feel lonely are not more likely to be alone than those who do not. In fact, one important scholarly article based on a random national sample of 2,248 adults age eighteen and over found: "Contrary to what would be predicted . . . unmarried persons who live alone are in no worse, and on some indicators are in better, mental health than unmarried persons who live with others." See Michael Hughes and Walter Gove, "Living Alone, Social Integration, and Mental Health," *American Journal of Sociology* 87 (1981), no. 1: 48–74. The authors look closely at the question of whether there is a selection bias that determines who lives alone—i.e., are people who live alone different from those who live with others, and are differences that are unrelated to their residential status the things that most affect their mental health. Their

conclusion: "The data clearly suggest that in a representative population, a process of social selection related to poor mental health does not appear to play a significant role in determining who will live alone" (p. 62).

14. This is an overstatement, since recent research shows that men over forty produce less sperm than their younger counterparts and that their children face higher risks of conditions such as autism and schizophrenia. See Roni Rabin, "It Seems the Fertility Clock Ticks for Men, Too," *New York Times*, February 26, 2007.

15. Erving Goffman, *Stigma: Notes on the Management of Spoiled Identity* (Englewood Cliffs, N.J.: Prentice-Hall, 1963).

16. Waite and Gallagher, *The Case for Marriage*, p. 77.

17. Gretchen Livingston and D'Vera Cohn, "Childlessness Up Among All Women; Down among Women with Advanced Degrees," Washington, D.C.: Pew Research Center, 2010.

18. See Richard Fry and D'Vera Cohn, "Women, Men, and the New Economics of Marriage," Washington, D.C.: Pew Research Center, 2010.

19. See Judith Jones, *The Pleasures of Cooking for One* (New York: Knopf, 2009).

20. Kari Bodnarchuk, "A Woman Traveling

Alone? The World Can Be Your Oyster, Too," *Boston Globe,* March 15, 2009.

21. Other hotels are also starting to market to solo tourists. The Fairmont Miramar hotel in Santa Monica has a "Single and the City" package, which includes tips on how to tour the city on your own, and the Westin St. John resort offers a three-night "solo-cation," complete with private pool. A number of new travel agencies offer group trips designed for those in search of romance as well as special offers, such as the Solo Super Saver from Singles Travel International, for those who just want a good deal when they are alone. These changes are outliers. Solo travelers see all the special things the travel industry does for couples and families and say that it has yet to make singles feel at home when they are away.

22. Ellen Rand, "When Single Women Buy Homes," *New York Times*, December 20, 1981.

23. Data on home buyers are from the National Association of Realtors, "Profile of Home Buyers and Sellers," 2009; the quote is from Liz Lemmer, "Singles Taking Stride in the Home Buying Market," Medill News Service, February 17, 2007.

24. Fry and Cohn, "Women, Men, and the New Economics of Marriage."

25. The National Consumer Survey data used in the Packaged Facts study show that 24 percent of singles self-report as "TV addicts," compared to 19 percent of married individuals ("Singles in the U.S.," p. 165).

26. According to its Web site, Single Mothers by Choice "is not an advocacy group. It is not fair to urge a woman who may not have the emotional or financial resources, or who does not feel she would be able to handle single parenting, to get into an impractical or overextended situation. Single parenting is difficult enough for the woman who is sure and prepared. In the absence of a good partnership, and with the rate of divorce as high as it is, we feel that being raised by a caring and competent single parent is definitely a viable option." See www.single mothersbychoice.org/about/philosophy/.

27. Katherine Grier, *Pets in America: A History* (Chapel Hill: University of North Carolina Press, 2006), p. 315; Alan Beck and N. Marshall Meyers, "Health Enhancement and Companion Animal Ownership," *Annual Review of Public Health* 17 (1996): 247–57.

28. The census data on pet ownership are available online at www.census.gov/compendia/statab/2010/tables/10s1204.xls.

29. For some who live alone, cats do occasionally substitute for human companions. On the

blog Onely, which promotes and affirms the solo lifestyle, a graduate student confesses: "I have two new men in my life . . . I spend all my non-work hours with Alvin or Theo. Several times in the last week I've postponed phone calls to friends and family so that I could hang out with, cook for, or cuddle with a new flame. I'm sleep deprived because we stay up too late laughing and talking. When people do call to find out where I've been, I barely ask about their lives, but instead I blather on and on about how handsome Theo is or how smart and funny Alvin seems . . . Alvin is adventurous and brings out my wild side, but Theo is more shy and has a chronic worried look on his face that makes me want to comfort him. I'm lucky I don't have to choose between them, because they seem to enjoy sharing my lap. Oh, my poor matchmaking coworkers, who don't have kittens . . . I will try to comfort and support them." See "OMG, I'm One of THEM" at http://onely.org/2010/02/06/omg-im-one-of-them/.

30. Donna Haraway, *The Companion Species Manifesto: Dogs, People, and Significant Otherness* (Chicago: Prickly Paradigm, 2003), p. 12.
31. Beck and Meyers, "Health Enhancement and Companion Animal Ownership," pp. 247–53.

32. Lee Rainie and Mary Madden, "Not Looking for Love: Romance in America," Washington, D.C.: Pew Research Center, 2006.

CHAPTER 3: SEPARATING
1. In 2008 about 30 million of the 93 million unmarried Americans were either divorced (25 million) or separated (5 million). Within five years, nearly one in four marriages in the United States results in separation or divorce. These data are from U.S. Census, "Number, Timing, and Duration of Marriages and Divorces: 2001," 2005, p. 6, available at www.census.gov/prod/2005pubs/p70-97.pdf.
2. Cherlin, *The Marriage-Go-Round*, p. 4.
3. The data on remarriage come from a 2002 report by the U.S. Centers for Disease Control and Prevention and are available online at www.cdc.gov/nchs/data/series/sr_23/sr23_022.pdf.
4. For one careful analysis, see Richard Peterson, "A Re-Evaluation of the Economic Consequences of Divorce," *American Sociological Review* 61 (1996): 528–36. Peterson shows that the typical decline in men's and women's standard of living after divorce is 10 percent and 27 percent, respectively, numbers that are substantial but actually lower than many previous estimates.
5. The survey, which was conducted by

Knowledge Networks, is based on a nationally representative sample of 1,147 people. See Xenia P. Montenegro, "The Divorce Experience: A Study of Divorce at Midlife and Beyond," Washington, D.C.: AARP, 2004. The statistics on frequency of sexual activity appear on pp. 45–49. An academic study of American sexual practices published in the *British Medical Journal* adds support for the AARP's findings. Drawing on two nationally representative samples of the U.S. population, scholars at the University of Chicago found that men and women who live with a partner are significantly more likely to report being sexually active in the previous six months than those who live alone, and the disparity increases with age. For instance, 72 percent of men ages twenty-five to fifty-four who do not live with a partner report sexual activity in the previous six months, compared to 58 percent of women. Among those ages sixty-five to seventy-four, 38 percent of solo-dwelling men but only 4 percent of solo-dwelling women report sexual activity in the previous six months. See Stacy Tessler Lindau and Natalia Gavrilova, "Sex, Health, and Years of Sexually Active Life Gained Due to Good Health," *British Medical Journal* 240 (2010): c810.

6. The study published in the *British Medical Journal* confirms that gender differences in interest in sex are widespread, and that they grow with age. Among those between fifty-five and sixty-four years old, 50 percent of men who live without a partner say they are "interested in sex," compared to 24 percent of women who live without a partner. Among those ages sixty-five to seventy-four, 31 percent of solo-dwelling men and 8 percent of solo-dwelling women say they are "interested in sex." Lindau and Gavrilova, "Sex, Health, and Years of Sexually Active Life," p. 5.
7. The data on remarriage come from Cherlin, *Marriage, Divorce, Remarriage*; and the AARP study "The Divorce Experience."
8. In their study of elderly Londoners, Haines and Hurlbert found that women with broad social networks were actually more likely to experience distressing events, such as the death or illness of a friend, than women with fewer ties. See Valerie Haines and Jeanne Hurlbert, "Network Range and Health," *Journal of Health and Social Behavior* 33 (1992): 254–66.
9. These numbers are based on an original analysis of the GSS data from 2002 to 2008, conducted by the sociologist Erin Cornwell. According to the psychologist Sonja

Lyubomirsky, "Studies have shown that, relative to married people, singles are closer to their friends and have more frequent contact with them and that lifelong single older women tend to have close to a dozen devoted decades-long friends." See Sonja Lyubomirsky, *The How of Happiness: The Scientific Approach to Getting the Life You Want* (New York: Penguin Press, 2007), p. 147.

10. The data on loneliness come from Cornwell's analysis of the GSS.
11. Ibid.
12. See T. M. Luhrmann, "The Art of Hearing God: Absorption, Dissociation, and Contemporary American Spirituality," *Spiritus: A Journal of Christian Spirituality* 5 (2005), no. 2: 133–57.
13. The data on church attendance are from Cornwell's analysis of the GSS. See Herbert Anderson and Freda Gardner, *Living Alone* (Louisville: Westminster John Knox, 1996), p. 24.
14. Support for this skepticism about the quality of life within marriage comes from the General Social Survey. One recent study found that "only one-third of all marriages were both happy and intact after sixteen years." Paul Amato, Alan Booth, David Johnson, and Stacy Rogers, *Alone Together*

(Cambridge: Harvard University Press, 2007), p. 2.

15. See Carol Gilligan, *In a Different Voice: Psychological Theory and Women's Development* (Cambridge: Harvard University Press, 1982); and Deborah Belle, "Gender Differences in Children's Social Networks and Supports," in Deborah Belle (ed.), *Children's Networks and Social Supports* (Hoboken, N.J.: Wiley, 1989), p. 179.

CHAPTER 4: PROTECTING THE SELF

1. William Deresiewicz, "The End of Solitude," *The Chronicle of Higher Education: Chronicle Review* 55 (2009), no. 21; and Dalton Conley, *The Elsewhere Society* (New York: Pantheon, 2009), p. 7.

2. See Sandra Smith, *Lone Pursuit: Distrust and Defensive Individualism among the Black Poor* (New York: Russell Sage Foundation, 2007), p. 22.

3. Phil's account of the benefits of going solo are reminiscent of the arguments made by the late psychologist Anthony Storr in his book *Solitude*. Storr's thesis was that solitude, used wisely, allows a "return to the self" that enhances the creative abilities of great writers and artists. He quotes Edward Gibbon: " 'Conversation enriches the understanding, but solitude is the school of genius;

and the uniformity of a work denotes the hand of a single artist.'" Storr, who was careful to note that solitude can take a constructive or destructive course depending on the way it's used, reports that "many of the world's greatest thinkers have not reared families or formed close personal ties." Storr, *Solitude*, p. 1.

4. On the reluctance of employers to hire men with criminal records, particularly African Americans, see Devah Pager, *Marked: Crime, Race, and Finding Work in an Era of Mass Incarceration* (Chicago: University of Chicago Press, 2007).

5. See Porter and O'Donnell, "Facing Middle Age"; and Richard Fry and D'Vera Cohn, "Women, Men, and the New Economics of Marriage."

6. The University of Wisconsin sociologist Alice Goffman makes a similar observation in her ethnographic study of young black men with criminal records in Philadelphia: "Suspicious even of those closest to them, young men cultivate unpredictability or altogether avoid institutions, places, and relations on which they formerly relied." Few of these men actually live alone, but the fact that their survival strategies involve avoiding potentially helpful networks and institutions means that they are less likely to

get out of poverty. See Alice Goffman, "On the Run: Wanted Men in a Philadelphia Ghetto," *American Sociological Review* 74 (2009), no. 3: 339–57.

7. Psychologist Randy Frost and social work scholar Gail Steketee estimate that 2 percent to 5 percent of the American population— between 6 million and 15 million people— hoard enough to affect their lives, and argue that hoarding has become a significant problem in cities. They note that, like Mary Ann, hoarders shift their behavior to emphasize interaction with objects rather than people. See their book *Stuff: Compulsive Hoarding and the Meaning of Things* (New York: Houghton Mifflin Harcourt, 2010).

CHAPTER 5: TOGETHER ALONE

1. Ethan Watters discusses the problem of organizing around the stigmatized "singles" concept in chapter five of *Urban Tribes*.

2. Kris Marsh, William Darity Jr., Philip Cohen, Lynne Casper, and Danielle Salters, "The Emerging Black Middle Class: Single and Living Alone," *Social Forces* 86, no. 2: 750, 753.

3. Natalie Nitsche and Hannah Brückner, "Opting Out of the Family? Social Change in Racial Inequality in Family Formation Patterns and Marriage Outcomes among

Highly Educated Women," presentation at the convention of the American Sociological Association, 2009.

4. Marsh et al., "The Emerging Black Middle Class," p. 740.

5. Page Gardner, "Twenty Million Women, Twenty Million Reasons," *Huffington Post*, November 8, 2007.

6. The Women's Voices, Women Vote report on the 2008 trends, "Unmarried Women in the Electorate: Behind the Numbers," is available at www.wvwv.org/assets/2010/1/19/Unmarried_Women_in_the_Electorate_-_Behind_the_Numbers.pdf.

7. Women's Voices, Women Vote/Greenberg Quinlan Rosner Research, "Unmarried Women Change America," November 2008.

8. See Women's Voices, Women Vote, "Unmarried Women in the Electorate: Behind the Numbers."

9. Packaged Facts, "Singles in the U.S.," p. 16.

10. Euromonitor International, "Single Living."

11. See David Brooks, "The Sandra Bullock Trade," *New York Times*, March 29, 2010. The response on DePaulo's *Psychology Today* blog, Living Single, appeared later the same day. See "David Brooks + Sandra Bullock = Matrimonia" at www.psychologytoday.com/blog/living-single/201003/david-brooks-sandra-bullock-matrimania.

12. Available at http://content.healthaffairs.org/ content/26/3/836.short.

CHAPTER 6: AGING ALONE
1. See the U.S. Administration on Aging report, "A Profile of Older Americans 2009," at www.aoa.gov/AoARoot/Aging_Statistics/ Profile/2009/6.aspx; the European Commission report, "Independent Living for the Ageing Society," at http://ec.europa.eu/ information_society/activities/policy_link/ brochures/documents/independent_living.pdf; and the *Japan Times* report at http://search. japantimes.co.jp/cgi-bin/nn20100514x2.html; on China, see Xin Meng and Chuliang Luo, "What Determines Living Arrangements of the Elderly in Urban China," 2004, http://people.anu.edu.au/xin.meng/living-arrange.pdf; on South Korea, see Young Jin Park, "The Rise of One-Person House-holders and their Recent Characteristics in Korea," *Korea Journal of Population and Development* 23 (1994), no. 1: 117–29.
2. The data on aging in Europe come from Henry Aaron, "Longer Life Spans: Boon or Burden?" *Daedalus*, Winter 2006: 9–19. And see Robert William Fogel, *The Escape from Hunger and Premature Death, 1700–2100: Europe, America, and the Third World* (Cambridge: Cambridge University Press, 2004), p. 1.

3. The classic study of increased mortality among the recently widowed is C. Murray Parkes, B. Benjamin, and R. G. Fitzgerald, "Broken Heart: A Statistical Study of Increased Mortality Among Widowers," *British Medical Journal* 1, no. 5646 (March 22, 1969): 740–43.

4. About 1.5 million Americans live in a nursing home on any given day, and about 3 million people reside in them over the course of a typical year. Although many nursing homes maintain a high level of quality care, many others—including a disproportionately high number of those recently acquired by private equity groups—do not; federal oversight of them has been criticized by the U.S. Government Accountability Office. See Charles Duhigg, "At Many Homes, More Profit and Less Nursing," *New York Times*, September 23, 2007.

5. See Benjamin Cornwell, Edward Laumann, and L. Philip Schumm, "The Social Connectedness of Older Adults: A National Profile," *American Sociological Review* 73 (2008): 185–203. The paper showing constant rates of reported loneliness in England is Christina Victor, Ann Bowling, John Bond, and Sasha Scambler, "Loneliness, Social Isolation, and Living Alone in Later Life," Research Findings no.

17, Growing Older Programme. Economic & Social Research Council, 2003, www.growing older.group.shef.ac.uk/ChristinaVic_F17.pdf; the study on the health of people aging alone is Steven Iliffe et al., "Health Risk Appraisal in Older People II: The Implications for Clinicians and Commissioners of Social Isolation Risk in Older People," *British Journal of General Practice* 57 (2007), no. 537: 277–82.

6. On the gender disparity in aging, see Deborah Carr, "Widows and Widowers," in Dennis Peck and Clifton Bryant (eds.), *Encyclopedia of Death and the Human Experience* (Thousand Oaks, Calif.: Sage, 2009), pp. 989–95. On the desire to date, see Deborah Carr, "The Desire to Date and Remarry among Older Widows and Widowers," *Journal of Marriage and Family* 66 (2006), no. 4: 1051–68.

7. Paula Span, "They Don't Want to Live with You, Either," *New York Times*, March 24, 2009. The data on widows living with children are from V. Joseph Hotz, Kathleen McGarry, and Emily Wiemers. "Living Arrangements among Elderly Women in the Panel Study of Income Dynamics," PSID Conference on Pensions, Private Accounts, and Retirement Savings over the Life Course, November 20–21, 2008.

8. Deborah Carr, "The Desire to Date and Remarry."

9. Yvonne Michael, Lisa Berkman, Graham Colditz, and Ichiro Kawachi, "Living Arrangements, Social Integration, and Change in Functional Health Status," *American Journal of Epidemiology* 153 (2001), no. 2: 123–31.

10. This is consistent with findings from some qualitative research on the dating practices of elderly women. See Kate Davidson, "Gender Differences in New Partnership Choices and Constraints for Older Widows and Widowers," *Ageing International* 27 (2002): 43–60.

11. The Stanford psychologist Laura Carstensen has developed the socioemotional selectivity theory to explain this transformation among the elderly. See Laura Carstensen, "Social and Emotional Patterns in Adulthood: Support for Socioemotional Selectivity Theory," *Psychology and Aging* 7 (1982) no. 3: 331–38.

12. See Martha Albertson Fineman, *The Autonomy Myth: A Theory of Dependency* (New York: New Press, 2005).

13. For instance, in his classic study of urban social networks, Claude Fischer reports that "old men were the most isolated" of all social groups. Claude Fischer, *To Dwell Among*

Friends: Personal Networks in Town and City (Chicago: University of Chicago Press, 1982), p. 253. Erin Cornwell's analysis of recent General Social Survey data reveals the same pattern.

14. The Commonwealth Fund Commission on Elderly People Living Alone, "Aging Alone: Profiles and Projections." Baltimore, Md., 1987.

15. Among elderly women, roughly 4 in 10 Latinas and African Americans who live alone are impoverished, compared to about 2.5 Asians and 1.5 whites. The trends are similar for solo-dwelling elderly men: 3.5 in 10 Latinos are poor, compared to about 3 African Americans, 2 Asians, and 1 white. These figures are from the 2009 American Community Survey and are reported in Deborah Carr, "Golden Years? Poverty Among Older Americans," *Contexts*, Winter 2010: 62–63.

16. Neal Krause, "Neighborhood Deterioration and Social Isolation in Later Life," *International Journal of Aging and Human Development* 36 (1993): 9–38.

CHAPTER 7: REDESIGNING SOLO LIFE

1. Dolores Hayden, *Redesigning the American Dream: Gender, Housing, and Family Life*, 2d ed. (New York: Norton, 2002).

2. See, for instance, the ratings available on the *U.S. News and World Report* Web site: http://health.usnews.com/senior-housing.

3. See "Nursing Homes: Business as Usual," *Consumer Reports,* 2006, www.consumer reports.org/health/healthy-living/health-safety/nursing-homes-9-06/overview/0609_nursing-homes_ov.htm. The report on Illinois nursing homes is David Jackson and Gary Marx, "Illinois Nursing Homes Mix Felons, Seniors," *Chicago Tribune*, September 29, 2009. In *Heat Wave*, I reported on a similar practice in Chicago's public housing for seniors. Residents I interviewed complained that the presence of violent neighbors discouraged them from using public spaces and kept them locked in at home.

4. Duhigg, "At Many Homes, More Profit and Less Nursing."

5. Nicholas Roy, Gregory Baltus, Dieter Fox, Francine Gemperle, Jennifer Goetz, Tad Hirsch, Dimitris Margaritis, Mike Montemerlo, Joelle Pineau, Jamie Schulte, and Sebastian Thrun, "Towards Personal Service Robots for the Elderly," 2000, available at several Web sites, including http://www.ri.cmu.edu/publication_view.html?pub_id=3390.

6. Robert Sparrow and Linda Sparrow, "In the Hands of Machines? The Future of Aged

Care," *Minds and Machines* 16 (2006) no. 2: 141–61.

7. Ibid.

8. The Kompaï is profiled in Brian Horowitz, "Will Robots Help the Elderly Live at Home Longer?" *Scientific American*, June 21, 2010.

9. See George Ford and Sherry Ford, "Internet Use and Depression among the Elderly," The Phoenix Center, 2009, Policy Paper 38, www.phoenix-center.org/DepressionOct15 2009.pdf.

10. See Jim Moore, "Deep Economic Impact," *Assisted Living Executive*, January–February 2008: 10–15; and Paula Span, "Assisted Living: Back to the Future," *New York Times*, December 28, 2009.

11. Jane Gross, "The $500,000 Dilemma," *New York Times*, July 2, 2009.

12. Ibid.

13. See, for instance, Debra Dobbs, J. Kevin Eckert, Bob Rubinstein, Lynn Keimig, Leanne Clark, Ann Christine Frankowski, and Sheryl Zimmerman, "An Ethnographic Study of Stigma and Ageism in Residential Care or Assisted Living," *The Gerontologist* 48 (2008), no. 4: 517–26. The fact that there is cruelty in these cultural practices should not call into question the extent to which these residential communities also provide care and support. But it does mean we

shouldn't romanticize them. See Arlie Hochschild, *The Unexpected Community: Portrait of an Old Age Subculture* (Berkeley: University of California Press, 1973); and Barbara Myerhoff, *Number Our Days: A Triumph of Continuity and Caring among Jewish Old People in an Urban Ghetto* (New York: Touchstone, 1980).

14. See the 2009 report "Coming Home: Affordable Assisted Living" by the Robert Wood Johnson Foundation.

15. Jo Williams, "Innovative Solutions for Averting a Potential Resource Crisis—The Case of One-Person Households in England and Wales," *Environmental Development and Sustainability* 9 (2007): 325–54.

16. David Owen, "Green Manhattan: Why New York Is the Greenest City in the U.S.," *The New Yorker*, October 18, 2004.

CONCLUSION

1. There is a myth that Sweden has a high suicide rate, and another that the high rates of living alone there are partly responsible. But the most recent World Health Organization statistics debunk them. The reported Swedish suicide rate, 26 per 100,000 residents, places it far below the top twenty-five high-risk nations. The nations where suicide is reported to be more common include Austria,

Belgium, China, Finland, France, Japan, Poland, Russia, South Korea, Sri Lanka, and Uruguay. See www.who.int/mental_health/prevention/suicide_rates/en/.

2. David Popenoe, "Beyond the Nuclear Family: A Statistical Portrait of the Changing Family in Sweden," *Journal of Marriage and Family* 49 (1987), no. 1: 180.

3. See Lars-Erik Borgegård and Jim Kemeny, "Sweden: High-Rise Housing for a Low-Density Country," in Richard Turkington, Ronald van Kempen, and F. Wassenberg (eds.), *High-Rise Housing in Europe: Current Trends and Future Prospects* (Delft: Delft University Press, 2004), pp. 31–48.

4. All the major Swedish political parties, including the neoliberals, who advocate more laissez-faire economic policies, support sustaining a welfare state that is far more generous than those found in nations in Europe and North America where collective living is more common. They have to, since the overwhelming majority of Swedish voters believe that robust public programs (for housing, health, education, and the like) allow them to become strong and autonomous individuals, and they demand that their political representatives, even the conservative and libertarian ones, promote the common good.

5. A news story about the report is here: www.dn.se/sthlm/s-lovar-50000-nya-bostader-i-stockholms-lan.

6. See the building's site at www.fard knappen.se/fardknappen.se/In_English.html.

7. The study of supportive housing in San Francisco is Tia Martinez and Martha Burt, "Impact of Permanent Supportive Housing on the Use of Acute Care Health Services by Homeless Adults," *Psychiatric Services* 57 (2006): 992–99. The study in Seattle is Mary E. Larimer, Daniel K. Malone, Michelle D. Garner, et al., "Health Care and Public Service Use and Costs Before and After Provision of Housing for Chronically Homeless Persons with Severe Alcohol Problems," *JAMA* 301 (2009), no. 13: 1349–57.

8. The New York City study is "The Impact of Supportive Housing on Surrounding Neighborhoods: Evidence from New York City," Furman Center for the Study of Real Estate and Urban Policy, New York, 2008.

9. See "Medicaid Payment for Assisted Living: Current State Practices and Recommendations for Improvement," National Senior Citizens Law Center, 2010.

10. The quote and the claim that there are about 38 million uncompensated family caregivers come from the White House Middle Class

Task Force, www.whitehouse.gov/sites/ default/files/Fact_Sheet-Middle_Class_Task_ Force.pdf. Advocacy groups estimate that the annual value of the care given by family members is approximately $375 billion.

11. For instance, the commentator Paul Begala calls baby boomers "the most self-centered, self-seeking, self-interested, self-absorbed, self-indulgent, self-aggrandizing generation in American history." See Paul Begala, "The Worst Generation," *Esquire*, April 2000.

12. These numbers are based on an original analysis of the GSS data from 2002 to 2008 conducted by the sociologist Erin Cornwell, and on the data in the Packaged Facts report "Singles in the U.S."

13. Cacioppo and Patrick, *Loneliness*, p. 13.

14. Christakis and Fowler, *Connected*, pp. 292, 305.

SELECT BIBLIOGRAPHY

Aaron, Henry. "Longer Life Spans: Boon or Burden?" *Daedalus*, Winter 2006: 9–19.

Adams, John. *Housing America in the 1980s.* New York: Russell Sage Foundation, 1988.

Alwin, Duane, Philip Converse, and Steven Martin. "Living Arrangements and Social Integration." *Journal of Marriage and the Family* 47 (1988), no. 2): 319–34.

Amato, Paul, Alan Booth, David Johnson, and Stacy Rogers. *Alone Together.* Cambridge, Mass.: Harvard University Press, 2007.

Anderson, Herbert, and Freda Gardner. *Living Alone.* Louisville, Ky.: Westminster John Knox, 1996.

Aristotle. *Politics.* Trevor J. Saunders, trans. New York: Oxford University Press, 1995.

Beck, Alan, and N. Marshall Meyers. "Health Enhancement and Companion Animal Ownership." *Annual Review of Public Health* 17 (1996): 247–57.

Beck, Ulrich, and Elisabeth Beck-Gernsheim. *Individualization: Institutionalized Individualism and Its Social and Political Consequences.* London: Sage, 2002.

Beck-Gernsheim, Elisabeth. *Reinventing the*

Family: In Search of New Lifestyles. Oxford, UK: Polity, 2002.

Begala, Paul. "The Worst Generation." *Esquire,* April 2000.

Bellah, Robert, Richard Madsen, William Sullivan, Ann Swidler, and Steven Tipton. *Habits of the Heart: Individualism and Commitment in American Life.* Berkeley: University of California Press, 2007 [1981].

Belle, Deborah. "Gender Differences in Children's Social Networks and Supports," in Deborah Belle (ed.), *Children's Networks and Social Supports,* pp. 173–90. Hoboken, N.J.: Wiley, 1989.

Bloom, Harold. *Ralph Waldo Emerson.* New York: Chelsea House, 1985.

Borgegård, Lars-Erik, and Jim Kemeny. "Sweden: High-Rise Housing for a Low-Density Country," in Richard Turkington, Ronald van Kempen, and F. Wassenberg (eds.), *High-Rise Housing in Europe: Current Trends and Future Prospects,* pp. 31–48. Delft, Netherlands: Delft University Press, 2004.

Bramlett, Matthew, and William Mosher. "First Marriage Dissolution, Divorce, and Remarriage: United States." U.S. Centers for Disease Control and Prevention, 2001.

Brown, Helen Gurley. *Sex and the Single Girl.* New York: Bernard Geis, 1962.

Brown, Peter. "The Rise and Function of the Holy Man in Late Antiquity." *Journal of Roman Studies* 61 (1971): 82–83.

Brown, Waln, and Thomas Newman. "Latchkey Kids." Tallahassee, Fla.: William Gladden Foundation, 2005.

Cacioppo, John, and William Patrick. *Loneliness: Human Nature and the Need for Social Connection*. New York: Norton, 2008.

Carr, Deborah. "Golden Years? Poverty among Older Americans." *Contexts*, Winter 2010: 62–63.

———. "Widows and Widowers," in Dennis Peck and Clifton Bryant (eds.), *Encyclopedia of Death and the Human Experience*, pp. 989–95. Thousand Oaks, Calif.: Sage, 2009.

———. "The Desire to Date and Remarry among Older Widows and Widowers." *Journal of Marriage and Family* 66 (2006), no. 4: 1051–68.

Carstensen, Laura. "Social and Emotional Patterns in Adulthood: Support for Socioemotional Selectivity Theory." *Psychology and Aging* 7 (1982), no. 3: 331–38.

Chapin, Anna Alice. *Greenwich Village*. New York: Dodd, Mead, 1917.

Chauncey, George. *Gay New York: Gender, Urban Culture, and the Making of the Gay Male World, 1890–1940*. New York: Basic Books, 1991.

Cherlin, Andrew. *The Marriage-Go-Round: The State of Marriage and the Family in America Today*. New York: Knopf, 2009.

———. *Marriage, Divorce, Remarriage*, 3d ed. Cambridge, Mass.: Harvard University Press, 1992.

Christakis, Nicholas, and James Fowler. *Connected: The Surprising Power of Our Social Networks and How They Shape Our Lives*. New York: Little, Brown, 2009.

Chudacoff, Howard. *The Age of the Bachelor: Creating an American Subculture*. Princeton, N.J.: Princeton University Press, 1999.

Colegate, Isabel. *A Pelican in the Wilderness: Hermits, Solitaries, and Recluses*. Washington, D.C.: Counterpoint, 2002.

Commonwealth Fund Commission on Elderly People Living Alone. "Aging Alone: Profiles and Projections." Baltimore, Md., 1987.

Conley, Dalton. *The Elsewhere Society*. New York: Pantheon, 2009.

Cornwell, Benjamin, Edward Laumann, and L. Philip Schumm. "The Social Connectedness of Older Adults: A National Profile." *American Sociological Review* 73 (2008): 185–203.

Costa, Dora. *The Evolution of Retirement: An American Economic History, 1880–1990*. Chicago: University of Chicago Press, 1998.

Crawford, Matthew. *Shop Class as Soulcraft: An Inquiry into the Value of Work*. New York: Penguin Press, 2009.

Davidson, Kate. "Gender Differences in New Partnership Choices and Constraints for Older Widows and Widowers." *Ageing International* 27 (2002): 43–60.

DePaulo, Bella. *Singled Out: How Singles Are Stereotyped, Stigmatized, and Ignored, and Still Live Happily Ever After*. New York: St. Martin's, 2006.

Deresiewicz, William. "The End of Solitude." *The Chronicle of Higher Education: Chronicle Review* 55 (2009), no. 21.

Dobbs, Debra, et al. "An Ethnographic Study of Stigma and Ageism in Residential Care or Assisted Living." *The Gerontologist* 48 (2008), no. 4: 517–26.

Ehrenreich, Barbara. *The Hearts of Men*. New York: Vintage, 1983.

Ellickson, Robert. *The Household: Informal Order Around the Hearth*. Princeton, N.J.: Princeton University Press, 2008.

Euromonitor International. "Single Living: How Atomisation—The Rise of Singles and One-Person Households—Is Affecting Consumer Purchasing Habits," 2008.

Ferber, Richard. *Solve Your Child's Sleep Problems*. New York: Simon & Schuster, 1986.

Fineman, Martha Albertson. *The Autonomy Myth: A Theory of Dependency*. New York: New Press, 2005.

Fischer, Claude. *Made in America: A Social History of American Culture and Character*. Chicago: University of Chicago Press, 2010.

———. "The 2004 Finding of Shrunken Social Networks: An Artifact?" *American Sociological Review* 74 (2009): 657–69.

———. *To Dwell Among Friends: Personal Networks in Town and City*. Chicago: University of Chicago Press, 1982.

Fischer, Claude, and Michael Hout. *Century of Difference: How America Changed in the Last One Hundred Years*. New York: Russell Sage Foundation, 2006.

Fogel, Robert William. *The Escape from Hunger and Premature Death, 1700–2100: Europe, America, and the Third World*. Cambridge, UK: Cambridge University Press, 2004.

Ford, George, and Sherry Ford. "Internet Use and Depression Among the Elderly." Policy Paper 38, The Phoenix Center, 2009.

Friedan, Betty. *The Feminine Mystique*. New York: Norton, 1963.

Frost, Richard, and Gail Steketee. *Stuff: Compulsive Hoarding and the Meaning of Things*. New York: Houghton Mifflin Harcourt, 2010.

Fry, Richard, and D'Vera Cohn. "Women, Men, and the New Economics of Marriage."

Washington, D.C.: Pew Research Center, 2010.

Fussell, Elizabeth, and Frank Furstenberg Jr. "The Transition to Adulthood During the Twentieth Century," in Richard Settersten Jr. et al. (eds.), *On the Frontier of Adulthood: Theory, Research, and Public Policy*, pp. 29–75. Chicago: University of Chicago Press, 2005.

Giddens, Anthony. *Modernity and Self-Identity: Self and Society*. Palo Alto, Calif.: Stanford University Press, 1991.

Gilligan, Carol. *In a Different Voice: Psychological Theory and Women's Development*. Cambridge, Mass.: Harvard University Press, 1982.

Goffman, Alice. "On the Run: Wanted Men in a Philadelphia Ghetto." *American Sociological Review* 74 (2009), no. 3: 339–57.

Goffman, Erving. *Stigma: Notes on the Management of Spoiled Identity*. Englewood Cliffs, N.J.: Prentice-Hall, 1963.

Goldin, Claudia, Lawrence F. Katz, and Ilyana Kuziemko. "The Homecoming of American College Women: The Reversal of the College Gender Gap." National Bureau of Economic Research, Working Paper 12139, 2006.

Gornick, Vivian. *Approaching Eye Level*. Boston: Beacon Press, 1996.

Gottlieb, Lori. "Marry Him! The Case for

Settling for Mr. Good Enough." *Atlantic Monthly*, March 2008.

———. *Marry Him! The Case for Settling for Mr. Good Enough*. New York: Dutton, 2010.

Grier, Katherine. *Pets in America: A History*. Chapel Hill: University of North Carolina Press, 2006.

Groth, Paul. *Living Downtown: The History of Residential Hotels*. Berkeley: University of California Press, 1994.

Grundy, Emily, and Michael Murphy. "Marital Status and Family Support for the Oldest-Old in Great Britain," in Jean-Marie Robin et al. (eds.). *Human Longevity, Individual Life Duration, and the Growth of the Oldest-Old Population*, Volume 4, pp. 415–36. New York: Springer, 2006.

Gura, Philip. *American Transcendentalism: A History*. New York: Hill and Wang, 2008.

Haines, Valerie, and Jeanne Hurlbert. "Network Range and Health." *Journal of Health and Social Behavior* 33 (1992): 254–66.

Hampton, Keith, Lauren Sessions, Eun Ja Her, and Lee Rainie. "Social Isolation and New Technology: How the Internet and Mobile Phones Impact Americans' Social Networks." Washington, D.C.: Pew Internet & American Life Project, 2009.

Haney, Craig. "Mental Health Issues in Long-Term Solitary and 'Supermax' Confinement."

Crime & Delinquency 49 (2003), no. 1: 124–56.

Haney, Craig, and Mona Lynch. "Regulating Prisons of the Future: The Psychological Consequences of Solitary and Supermax Confinement." *New York University Review of Law and Social Change* 23 (1997): 477–570.

Haraway, Donna. *The Companion Species Manifesto: Dogs, People, and Significant Otherness*. Chicago: Prickly Paradigm, 2003.

Harris, Luther. *Around Washington Square: An Illustrated History of Greenwich Village*. Baltimore: Johns Hopkins University Press, 2003.

Hayden, Dolores. *Redesigning the American Dream: Gender, Housing, and Family Life*, 2d ed. New York: Norton, 2002.

Hochschild, Arlie. *The Time Bind: When Home Becomes Work and Work Becomes Home*. New York: Metropolitan, 1997.

———. *The Unexpected Community: Portrait of an Old Age Subculture*. Berkeley: University of California Press, 1973.

Hotz, V. Joseph, Kathleen McGarry, and Emily Wiemers. "Living Arrangements among Elderly Women in the Panel Study of Income Dynamics." PSID Conference on Pensions, Private Accounts, and Retirement Savings over the Life Course, November 20–21, 2008.

Hughes, Michael, and Walter Gove. "Living Alone, Social Integration, and Mental Health." *American Journal of Sociology* 87 (1981), no. 1: 48–74.

Iacovou, Maria, and Alexandra Skew. "Household Structure in the EU," in Anthony B. Atkinson and Eric Marlier, *Income and Living Conditions in Europe*, pp. 79–100. Luxembourg: Eurostat Statistical Books, 2010.

Iliffe, Steven, et al. "Health Risk Appraisal in Older People II: The Implications for Clinicians and Commissioners of Social Isolation Risk in Older People." *British Journal of General Practice* 57 (2007), no. 537: 277–82.

Iliffe, Steven, et al. "Are Elderly People Living Alone an At-Risk Group?" *British Medical Journal* 305 (1992): 1001–4.

Jones, Judith. *The Pleasures of Cooking for One*. New York: Knopf, 2009.

Kipnis, Laura. *Against Love: A Polemic*. New York: Pantheon, 2003.

Klinenberg, Eric. *Heat Wave: A Social Autopsy of Disaster in Chicago*. Chicago: University of Chicago Press, 2002.

Krause, Neal. "Neighborhood Deterioration and Social Isolation in Later Life." *International Journal of Aging and Human Development* 36 (1993): 9–38.

Kreider, Rose M., and Jason M. Fields. "Number, Timing, and Duration of Marriages and Divorces: 1996." U.S. Census Reports, 2002.

Lareau, Annette. *Unequal Childhoods: Class, Race, and Family Life.* Berkeley: University of California Press, 2003.

Larimer, Mary E., Daniel K. Malone, Michelle D. Garner, et al. "Health Care and Public Service Use and Costs Before and After Provision of Housing for Chronically Homeless Persons with Severe Alcohol Problems." *JAMA* 301 (2009), no. 13: 1349–57.

Lindau, Stacy Tessler, and Natalia Gavrilova. "Sex, Health, and Years of Sexually Active Life Gained Due to Good Health." *British Medical Journal* 240 (2010): c810.

Livingston, Gretchen, and D'Vera Cohn. "Childlessness Up among All Women; Down among Women with Advanced Degrees." Washington, D.C.: Pew Research Center, 2010.

Luhrmann, T. M. "The Art of Hearing God: Absorption, Dissociation, and Contemporary American Spirituality." *Spiritus: A Journal of Christian Spirituality* 5 (2005), no. 2: 133–57.

Lyubomirsky, Sonja. *The How of Happiness: The Scientific Approach to Getting the Life You Want.* New York: Penguin Press, 2007.

Marcus, Sharon. "Placing Rosemary's Baby." *Differences: A Journal of Feminist Cultural Studies* 5 (1993), no. 3: 121–40.

Marsh, Kris, William Darity, Jr., Philip Cohen, Lynne Casper, and Danielle Salters. "The Emerging Black Middle Class: Single and Living Alone." *Social Forces* 86, no. 2: 735–62.

Martinez, Tia, and Martha Burt. "Impact of Permanent Supportive Housing on the Use of Acute Care Health Services by Homeless Adults." *Psychiatric Services* 57 (2006): 992–99.

McPherson, Michael, Lynn Smith-Lovin, and Matthew Brashears. "Social Isolation in America: Changes in Core Discussion Networks over Two Decades." *American Sociological Review* 71 (2006): 353–75.

Michael, Yvonne, Lisa Berkman, Graham Colditz, and Ichiro Kawachi. "Living Arrangements, Social Integration, and Change in Functional Health Status." *American Journal of Epidemiology* 153 (2001), no. 2: 123–31.

Michel, Robert, Victor Fuchs, and Sharon Scott. "Changes in the Propensity to Live Alone: 1950–1976." *Demography* 17 (1980), no. 1: 39–56.

Montenegro, Xenia P. "The Divorce Experience: A Study of Divorce at Midlife and Beyond."

Washington, D.C.: The American Association of Retired People, 2004.

Murdock, George Peter. *Social Structure.* Oxford, UK: Macmillan, 1949.

Myerhoff, Barbara. *Number Our Days: A Triumph of Continuity and Caring among Jewish Old People in an Urban Ghetto.* New York: Touchstone, 1980.

Ogden, Philip, and François Schnoebelen. "The Rise of the Small Household: Demographic Change and Household Structure in Paris." *Population, Space, and Place* 11 (2005): 251–68.

Olds, Jacqueline, and Richard Schwartz. *The Lonely American: Drifting Apart in the Twenty-first Century.* Boston: Beacon Press, 2008.

Osgerby, Bill. "The Bachelor Pad as Cultural Icon." *Journal of Design History* 18 (2005), no. 1: 99–114.

Owen, David. "Green Manhattan: Why New York Is the Greenest City in the U.S." *The New Yorker,* October 18, 2004.

Packaged Facts. "Singles in the U.S.: The New Nuclear Family." Rockville, Md., 2007.

Pager, Devah. *Marked: Crime, Race, and Finding Work in an Era of Mass Incarceration.* Chicago: University of Chicago Press, 2007.

Park, Young Jin. "The Rise of One-Person House-holders and their Recent Characteristics in Korea." *Korea Journal of Population and Development* 23 (1994), no. 1: 117–29.

Parkes, C. Murray, B. Benjamin, and R. G. Fitzgerald. "Broken Heart: A Statistical Study of Increased Mortality Among Widowers." *British Medical Journal* 1, no. 5646 (March 22, 1969): 740–43.

Peterson, Richard. "A Re-Evaluation of the Economic Consequences of Divorce." *American Sociological Review* 61 (1996): 528–36.

Pink, Daniel. *Free Agent Nation: How America's New Independent Workers Are Transforming the Way We Live.* New York: Warner, 2001.

Popenoe, David. "Beyond the Nuclear Family: A Statistical Portrait of the Changing Family in Sweden." *Journal of Marriage and Family* 49 (1987), no. 1: 173–83.

Potter, David. "American Individualism in the Twentieth Century," in Ronald Gross and Paul Osterman (eds.), *Individualism: Man in Modern Society*, pp. 51–69. New York: Dell, 1971.

Putnam, Robert. *Bowling Alone: The Collapse and Revival of American Community.* New York: Simon & Schuster, 2000.

Rainie, Lee, and Mary Madden. "Not Looking for Love: Romance in America." Washington, D.C.: Pew Research Center, 2006.

Richards, Toni, Michael White, and Amy Ong Tsui. "Changing Living Arrangements: A Hazard Model of Transitions Among Household Types." *Demography* 24 (1987), no. 1: 77–97.

Ronald, Richard, and Yosuke Hirayama. "Home Alone: The Individualization of Young, Urban Japanese Singles." *Environment and Planning A* 41 (2009), no. 12: 2836–54.

Rose, Nikolas. *Powers of Freedom*. Cambridge, UK: Cambridge University Press, 1999.

Rosenfeld, Michael. *The Age of Independence: Interracial Unions, Same-Sex Unions, and the Changing American Family*. Cambridge, Mass.: Harvard University Press, 2007.

Scanlon, Jennifer. *Bad Girls Go Everywhere: The Life of Helen Gurley Brown*. New York: Oxford University Press, 2009.

Schumpeter, Joseph. *Capitalism, Socialism, and Democracy*. New York: Harper Perennial, 1962 [1942].

Sennett, Richard. *The Fall of Public Man*. New York: Norton, 1974.

Shain, Barry Alan. *The Myth of American Individualism: The Protestant Origins of American Political Thought*. Princeton, N.J.: Princeton University Press, 1994.

Simmel, Georg. "The Metropolis and Mental Life," in Donald Levine (ed.), *On Individuality and Social Forms*. Chicago:

University of Chicago Press, 1971 [1903].

Smith, Sandra. *Lone Pursuit: Distrust and Defensive Individualism among the Black Poor*. New York: Russell Sage Foundation, 2007.

Soons, Judith, Aart Liefbroer, and Matthijs Kalmijn. "The Long-Term Consequences of Relationship Formation for Subjective Well-Being." *Journal of Marriage and the Family* 71 (2009), no. 5: 1254–70.

Sparrow, Robert, and Linda Sparrow. "In the Hands of Machines? The Future of Aged Care." *Minds and Machines* 16 (2006), no. 2: 141–61.

Spock, Benjamin. *Dr. Spock's Baby and Child Care*, 7th ed. New York: Pocket, 1998.

Stansell, Christine. *American Moderns: Bohemian New York and the Creation of a New Century*. New York: Metropolitan, 2000.

Storr, Anthony. *Solitude: A Return to the Self*. New York: Free Press, 1988.

Thistle, Susan. *From Marriage to Market: The Transformation of Women's Lives at Work*. Berkeley: University of California Press, 2006.

Toossi, Mitra. "A Century of Change: The U.S. Labor Force, 1950–2000." *Monthly Labor Review*, May 2002: 15–28.

Umberson, Debra, Kristi Williams, Daniel Powers, Hui Liu, and Belinda Needham.

"You Make Me Sick: Marital Quality and Health over the Life Course." *Journal of Health and Social Behavior* 47 (March 2006): 1–16.

U.S. Census Bureau. "Number, Timing, and Duration of Marriages and Divorces: 2001," 2005.

Vervoorn, Aat. *Men of the Cliffs and Caves: The Development of the Chinese Eremitic Tradition to the End of the Han Dynasty.* Hong Kong: Chinese University Press, 1990.

Victor, Christina, Ann Bowling, John Bond, and Sasha Scambler. "Loneliness, Social Isolation, and Living Alone in Later Life." Research Findings no. 17, The Growing Older Programme. Sheffield, UK: Economic & Social Research Council, 2003.

Waite, Linda, and Maggie Gallagher. *The Case for Marriage: Why Married People Are Happier, Healthier, and Better Off Financially.* New York: Doubleday, 2000.

Walkowitz, Judith. *City of Dreadful Delight: Narratives of Sexual Danger in Late-Victorian London.* Chicago: University of Chicago Press, 1992.

Ware, Caroline. *Greenwich Village, 1920–1930.* New York: Octagon, 1935.

Waswo, Ann. *Housing in Postwar Japan: A Social History.* London: Routledge Curzon, 2002.

Watters, Ethan. *Urban Tribes: A Generation Redefines Friendship, Family, and Commitment*. New York: Bloomsbury, 2003.

Wetzsteon, Ross. *Republic of Dreams: Greenwich Village: The American Bohemia, 1910–1960*. New York: Simon & Schuster, 1998.

Whitehead, Barbara Dafoe. *The Divorce Culture: Rethinking Our Commitments to Marriage and Family*. New York: Knopf, 1996.

Whitman, Walt. *New York Dissected*, Emory Holloway and Ralph Adimari (eds.). New York: Rufus Rockwell Wilson, 1936 [1856].

Williams, Jo. "Innovative Solutions for Averting a Potential Resource Crisis—The Case of One-Person Households in England and Wales." *Environmental Development and Sustainability* 9 (2007): 325–54.

Zorbaugh, Harvey. *The Gold Coast and the Slum: A Sociological Study of Chicago's Near North Side*. Chicago: University of Chicago Press, 1983 [1929].

ACKNOWLEDGMENTS

Must I say that this book was by no means a solitary endeavor?

Thanks go first to the Robert Wood Johnson Foundation and to the staff at the RWJF Investigator Awards in Health Policy program, which not only funded the research but also patiently withstood various interruptions along the way. A year at the Stanford Center for Advanced Study in the Behavioral Sciences provided ideal conditions for conceiving and developing the book, and New York University gave me time and space to finish it.

The project could not have happened without the extraordinary team of graduate students who, at various stages of the project, did fieldwork, conducted interviews, crunched numbers, designed graphics, coded transcripts, scoured archives, and let me know what we had failed to learn. Jenna Appelbaum, Heather Barry, Jill Conte, Max Holleran, Jane Jones, Sarah Kaufman, Isadora Levy, Allison McKim, Laura Noren, Nerea Puzole, Elena Portacolone, Jason Stanley, and Abigail Weitzman: Thanks to each of you for collaborating. I'm also grateful to Erin Cornwell, who helped me analyze data from the General Social Survey that shows what is and is not distinctive about living alone.

Gentle, generous, yet unabashedly critical readers made this book much better than it would have been had I done it independently. Eric Bates, Max Besbris, Deborah Carr, Chelsea Clinton, Claude Fischer, Edward Klinenberg, Andrew Lakoff, Jeff Manza, Sharon Marcus, Vanessa Mobley, Bob Shrum, Anna Skarpalis, Rona Talcott, Fred Turner, Matt Wray, and Caitlin Zaloom reviewed drafts, pointed out the most glaring weak spots, and stayed on my case until I made them stronger. They didn't always tell me what I wanted to hear, but they were consistently helpful, not to mention right.

I'm lucky to have the support of superagent Tina Bennett and her ace assistant Svetlana Katz. I'm also grateful that they ushered this book to The Penguin Press, where Eamon Dolan always understood when to let me go solo and when I needed an editor's hand, and Scott Moyers, Emily Graff, and Ann Godoff provided crucial support on the last and most difficult steps.

Above all, I'm fortunate to be part of a family that values companionship as well as personal time; for me, at least, a good life—not to mention the capacity to write!—requires both. My greatest thanks go to Kate, Cyrus, and Lila: I treasure each day and night we share together at home.

Center Point Large Print
600 Brooks Road / PO Box 1
Thorndike ME 04986-0001 USA

(207) 568-3717

US & Canada:
1 800 929-9108
www.centerpointlargeprint.com